SEVENTEEN CENTURIES
ON THE ROAD
FROM CENTER PLACE

UNIVERSITY OF NEW MEXICO PRESS / ALBUQUERQUE

ANASAZI AMERICA

David E. Stuart

WITH THE RESEARCH ASSISTANCE OF
Susan Moczygemba-McKinsey

Library of Congress Cataloging-in-Publication Data:

Stuart, David E.
  Anasazi America : seventeen centuries on the road from center place / David E. Stuart ; with the research assistance of Susan Moczygemba-McKinsey.
    p. cm.
Includes bibliographical references and index.
  ISBN 0-8263-2178-X (cloth : alk. paper) — ISBN 0-8263-2179-8 (pbk. : alk. paper)
  1. Pueblo Indians — Antiquities. 2. Chaco Canyon (N.M.) — Antiquities. 3. Pueblo Indians — Social life and customs. 4. Human ecology — Case studies. 5. Social change — Case studies. I. Moczygemba-McKinsey, Susan
B. II. Title.
  E99.P9 S83 2000
  978.9'82 — dc21   99-006973

Cover photograph: American Flag "Dance" at Taos Pueblo, Winter 1905, photographer B. G. Randall. © 1996 Cliff Mills Studio, Santa Fe (http://cliffmills.tripod.com).

Title page photograph: Winter view of Taos Pueblo, 1905. © 1996 Cliff Mills Studio.

To the students in "Ancient New Mexico," Spring 1998.
Thank you for the journey.
—David E. Stuart

To Brian, for shouldering my part of the load,
and to the memory of my dad, Felix C. Moczygemba,
who made my mountains more manageable.
—Susan Moczygemba-McKinsey

Contents

	List of Illustrations	IX
	Acknowledgments	XI
	Preface	XIII
	Prologue: Daniel's Question	3
1	The Rhythms of Civilization	7
2	The Roots of Anasazi Society	13
3	The Role of Agriculture	35
4	The Rise of the Chaco Anasazi	51
5	The Chaco Phenomenon	65
6	The Fall of Chacoan Society	107
7	The Upland Period	125
8	The Creation of Pueblo Society	147
9	Enduring Communities	179
	Epilogue: The Spirit of Community	203
	Notes	205
	Glossary	217
	Suggested Readings	219
	References Cited	221
	Index	239
	Biographical Note	249

Illustrations

Maps

1	The Four Corners	10
2	A Trip Through Chaco Country	71
3	The Heart of Chaco	76
4	The Pueblos of Modern Times	182

Figures

1	Child Poverty Rates in the United States, 1959–1996	194
2	Child Poverty before and after Government Intervention	195
3	Tax Revenue as a Percentage of Gross Domestic Product, 1994	196

Photographs

The Land and its Farmers	25–33
The Chaco Phenomenon	89–106
Puebloan Descendants	169–178

Acknowledgments

FIRST AND FOREMOST, I WANT TO THANK THE STUDENTS IN MY spring 1998 "Ancient New Mexico" course for the most stimulating episode of my teaching career. They are Ryan Bartell, Tod Dikeman, Kenneth Duncan, Sam Duran, Kevin Eklund, Emily Fowler, Alan Garrett, Chris Gibson, Ana Gomes, Jake Ingram, Peter Kalberer, Juliette Lagassé-Martínez, Carmen Land, Margaret McKenney-Fuller, Susan Moczygemba-McKinsey, Daniel Moya, Malinda Moyers, John Myers, Marilyn Salas, Joseph Sandberg, Jeffery Shaner, Turza Shows, Kristin Taylor, Justin Tibbitts, Joan Turietta, Debralee Whalen, Eric Wheeler, and Heidi Wohle.

Second, I owe an enormous debt of gratitude to Elizabeth Rohne for rendering my handwritten manuscript into a clean typescript and for enduring with good grace the inevitable revisions. Susan Moczygemba-McKinsey, too, invested an enormous amount of work in researching and referencing this book. Given my role as a full-time university administrator, I could not have written this book without their assistance. I am equally grateful to my wife, Cynthia M. Stuart, who gave me up as lost nearly every evening and weekend between May 1998 and mid-March 1999.

I am also pleased by the support and encouragement I received from Elizabeth Hadas and her team at the University of New Mexico Press. They are *the* cultural voice of the American Southwest, and their imprimatur on this book means a great deal to me.

Others also gave generously of themselves. Regge N. Wiseman, a fine archaeologist and colleague at the Museum of New Mexico, dug up a number of scarce excavation reports for Susan and me on short notice. Peter McKenna and G. B. Cornucopia of the National Park Service helped us answer a number of questions, as did Karen Sandefur at Salmon Ruin. Stanley Rhine, a forensic anthropologist at the University of New Mexico, consulted on the interpretation of several Chacoan burials. Frances Joan Mathien of the National Park Service's Chaco Research Center at UNM helped us find important reference material and answered questions about the ancient turquoise trade. Garland Bills, chair of the Department of Linguistics at UNM, answered our questions about Puebloan languages. Annotated illustrations were cheerfully and efficiently provided by Joyce Raab with assistance from Heidi Reed and Angela Rogers of the Chaco Archive, a remarkably valuable facility housed at UNM's Zimmerman Library. The superb maps were created by Carol Cooperrider of Albuquerque, and copyeditor Jane Kepp in Santa Fe added much to the quality of the finished text. Thomas Mortenson provided the figures for chapter 9. Cliff and Nancy Mills of Santa Fe graciously provided the arresting cover and title page views of Taos Pueblo from their important collection of Territorial New Mexico photographs (taken by Cliff's great-grandfather, B.G. Randall). On sunny days their display table can be found on Santa Fe's charming plaza.

Finally, I am enormously grateful to Linda S. Cordell, who formally reviewed this volume for UNM Press. She suggested remedies for many errors of fact, tone, and interpretation. Nonetheless, I plotted my own intellectual course on a number of points. Since I consider Cordell to be one of the "best in the business," I have done this at some peril to my reputation, rather than to hers. She warned particularly that I not use definite dates for a number of events (such as the drought of A.D. 1090), because new research might change them by a few years one way or the other. This warning I pass along to the reader—archaeology is a dynamic field, and what we know or think we know today will change.

Preface

THE GENERAL THEME OF THIS BOOK BEGAN AS A BRIEF KEYNOTE address made at the seventieth annual Pecos Conference, held at Chaco Canyon in August 1997. I delivered that address, "The Rise and Fall of the Chaco Anasazi: Lessons Learned," with some trepidation. First, it stressed the present as well as the past—a distinct departure from standard archaeological themes. And in the audience of nearly 700 sat many of the world's finest archaeologists, including a number of my own mentors. Nervously, I described the failure of the Chacoans to change course and adapt in order to avert the collapse of the impressive regional society they had created in the tenth and eleventh centuries. Foremost among Chacoan problems were misuse of farmland, the desperate economic and nutritional status of small farmers, the loss of community, and an inability to deal with climatological catastrophe. The parallels to modern America seemed obvious. I also argued that the Puebloan society which succeeded the Chacoans had adapted intelligently and strategically to minimize a recurrence of these problems. Finally, I ended the address with a simple query: "As we approach the millennium in modern America, can't we recognize our own problems and adapt as well as the Puebloans did, without first having to suffer the dramatic consequences of myopia in our own society?" Thankfully, the response was positive.

Nothing encourages a scholar so much as the approval of his colleagues, even if it is merely polite approval. Whether polite or heartfelt, this approbation spurred me to revise my "Ancient New Mexico" course at the University of New Mexico and to focus more on "past and present."

The 1997-1998 academic year was memorable. Favored by this new theme and an interesting mix of enthusiastic traditional and nontraditional undergraduate students, "Ancient New Mexico" hit its stride in the spring semester of 1998. At the end of the first lecture, the class erupted in applause. This response was absolutely stunning. From time to time, students had applauded the final lecture of a semester—a sweet experience in itself—but in 34 semesters of teaching this had never before happened to me at the beginning of a term. Had these students taken a psychology class on how to motivate the lecturer? At first, it seemed so, but soon it was obvious that the students were pushing themselves as hard as they were pushing me. By the end of the fourth week, this was no longer just a class—it had become a shared journey.

The semester ended with applause, as it had begun. At the farewell dinner, held before graduation day, the students were still asking questions and raising possibilities about the parallels between Chacoan society and modern America. As I describe in the prologue, one of those after-dinner questions led directly to this book's being written, and a few weeks after term's end, another student in the class accepted the role of research assistant for the book.

In explaining the importance of research to university students, academicians often point out that their research and publications help them teach better undergraduate classes. It is rarely phrased the other way around. We simply do not expect our undergraduate classes to help us conceive our research or to directly motivate us to write our books. But that is precisely what happened in this case. Any reader among you who is a teacher will understand that I have not merely seen the promised land during this experience but have actually walked in it, smelled its gentle essence, and felt the precious warmth of its sunlight.

In other respects, this book is as unusual as the experience that wrought it. In the first place, several of its intellectual themes are distinctive—the products of my own broad training in anthropology. They began many years ago with the publication of *Prehistoric New Mexico*, a reference work I wrote with Rory P. Gauthier. I argued then that evolution, both biological and cultural, is the process that continually and selectively separates metabolically more powerful from metabolically more efficient organisms or societies. The idea was that captured energy is the essence of life itself. Even men and women are metabolically different. Women metabolize more slowly and efficiently than men and are a bit smaller, but they live longer. Men metabolize more rapidly and are larger on average, but die younger. In any large group of children born in a given year, the males and females, absent catastrophe, will each consume the same number of calories in basal metabolism over the natural life span of the cohort—but they will use those calories differently. Those differences have enormous evolutionary consequences.

Similarly, a powerful society (or organism) captures more energy and expends (metabolizes) it more rapidly than an efficient one. Such societies tend to be structurally more complex, more wasteful of energy, more competitive, and faster paced than an efficient one. Think of modern urban America as power-ful, and you will get the picture. In contrast, an efficient society "metabolizes" its energy more slowly, and so it is structurally less complex, less wasteful, less competitive, and slower paced. Think of Amish farmers in Pennsylvania or con-temporary Pueblo farmers in the American Southwest.

In competitive terms, the powerful society has an enormous short-term ad-vantage over the efficient one *if* enough energy is naturally available to "feed" it, or if its technology and trade can bring in energy rapidly enough to sustain it. But when energy (food, fuel, and resources) becomes scarce, or when trade and technology fail, an efficient society is advantageous because its simpler, less wasteful structure is much more easily sustained in times of scarcity. Since both "power" and "efficiency" offer enormous advantages under the right circum-stances, most human societies are engaged in a constant and complex balanc-ing act between the two. Being human, we want to have it both ways.

Having it both ways gives us the capacity to continually refashion society as either more powerful or more efficient and is the primary reason we humans have become ascendant over other species. In other words, human culture re-sponds more rapidly to new circumstances than does genetic change, and hence culture is an inherently more powerful (but riskier) evolutionary mechanism. Our cultural ability to transform ourselves has allowed our species to change the metabolic signature of its societies at will and dodge many of the evolutionary "bullets" that have extinguished other species. The metabolic-energetic signa-ture of animals is "hard-wired" in, genetically. In a human society, the energetic signature is encoded in cultural "software." We just rewrite the program as needed. But the rewrite, like our perceptions of a given problem, is often imper-fect. So failure, transformation, and survival are themes of this book.

In the second place, this book is not an archaeological text per se. Rather, I use archaeological data along with ethnographic data, historical records, and contemporary sources to chronicle the rise and fall of one remarkable South-western society (Chacoan) and its replacement by another (Puebloan), and to point out the parallels between those two societies and modern America.

The fundamental threads that tie Chacoan, Puebloan, Spanish, Mexican, and American societies together in the Southwest are time and place. Each succeeded the other in what is now New Mexico. Each has struggled, surprisingly, with similar issues surrounding farmland, water, climate, economy, and community. And among them, only industrial America has not yet struggled with the issue of cultural survival. I argue that this struggle will come if Americans are not both wiser and more adaptable in the future than they have been in the recent past.

It is my hope that this book will both inform readers and provide them with food for thought. The American Southwest is distinctive, colorful, and delightful. But most important of all, it offers a parable from the past that can inform our own present, if not our future. I predict that this parable will dismay some readers. History is not elegant. Failure is not glorious. Success is not permanent. Knowledge is not absolute. And survival is not a birthright. Instead, it turns out to be hard, gritty work.

For at least 17 centuries this gritty work of survival was done by the prehistoric farmers that archaeologists have labeled "Anasazi" and by their Puebloan descendants, who excelled at it. The Anasazi do have lessons to offer America—hence the title of this book.

ANASAZI
AMERICA

Prologue

Daniel's Question

MANY READERS MAY SUPPOSE THAT ARCHAEOLOGY IS ABOUT mounting expeditions to exotic places, assembling fabulous museum exhibits of priceless antiquities, or reconstructing ancient societies. Archaeology does involve all of these at one time or another, but the plain fact is that people like to romanticize archaeology—and archaeologists. After all, the Indiana Jones movies are about a flamboyant and fictional archaeologist—not an accountant, an engineer, or an insurance actuary. Those professions are important and necessary, but they just don't stir the public's imagination as do things archaeological.

The pure emotional aura of ancient civilizations and abandoned cities inflames the human imagination. Nearly every archaeologist understands this. It is, after all, what drew most of us to an unusual profession in the first place. But archaeologists are not the only ones fascinated with antiquity. Every tribal society that continues to survive at the edges of the modern world has its oral history about how the world was created and how the ancient ones behaved. Australian Aborigines have their "dreamtime." Herodotus later had his history of cities and civilizations far more ancient than his own classical Greece. And as every student of history knows, the later Romans aped both Greece and ancient Egypt. Even we "modern" Judeo-Christians have our Genesis story.

Here in the contemporary American Southwest, many Indian men—Pueblo, Navajo, and Apache—still own "medicine bundles" that often contain ancient objects such as lance points made thousands of years ago by hunters and gatherers who once roamed these parts. These bundles have power, partly because they connect the owner to the past. Is it a deep human hunger for connection to the past that generates near-universal fascination with archaeology? Yes, partly. But it is also something more. Much more.

3

Daniel, a Pueblo Indian potter and a student in my "Ancient New Mexico" class at the University of New Mexico, captured it all in a recent conversation. "Professor," he said, "I need to talk to you about the Folsom points we studied last semester." He was referring to a type of exquisitely made spear point common between 8500 and 9000 B.C. He went on: "They baffle me. I cannot *understand* them. I have made copies of all the rest that we studied and I understand these. But the Folsom is different— trying to make one, I have driven flakes of obsidian into my fingers until the tips were hard and bloody. But I cannot do it. I think it is a *spiritual* thing—some spiritual thing that I do not command. I need to understand this part of my past in order to become both the artist and the historian of my people that I wish to be."

I couldn't solve Daniel's immediate problem, having neither the technical skill nor, perhaps, the spirituality to make a magnificent fluted Folsom point. But his quest captures the very essence of our collective human fascination with archaeology. It is all about who we were, who we are, and who we hope to be.

This sense of our connectedness to the whole flow of the human saga is deeply intoxicating. Archaeology is about much more than antiquities on a museum shelf. It is about the hypnotic rhythms of civilization—the rise and fall of humankind's cultural breast, from which issues the collective breath of human triumph and folly, of greatness and ruin, of kindness and cruelty. It is about both past and present, about power and decline.

But Daniel's quest is more focused and urgent than most of ours. As a descendant of the ancient farmers of the Four Corners popularly called the "Anasazi," he needs to learn his people's story. The precious legacy of their survival is his inheritance. Bequeathed to him at great human cost, the structured knowledge of his Anasazi-Puebloan ancestors and the collective arts of survival they acquired over the course of 17 centuries allowed his people to win the greatest of all human battles—evolution. Puebloan survival itself is absolute proof of this Homeric victory.

Daniel's task will be even more complex than that of his ancestors. He must first understand and recapitulate their lessons if his own world is to last for yet another millennium. At the same time, he must adapt to the "modern" world that now surrounds his. Like all powerful societies, it unthinkingly threatens to swallow up all that is traditional. These lessons are essential to the rest of us, too. Through them, modern industrial and information-based societies may also find the means to survive another millennium. This, then, is why we do archaeology. Archaeologists are detectives in the game of evolution and keepers of the tally in the human saga of survival. Archaeology is about people and almost always about the present as well as the past, though we often fail to make that obvious.

Since Daniel's question prompted me, his thoroughly American professor, to write this book as an answer, I have written it as if addressed to him. It is his people's story. I have not told it the way his elders would tell it, and it won't help him make a perfect Folsom point. But I tell it as a fundamental part of the grand rhythm of human civilization, with the fervent hope that its telling will speed Daniel on his quest, his spirit strengthened by the wisdom of the Anasazi, so that he and his society flow ever forward on the winds of time.

DAVID E. STUART
ALBUQUERQUE, MARCH 1999

CHAPTER ONE

The Rhythms of Civilization

T HIS BOOK RECONSTRUCTS THE RISE AND FALL OF THE CHACO ANASAZI of New Mexico. It is about how ancient farmers in the American Southwest gathered the knowledge and power to create the grandest regional social and political system in prehistoric North America during the tenth and eleventh centuries A.D., only to lose nearly all that they had created in the twelfth.

At their height in the late eleventh century, the Chaco Anasazi dominated 40,000 square miles of the scrubby, semiarid Four Corners region.[1] This was an area nearly the size of Scotland—and considerably larger than any one European principality of the time. A vast and powerful alliance consisted of 10,000 to 20,000 farming hamlets and nearly 100 spectacular district towns, called "great houses" by archaeologists, that integrated the surrounding farmsteads through economic and religious ties. Hundreds of miles of formal roadways interconnected the whole system.[2] Chaco Canyon, now a national park and, like the great pyramids at Giza, a World Heritage Site, was both the heart and soul of this domain.

It took these Anasazi farmers more than seven centuries to lay the agricultural, organizational, and technological groundwork for the creation of the classic Chacoan period, which lasted about 200 years—only to collapse spectacularly in a mere 40.[3]

Why did such a great society collapse? Who survived? Why? How did the survivors behave? What has that to do with modern Pueblo descendants of the Anasazi? What has it to do with the rest of us?

Past and Present

When Chacoan society collapsed, different clans and families experienced different fates—each according to their wealth, their station, and the knowledge they possessed. Some stayed on in the great houses while others moved away, abandoning their farmsteads. Among each, some perished. In complex eleventh-century Chacoan society, there were many differences among people, and those critical differences were grist for the mill of evolution during the collapse. Some were ground down and perished. Others, though not left whole, survived.

Those who perished became the past. Those who survived left more descendants and became the present. If we can understand both, we will have retrieved a saga worthy of the telling. We will also know much about how the Anasazi once created a great but fragile society, and how catastrophe forced them to dramatically transform it into a far more modest but durable one. That transformation allowed them to survive and has brought their descendants face-to-face with our own modern version of a powerful society.

Because non-Indian Americans dominate the social landscape that surrounds current Puebloan society in New Mexico, both of our "presents" have become intertwined. In some ways, Pueblo people and the rest of us are quite alike—we hope, dream, work, joke, make families, believe in a higher order, and expect to pass our societies on to our children and our children's children.

In other ways, though we live near one another, work in many of the same places, and often share communities, our differences are great. Just what are these differences? Are they destined to be more grist for the mill of evolution should another catastrophe befall us in our own time? Who would perish and become the "past" of an evolving saga? Who would survive and become the future—a new "present?" Now that much of the world, both traditional and industrial, is so deeply intertwined, Pueblo people are not the only ones who need to know the fundamentals of survival. We all do.

In today's world, an economic disturbance in one nation can within days cascade into direct financial consequences for others half the world away. A famine in one country can trigger a war in another. A plague in one faraway place can become a pandemic in weeks. And one small person with a very big bomb could end the entire human saga in mere hours. What have the Chaco Anasazi got to do with all this? Perhaps nothing. They are not responsible for us; they could not even have imagined us. And yet in another sense, their survival as Pueblo people means everything—for if we do the necessary detective work and listen carefully to their past, we can retrieve an important message for all surviving traditional societies, for the rest of us, and for all of twenty-first-century society to come.

Enter the Anasazi

What is currently called the Four Corners region of the American Southwest was homeland to the ancient American Indian farmers popularly called "Anasazi." Actually, "Anasazi" is a Navajo name that is usually, and romantically, translated as "the ancient ones." A better translation would be "ancestors of our enemies,"[4] a frank description of the social relationships that once prevailed between local Navajo bands and the village-dwelling farmers of the late prehistoric Southwest. I use "Anasazi" in this book simply because library catalogues and Internet databases the world over still use it. Pueblo Indians do *not* use this term for their own ancestors; they prefer, in English, "the ancient ones."

Though long known to the Navajo, the Anasazi first attracted the attention of a young, expanding American nation in 1849. In that year, an American military expedition accompanied by Lieutenant J. H. Simpson filed into the broad, jagged canyon of the dried-out Chaco River and, under a blazing August sun, beheld a number of magnificent, abandoned sandstone citadels in partial ruin.[5] Though these empty villages had long been known to the New Mexican and Indian guides accompanying the expedition, they were new to Simpson and fascinated him. He began to romanticize them immediately, choosing "Pueblo Pintado" (Painted House), the more lyrical Spanish name, over the more prosaic Jemez name, "Pueblo of the Rats," to identify the first-met, easternmost of these intricately constructed communal settlements.[6]

Simpson speculated that these large ruins evidenced an earlier and "higher" civilization than that which existed among Indian nations in his own day.[7] This is pertinent to the theme of this book on several counts.

First, it downgraded the status of then-contemporary Southwestern Indian societies, denying them equal cultural footing with white Americans while romanticizing these impressive ruins whose vanished inhabitants seemed to Simpson more like members of his own "civilized" society.

Second, this line of reasoning may have unconsciously assuaged some guilt and ambivalence over the potential fate of contemporary Indians as America expanded westward. Simpson was, after all, part of a military reconnaissance sent to contain Navajo raiding on Hispanic and Indian settlements along the Rio Grande.[8] He arrived in the Four Corners less than a year after the treaty of Guadalupe Hidalgo was forced on Mexico, ceding all these lands to the United States.[9] The growing nation was keen to assert its rights and eliminate threats to its emerging power. In the ensuing 25 years, it often viewed contemporary Indian peoples as a threat, and nearly as often eliminated them.[10]

Third, Simpson, the soldier, civil engineer, and native of New Jersey, quintessentially American, knew "power" when he saw it — and he clearly saw its vestiges in these immense ruins.

THE FOUR CORNERS

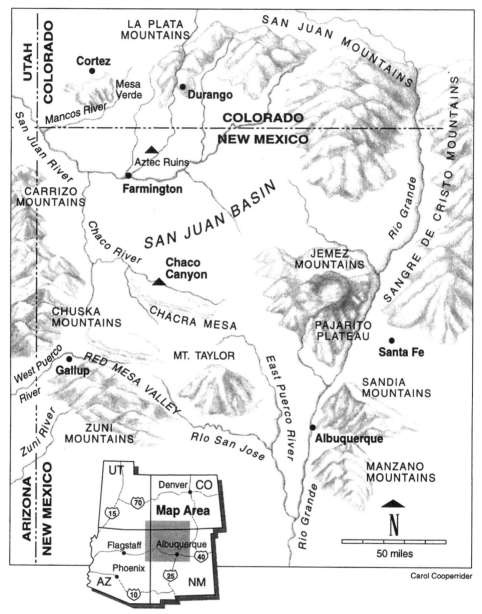

Carol Cooperrider

Before leaving Chaco Canyon that day, Simpson, along with others, carved his name into one of the inner walls of the great house now called Pueblo Bonito ("pretty house").[11] He was, in a sense, "marking his territory"—staking a claim that the Chaco Anasazi were somehow kindred to an expanding American identity.

It is no accident that the most powerful epoch in all of Anasazi prehistory created the great houses that made such an impression on Simpson and succeeding generations of Americans, scholars and tourists alike. Simpson probably did not realize how rapidly the great houses had been built and then abandoned. Powerful societies do often rapidly create vast amounts of infrastructure and remarkable quantities of manufactured objects. But as Simpson rode away with his companions to explore other terrain, he could not have known that the Anasazi had started out much less impressively. It had taken them many centuries of development before they were able to create all that he had just seen.

Nor did it likely occur to Simpson that his own Jemez Indian guides might be direct descendants of those who had raised the wall into which he had just impulsively engraved his name. Like many who were to come after him, he was unable to associate any more modest beginnings—or endings—with the brief but impressive period of power during which the great houses were erected. Simpson, product of his time, grasped only a chapter instead of the whole story.

Now let us begin with the roots of Anasazi society and set forth the entire saga, with all the majesty of its remarkable rhythms—from modest to powerful to catastrophic, and finally to efficient and enduring.

CHAPTER TWO

The Roots of Anasazi Society

N̲O ONE KNOWS PRECISELY WHEN THE ANCIENT INDIAN PEOPLE WHO would one day be called Anasazi first arrived in the Four Corners. To determine that, one would have to know much more about the early peopling of the Americas, which is not really the subject of this book. What we do know is that several waves of early hunters and gatherers crossed the strait that connects Siberia to Alaska at a time when it was dry land. Archaeologists refer to this land bridge as Beringia.[1] Now it is shallowly submerged under the Bering Sea, as it has been for nearly 10,000 years.

When Lieutenant Simpson visited Chaco Canyon, scholars believed that the Americas had first been inhabited only a bit before the common, or "Christian," era. They clung to that belief until so-called Folsom-period lance points were discovered with the skeletons of extinct bison in New Mexico in 1926 and their great antiquity was formally confirmed in 1927.[2] Soon, other important and even older finds were made in New Mexico. From 1930 to 1998, most archaeologists relied on the earliest well-dated archaeological remains in New Mexico—the camps and artifacts of ancient hunters that dated about 9200 B.C.—to roughly date the peopling of the Americas.

These camps are called "Clovis" after the eastern New Mexico town of the same name where the distinctive fluted lance and dart points of these early plant gatherers and mammoth hunters were first found.[3] We now know, from confirmed finds in Chile, that the Americas were settled long before Clovis hunters roamed New Mexico. We have few skeletal remains from these time periods, so we still have much to learn, but sites such as Monte Verde in Chile are now well dated at 10,500 B.C.[4] All of these early peoples are known as Paleo-Indians.

Judging from both linguistic and DNA studies, Paleo-Indians were descended primarily from ancient Asian-Mongoloid populations.[5] Some recent but controversial evidence suggests that lesser numbers of ancient people with some "Caucasoid" traits may also have arrived in the Americas from northern Asia long before 10,000 B.C.[6]

These people were fully modern humans. They knew fire, had small domesticated dogs, made a variety of simple tools (knives, lance points, dart tips, scrapers, gravers, burins, awls) from stone, bone, and wood, and fashioned clothing from hide. From the finds at Monte Verde, where preservation was good, we know they had skin shelters and an intimate knowledge of animal life and of local plants for food and medicine, as well as orderly living arrangements.[7]

They had not yet invented the bow and arrow. Instead, they used the atlatl, or dart thrower, which remained in use in some parts of the Americas through the A.D. 1500s.[8] In most respects the Clovis hunters in New Mexico were similar, so let us return there now.

For 5,000 years, from roughly 10,000 to 5000 B.C., small bands of Clovis hunters and gatherers and their successors — each group known by the name given to its characteristic spear point: Folsom, Midland, Belen, Cody, Plainview — roamed the Southwest. At the beginning of this period, in Clovis times, a cooler, wetter, late-Ice-Age climate prevailed. Giant game animals — among them mammoths, huge bison, camels, horses, and exotically horned elk — provided meat to supplement the small game and edible plants that these people sought in their ceaseless trek.[9]

As the Ice Age waned, the climate became drier and warmer, assuming essentially modern conditions. When the climate changed, the great Ice Age mammals vanished, to be replaced by smaller ones, the ancestors of today's bison, deer, elk, pronghorn antelope, bear, and desert bighorn sheep.

Paleo-Indian hunters adapted to these changes in a variety of ways. Their lance and dart points became a bit more specialized over time as they refined their modest tool kits of stone and bone implements to focus on the habits of the available game. As climate continued to change, so did the Paleo-Indians. Those who successfully hunted large herds of more modern bison about 6000 B.C. managed surprisingly large camps during the fall and spring hunting seasons. Population had grown, and judging from the complex "assembly-line" butchering of as many as 200 bison, society had become more complex. The Paleo-Indians of this time are known from their distinctive stone lance tips as "Cody" hunters.[10]

Like all hunters and gatherers in the Americas since the dawn of their time, Cody people spent most of their lives on trek, moving camp every few days to every few weeks. The raw expanses of the Southwest were vast. New Mexico alone encompasses more than 121,000 square miles[11] — larger than either Italy or Poland, a bit smaller than Germany. For the 5,000 years of the Paleo-Indian period, population in what is now New Mexico probably fluctuated between 2,000 and 6,000 persons at any one time—a density of one person per 20 to 60 square miles. For purposes of comparison, the contemporary Netherlands, a nation of 14,410 square miles and nearly 15 million people,[12] would have had, at the same density, a population of between 240 and 720 souls!

At these low population densities, technological and demographic change was agonizingly slow. Approximately one distinct new style of stone point for hunters' lances and long darts was created every 500 years. It must have seemed a timeless world to those who spent whole lives on trek in small bands. In a lifetime, one of these people might come face-to-face with several hundred other persons at most.

Judging from what we know of modern hunters and gatherers, these Paleo-Indians had few possessions and worked only enough to meet their basic needs—about 500 hours a year.[13] They considered the whole region in which they wandered, rather than a single place, to be home, and they were lavishly involved with tradition, doing things as they had always been done. Doing things precisely as one's forebears had was a formula for success. Those forebears had survived, and survival meant success. It all worked, so long as nothing changed dramatically.

The two great changes that typically confound hunter-and-gatherer society are climate change and population densities that exceed a foraging area's capacity to provide the essentials of life—food, water, and shelter. Paleo-Indian hunters could not control the climate, but it changed slowly enough in the Southwest from 10,000 B.C. to about 5000 B.C. that people probably perceived no change at all. It is we who now look back and analyze their stone tools, the placement of their campsites, and the bones left from their ancient meals in order to document adaptations to changing climate and regional ecology over the course of time.

Paleo-Indian people undoubtedly understood population dynamics, however, quite as well as contemporary hunters and gatherers—most of whom carefully manage sex, marriage, and procreation in order to maintain population within supportable limits for the territory available to them.[14] Total supportable population was reckoned not by periods of plenty—the occasional large bison hunt—but by how many could regularly survive on meager, widely scattered resources in seasons of want. In the Southwest, those seasons have always been midwinter and midsummer, when the respective extremes of cold and heat inhibit plant growth and scatter animal life. Temperature extremes in a normal year in the Four Corners are on the order of 100°F from high to low. In a hard year, make that 120°F.[15]

To sum it up, for five millennia the Paleo-Indians lived slow-paced, highly mobile, tradition-oriented lives. Nearly all the energy available to a foraging band was fixed, metabolically, in the living bodies of its members. Very little energy was fixed, stored in, or represented by artifacts and material goods. The food energy obtained on a given day was expended primarily in metabolism and in work done on that same day. We can describe Paleo-Indian people as *efficient:* their energy inputs and energy expenditures were balanced. Efficient human societies are like turtles in that neither is a good candidate for rapid evolution. They both move slowly, husband their reserves carefully, and last a comparatively long time. Still, Paleo-Indians may not have been the perfect conservationists we sometimes imagine them to be; research suggests that they overhunted the immense game animals of the late Ice Age and contributed to their extinction.[16] But five thousand years is a long time for a human society to last, and we can safely consider the Paleo-Indian way of life an enormous evolutionary success.

Nonetheless, had climate not begun to change more rapidly and radically after 5000 B.C., the story might have ended there without ever creating the Anasazi farmers as we now know them. The Four Corners saga might have been more like that of Australia, where slower, more moderate climatic changes in an even harsher landscape forced surviving hunters and gatherers to remain efficient and conservative. Had this been the scenario in the Four Corners, Lieutenant Simpson's Indian guides would likely have been carrying spear throwers, camping in small brush or skin shelters, and pursuing a Paleo-Indian way of life in 1849. Instead, they were descendants of a people who had known farming techniques for most of two millennia and who had already been living in complex, multistoried masonry or adobe pueblos, like the guides' own pueblo of Jemez, for the best part of a thousand years.

How did it happen that Simpson's guides and their ancestors developed their far more complex culture from such modest and change-resistant Paleo-Indian roots? In the Southwest, the climate changed rapidly and dramatically after 5000 B.C., becoming far more seasonal than the climate of Australia (the Southwest has four seasons, Australia only two). Climate change played a huge role in the development of later Southwestern societies, underlining other transformations that were to precede the Anasazi.

Archaic Society: The First Great Transformation

About 5000 B.C., the climate began to warm up, dry out, and become more notably seasonal. The lush grasslands that had once supported vast herds of bison, and with them the Cody people's great fall hunting camps, came under enormous climatological pressure. The Four Corners became even hotter and drier than it is today with the onset of a period known to paleoclimatologists as the Altithermal.[17] Today, 8 to 10 inches of precipitation fall on the Four Corners region yearly, and summer temperatures typically peak at about 105°F.[18] In an unusually harsh year—about once every 10 or 15 years—only 4 to 6 inches of precipitation fall, and late June or July temperatures might temporarily reach 110°F–112°F. In the ancient, stabilized sand dunes of the Four Corners, where plant seeds were regularly harvested, air temperatures at ground surface could reach 135°F at such times.

By 4000 B.C., nearly every year was such a year. Grass was sparse. Buffalo herds stayed to the north, wintering in what is now Colorado, Nebraska, and Wyoming and summering on the plains of Alberta and Saskatchewan. This left the Southwest parched and game poor. The period from about 5500 to 4000 B.C. was one of significant technological and social change. Early in this period, "Jay" lance points came to the Four Corners still carrying the Paleo-Indian signature of basal grinding, a way of dulling the edges of the point near its base so that it would not cut its rawhide binding.[19] Jay points resembled ones first made a thousand years earlier at ancient hunting sites such as Hell Gap in Wyoming, where bison herds prospered. But archaeologists find them alongside a much modified secondary tool kit: fist-shaped cobble grinding stones, fewer finely made scrapers for preparing hides, and many more coarse scrapers and simple, sharpened stone choppers that showed microscopic wear patterns typical of those created when such tools are used to strip seeds from various plants.

This modified tool kit is called "Archaic," and by extension, this is the label archaeologists apply to an entire developmental stage in Southwestern Native American history. The Archaic tool kit contained many more grinding and chopping tools and far fewer finely made hunting implements (knives, hide scrapers, lance and dart points) than had earlier Paleo-Indian tool assemblages.[20] These Archaic people were pressured by circumstances of climate into becoming more focused on gathering than on hunting. This represented a significant shift in daily economic emphasis. With a modified tool kit, these foragers were well equipped to process edible plants.

At first this might seem an unlikely response to unremitting heat and aridity. One could argue that the deteriorating climate might first have forced people to reduce their numbers by restricting sex, marriage, and child-bearing so that survivors would have enough game. That might well have been the short-term solution following the heyday of the Cody buffalo hunters at the end of the Paleo-Indian period. By then, Paleo-Indian hunters had likely resorted to such a strategy temporarily on several occasions. The first may have been in the Rio Grande Valley during an earlier dry interval preceding the Cody Period. The evidence for this lies in small, scattered Paleo-Indian sites there called "Belen," after Belen, New Mexico, and "Plainview," after a town in west Texas.[21] These Paleo-Indian camps show little evidence of large game hunting, and when once-plentiful game becomes scarce, hunter-gatherers typically become extremely conservative about sex and reproduction. Paleo-Indian populations may have risen and declined in several cycles even before the Altithermal first strengthened its hold. But by early Archaic times, the change in focus to plant resources—undoubtedly out of necessity—had actually produced a moderately growing population in the San Juan Basin and its margins in spite of climatic adversity. How did this happen?

It certainly took a while for the late Paleo-Indian and earliest Archaic people to build up additional knowledge about plant life. True, they had recognized and known the basic attributes of hundreds of species for millennia. But the kind of knowledge earned during this period focused on new ways to process, prepare, and cook plant species that were previously unusable. Foremost among these was yucca root.

We know that this was so because Jay campsites, typically in higher-elevation canyon-head settings just below a canyon rim, are marked by surprising numbers of scooped-out hearths.[22] These are easily seen by archaeologists on field survey because they contain masses of reddened, fire-cracked rock. The fundamental cooking technique was to heat stones over coals in the larger fire pits before transferring them to a smaller clay-lined or skin-lined pit nearby, where the hot stones boiled water in which food was cooked. Many of the red-hot stones, particularly cobbles pulled from the intermittent streams in canyon bottoms, cracked upon contact with the cooler water in the boiling pit. If starchy yucca root was being prepared, the process would have been especially tedious, because the root was often separately roasted over coals as a first step in this complicated cooking process.

A large Jay campsite at 6,500 feet in elevation and dating to about 5000 B.C. might contain 10 to 15 such cooking areas. One might also find a half dozen broken lance points made of fine-grained black basalt from the volcanic rock often found nearby, and enough sharpened and casually used flakes of the same material to fill a shoebox or two. But it would take a pickup truck to carry away the fire-cracked rock.

Ecologically, these Archaic hunters and gatherers had moved one entire link *down* the food chain, thereby eliminating the approximately 90-percent loss in food value that occurs when one feeds on an animal that is a plant eater. In short, when we in the modern world eat corn-fed beef, we are being horribly inefficient. Only about 10 percent of the corn is "fixed," or transformed, into the calories we consume when we eat the beef.[23] Putting it another way, every ton of feed corn given to cattle could support roughly 10 times the number of humans if they ate the corn rather than the beef.

In short, though the climate was harsh and large game animals scarce compared with late Ice Age times, these Archaic folks went both wide and deep ecologically by broadening the number of plant species they could utilize. Most days they managed to eliminate the enormous waste of an extra link in the food chain through new dietary habits and better food processing. Thus, in a climatological era of scarcity, they actually expanded their effective ecosystem by exploiting more plant species. This is sound ecological behavior—they could not have found a better basic strategy even if they had had the advantage of a contemporary university education. Do I attribute this to their genius? No. It is simply that those who stubbornly clung to the traditional big game hunting of their Paleo-Indian forebears could not prosper, so they left fewer descendants. Those more willing to experiment, or more desperate, fared better, so their behavior eventually became traditional among their more numerous descendants. In this fashion the big game hunting that had gone on for five millennia was gradually supplanted by gathering. This was the Southwest's first great lesson on the merits of progress. As we shall see, it was not to be the last.

Unlike the situation in Paleo-Indian camps, few bones of large game animals have been excavated from Jay-period camps or those of the succeeding "Bajada" people. And by Bajada times (about 4800 to 3300 B.C.), the somewhat smaller, stemmed dart tips had lost all basal grinding.[24] The last technological echo of the Paleo-Indian period had faded away.

Yet other important changes can be inferred from the sizes, locations, and tool kits of the Jay and Bajada camps, which remained typical for more than a millennium during the Altithermal. Camps were generally larger and more numerous than in Paleo-Indian times, and judging from the evidence of often-reused hearths, people returned to them again and again. Virtually every upper canyon in northwestern New Mexico with access to water (springs, seeps, or intermittent streams) contains Jay and Bajada camps. Hunting and hide-processing implements are scarce in these camps, but grinding stones, coarse choppers, and fire pits are plentiful. In some of the upper canyons, especially those that enjoy warm evening drafts in the cooler seasons, ancient rows of scattered yuccas can still be seen growing 500 to 1,000 feet in elevation above the yucca's natural ecological niche in the lower valleys. This raises the possibility that yuccas were transplanted—whether first by design or by accident from dropped pods or excreted seeds, we will never know. In any case, they suggest that humans have been tinkering with the Southwestern landscape for a very long time.

Gradually, the Altithermal loosened its grip. Grasslands again became more abundant, and larger game returned. The Archaic period took on a new tone, and another ripple of change worked its way across the basin-and-range country of the greater Southwest. The first triangular, stemmed dart point found its way to the Four Corners. Called the San Jose point in the Southwest but by a variety of names across the American West, this wickedly serrated stone tip was the first one to really look like an arrowhead.[25] Actually, it wasn't that at all. Rather, it was a specialized stone tip for the 5- to 7-foot-long springy dart flung from an atlatl. The shafts of these long darts were thicker than an arrow but much thinner than a javelin or spear. Often made from a reed or young willow cane, the long shaft gave the stone tip enormous penetrating power—and what penetrated the poor animal was a stemmed and barbed triangular San Jose point. The serrations, just like modern knife edges, had tremendous cutting action, opening up a wound that would bleed profusely. The barblike corners of the triangle stuck fast in the animal and could not be dislodged. A well-placed dart left a grievously wounded animal and an easily followed trail of blood. Deer was the game animal of choice during San Jose times, although the bones of elk, bighorn sheep, antelope, and bison attest that they were occasionally hunted, too.[26]

This period is notable because the San Jose point and its many cousins spread over half the continent—a technological innovation that came from the west, crossing the driest valleys of what are now central California and Arizona as it moved east. Gone were the days when Paleo-Indian bands roamed a thousand square miles or Jay gatherers returned again and again to a few favored campsites. People and technology were on the move over unprecedented distances. Most archaeologists believe that population in coastal California had begun to increase even while the late Altithermal choked the still sweltering Southwest.

In the Four Corners, the survivalist knowledge gained during the Altithermal had enabled the regional population base to increase. When the game animals returned, the human population grew even larger. The more abundant game provided increased quantities of the critical fats, proteins, and mineral nutrients such as iron, zinc, and potassium that are lacking in most plant foods. This meant that more pregnant women received nutrients critical not only to carrying pregnancies to term but also to nursing their infants. Starving women do not ovulate regularly. Even if they do become pregnant and later bear a live child, they often cannot make milk. Hunters and gatherers often resort to plant-induced abortions or infanticide, especially female infanticide, in times of catastrophic food shortages.[27] The combination at roughly 3000 B.C. of reliable plant foods, increased knowledge of food preparation, a return of cooler, moister conditions and large game animals, and a superb dart point to bring down that game proved a powerful mix. It allowed San Jose hunters and gatherers to reproduce prolifically in comparison with earlier Paleo-Indians.

The happy coincidence of favorable climate, greater knowledge, and better technology yielded a more densely populated landscape. Some four to eight square miles were now needed to support each person. We can guess that 15,000 to 30,000 souls lived in what is now New Mexico at any one moment, a stunning increase over the 2,000 to 6,000 probable tenants during the Paleo-Indian period. Though still 4,000 to 8,000 times less densely populated than the modern Netherlands (where the population density is greater than 1,000 people per square mile),[28] this is nearly equal to the one person per 3 square miles of the ice-free zones of contemporary Greenland.[29]

And what did the San Jose period teach surviving hunters and gatherers? That if all went well, one did not have to curb sexual activity quite so harshly, induce abortions, or use infanticide to prevent modest population growth. Indeed, child labor had become an asset. Tiny hands could strip wild seeds from the stalks of wild grasses such as the blazing star. More child labor also freed men to hunt more frequently. From such small shifts in behavior arise major cultural changes.

The San Jose adaptation was a very successful one. Its widely used dart point was found with accompanying but varied stone tool kits in every inhabitable locale in northwestern New Mexico. This trend toward increasingly different local tool types (flakes, knives, scrapers, and so forth) accelerated as population increased and homelands shrank after the San Jose period ended in about 2500 B.C.[30]

A period of essentially modern climatic conditions followed the San Jose period. By this time, stone tool varieties had become so localized that virtually every distinctive set of tools goes by a different name. No longer did hunters employ a single, widespread style of dart tip. The world was much fuller, too, than it had once been. This is obvious from the repeated use of sites such as Armijo rock shelter, located in a remote part of the Rio Puerco Valley northwest of Albuquerque.[31] Population had grown again until nearly every choice campsite and rock overhang was put to use. With greater population density came restricted freedom of movement. Families could no longer forage over such large territories, and so they began to harvest plants regularly in areas of high plant diversity. Archaeologists find many specialized plant-processing sites littered with early grinding tools called *one-hand manos,* which were used to break up seeds. Often these sites lie in stabilized sand dunes where stands of Indian rice grass or blazing star could have been harvested in great quantities. Many more one-hand manos are found in these sites than in sites dating to the earlier Archaic.

In the mountainous areas surrounding the San Juan basin (the Chuska, Lukachukai, and Zuni mountains, Cebolleta Mesa, the Jemez Caldera, Bluebird Mesa, and the Mesa Verde country to the north), extensive stands of stunted mountain oak were, and are, a notable feature of upland vegetation. Gambel oak and other, closely related varieties succeed old-growth trees after forest fires and, once established, produce a remarkable abundance of acorns. At such localities, archaeologists sometimes find dozens of one-hand manos in places where large boulders sit adjacent to areas where acorns were once harvested. Late Archaic piñon and acorn collectors used these boulders as convenient grinding platforms (like a pestle, or *metate*), leaving dozens of depressions ground into the native rock. Sometimes one even finds the fist-sized manos in place, just as they were left three or four millennia ago. Complex food-processing technologies that were first developed during the harsh times of the Altithermal were refined and applied to new plant species yet again in order to sustain a denser regional population — one that depended heavily on a combination of plant foods and small game, from rabbits, prairie dogs, and other rodents to turtles and birds.

By the end of Armijo rock shelter's chief period of use (sometime after 2000 B.C.),[32] some localities in the region must have had population densities approaching one person per square mile. The "quality-of-life" gains first obtained after the Altithermal, with its shift to a more vegetarian diet, were undoubtedly deteriorating. By now, foraging territories had probably become quite restricted, thwarting the age-old hunter-and-gatherer tendency simply to walk away from local resource problems. The nutritional inventory of known plant species was being fully exploited. Fragments of yucca-fiber sandals, small woven or plaited goods, and wooden implements from dry rock shelters tell us that people were already adopting necessary alternatives to hide and bone. The body of technological and ecological knowledge shared by these late Archaic people was being tested.

Past and Present: Growth or Efficiency

By roughly 2000 B.C. the desert Archaic adaptation to local climate and geography, now more than 3,000 years in the making, was nearly used up. Population had been increasing in fits and starts for nearly 4,000 years. Far more energy than ever before was fixed in the living bodies of this larger population. Harvesting plant resources actually requires more labor per calorie gained than does big game hunting, so it took more labor and food to sustain this economy. In other words, these late Archaic people were not quite so efficient as their Paleo-Indian forebears had been. They had grown in numbers, and tensions calling for yet another cultural transformation were rising rapidly. Something had to give.

Though the late Archaic population had grown very slowly by our standards, more total food and *work* were required each century to sustain even that slow population growth. As their population grew, people inadvertently became ever hungrier for both food energy and the labor necessary to supply it. However modest, this was a shift away from the steady state of a highly efficient society. Indeed, it was a detectable shift toward a growth, or power-driven, economy.

Growth models, albeit on a much grander scale, are familiar to all of us in contemporary society. Much of modern Western economic theory is based on the unabashed growth models formulated by John Maynard Keynes.[33] We rarely even question the underlying meanings of growth and progress in contemporary society. One never hears a presidential candidate in any nation promising a more efficient society. Whether candidates represent developed, developing, or Third

World countries, they all promise to "grow this economy" and carry their nation to "a new level." In short, they promise power, not efficiency. But once on the growth treadmill, getting off is treacherous. When modern economies do not grow, people lose jobs, the quality of life ebbs, and opportunities for the future fade. When developing economies do not grow, governments topple or conflicts break out. When Third World economies do not grow, famine, disease, and death ensue.

By shortly after 2000 B.C., late Desert Archaic people, among them the ancestors of our Anasazi, were on the horns of an epic evolutionary dilemma—shrink and return to efficiency, or find new ways to sustain growth. Then providence intervened.

Photo 1. Canyon del Muerto in far northeastern Arizona, where sites of the Basketmakers, direct ancestors of the Chaco Anasazi, were first identified in the late 1800s by cowboy ruin hunter Richard Wetherill. (Courtesy National Park Service, Chaco Culture National Historical Park [NPS].)

Photo 2.   Aerial view of the seasonal Chaco River near the great house called
Kin Bineola ("whirlwind house" in Navajo). After emerging from higher
canyon country such as Canyon del Muerto during the A.D. 700s-800s, the
Anasazi farmed these lower, drier elevations where water was available.
(Courtesy NPS.)

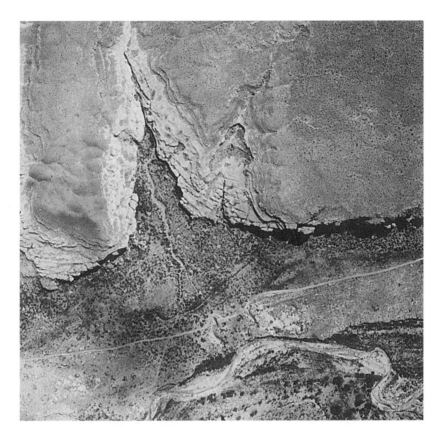

Photo 3.   Aerial view of the Chaco River (bottom) near the great house
called Peñasco Blanco at the rugged west end of Chaco Canyon. Anasazi
farmsteads dotted the canyon's south rim (top, center), where seasonal rains
created arroyos (center) and nourished sandy fields below the cliffs.
(Courtesy NPS.)

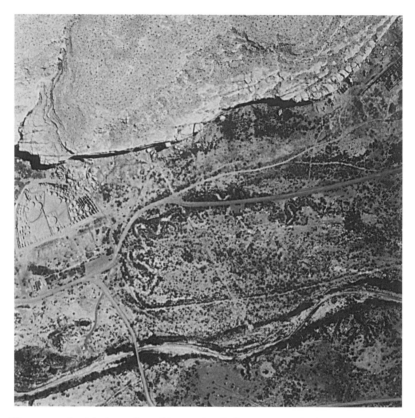

Photo 4.   Aerial view of Pueblo Bonito (left center) and Chetro Ketl (upper right) in central Chaco Canyon. These great houses of the tenth and eleventh centuries were all built on the north side of the seasonal Chaco River (near bottom), so that they faced south. The roads (right center) are modern. (Courtesy NPS.)

Photo 5 (*opposite*).   Aerial view of the huge kiva Casa Rinconada (right center) and partially excavated nearby farmsteads along Chaco Canyon's south rim, where another arroyo permitted farming. Pueblo Bonito lies just out of view (north) at bottom right. Closeups of several of these farmsteads follow. (Courtesy NPS.)

Photo 6.   A small farmstead on the south side of Chaco Canyon, excavated by the University of New Mexico archaeological field school in the 1930s. Three square masonry rooms are visible. Other rooms have eroded. (Courtesy NPS.)

Photo 7 *(center)*.   A medium-size farmstead of about 10 exposed rooms (center) and a possible pit house to the right of the simple masonry house block. A University of New Mexico flat-bed truck is in foreground (1930s). View to the north toward the Chaco River. (Courtesy NPS.)

Photo 8 *(far right)*.   A larger farmstead containing some 14 exposed, square rooms arranged in the shallow arc typical of Pueblo I sites. The circular structure (left center) is a pit house later renovated into a kiva. The dark scars (lower center) are archaeologists' trenches dug to determine the site's full dimensions. (Courtesy NPS.)

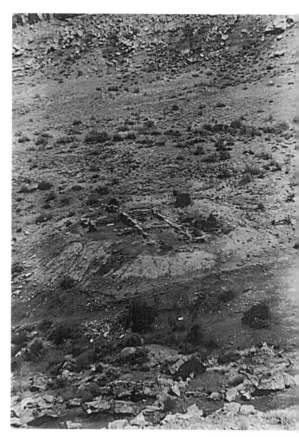

Photo 9. Views of BC58 (foreground) and BC57, two medium-size farmsteads of the A.D. 1000s, looking north (top) toward the canyon wall and great houses across the Chaco River (denser vegetation near top). Notice the square rooms and circular kiva in the right foreground. NPS archaeologists estimate that would have taken a skilled person 10 months of 12-hour days to construct it. (Courtesy NPS.)

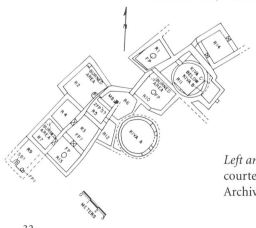

Left and opposite: Site diagrams courtesy of NPS Chaco Center Archives #692.

Photo 10.   Close-up view (looking west) of BC57 (also known as 29SJ397). This farmstead contained nine masonry rooms, two pit structures (left and bottom center of houseblock), and two circular kivas (bottom left and far right) added about A.D. 1120 as social conditions in Chaco Canyon deteriorated. Multiple construction and renovations at farmsteads were common. (Courtesy NPS.)

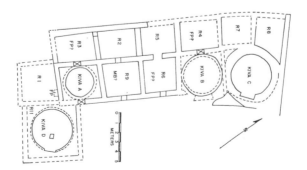

CHAPTER THREE

The Role of Agriculture

P

ROVIDENCE, ALBEIT MODEST, CAME IN TWO FORMS, ONE FROM THE HEAVENS
and one from neighbors to the south. First, the weather got wetter. Greater precipitation generally characterized the period from about 2000 B.C. to 500 B.C.[1] This
reduced some of the pressure on wild plant foods. Second, corn was introduced
from Mexico. It was to have only a modest impact at first, but later the entire rise
of the Chaco Anasazi would come to depend on it.

The exact date by which domesticated corn reached the Four Corners remains
in dispute. From excavations at Bat Cave in west-central New Mexico, we know
that a small-cobbed popcorn, called *chapalote,* was being cultivated there by approximately 1500 B.C. Bat Cave, first excavated by Herbert Dick in the late 1940s and
restudied more recently by a team from the University of Michigan, lies at the base
of a great rock overhang that stands guard over the southern margin of the Plains
of San Augustin in Catron County.[2] The floor of the plain was still an immense lake
when Paleo-Indian people first foraged the area, but it dried out as the late Ice Age
ended. Since it was under water in early times, no Clovis or Folsom artifacts are
to be found there. The cave, however, provides a nearly uninterrupted archaeological record from late Paleo-Indian to Puebloan times—a span of at least 6,000 years.
As a consequence, archaeologists consider it one of the most important sites in the
Americas.

Bat Cave, only a hard three-day walk south of the San Juan basin, tells us fascinating things about the introduction of domesticated food crops into New Mexico. The earliest corn was small, producing very little food energy per cob, but it
probably was drought and cold resistant. Because Bat Cave lies at an elevation of
6,800 feet,[3] small-cobbed corn was once argued to have come to the cooler uplands
of the Four Corners from the uplands and sierra of northern Mexico. It supple-

mented but did not immediately replace the traditional foraging and hunting economy.[4] By 1500 B.C. to 1000 B.C., however, several types of corn were being planted in mountains, uplands, and valleys scattered across the broader Southwest.[5] Squash came at the same time. Given the variety of garden settings and the several different food crops, multiple routes of introduction are likely.[6]

Late Archaic foragers in and around the San Juan basin planted small plots of *chapalote* and similar varieties of corn in the spring, apparently tended them intermittently, and then returned in the fall, adding the modest harvest to their food supply. Population continued to grow, but few dramatic changes took place. The appearance of corn long before villages were established means there really was no "agricultural revolution" as archaeologists once believed. For this reason the period from about 1500 B.C. to just after A.D. 1 has been called the En Medio period (Spanish for "in between"), in reference to a daily economy that was no longer pure hunter and gatherer and not yet truly horticultural.[7]

Why was there no rapid and widespread change to settled villages shortly after corn was first introduced? One reason was probably that precipitation and temperature from about 2000 B.C. to approximately 500 B.C. were somewhat kinder than they are now. The favorable climate somewhat muted the urgency of even greater dependency on horticulture. Moreover, stored corn probably helped sustain people through the winter, somewhat blunting the hunter-and-gatherer tendencies toward conflict and restricted population growth when food is scarce. Thus, the introduction of small-cobbed corn alone reinforced the general mode of change that was already going on in the late Archaic: more labor invested in a daily economy heavily reliant on plants, fewer sexual and reproductive restrictions, and modest increases in the efficiency of grinding and harvesting tools. In short, the introduction of corn and modestly improved climactic circumstances helped to stave off a regional crisis that could easily have resulted from population growth during the late Archaic.

That crisis—if triggered—could have set age-old cycles of conflict, wife-raiding, and abortion or infanticide into full motion.[8] The result would have been a late Archaic society that was forced back into classic hunter-gatherer behavior. There is evidence that episodes of conflict did break out during the end of this time period,[9] but none was profound enough or protracted enough to halt the overall move toward continued planting and harvesting. A few scattered brush houses and shallow pit dwellings have also been found, suggesting decreased mobility and higher population levels than in earlier Archaic times.[10]

Even though corn was a factor in the region's population growth, had regional population declined dramatically in the first few centuries after the introduction of corn, the survivors probably would have taken little further interest in the crop and avoided the extra labor required to plant, tend, and harvest it. There simply would have been no continuing advantage to using it under conditions of low population density and larger available foraging territories. In short, had climatic providence not been kind enough to prevent a regional famine, the San Juan basin could easily have become once again more determinedly traditional.

Instead, the introduction of corn led to an evolutionary holding action—albeit a tense one—by providing time for a steadily growing population to carefully explore the techniques and limitations of agriculture. Gathering knowledge and experience in order to perfect another economic option without assuming huge new risks can create an enormous long-term opportunity. The late Archaic people who benefited from this opportunity to perfect agricultural techniques were the ones who ultimately became Anasazi farmers. That transformation took less than another millennium of tinkering with agricultural strategies and one additional domesticated plant from Mexico—beans (*Phaseolus* species),[11] ancestral to today's pinto and related varieties.

Beans are harder to detect in the archaeological record than are corn and squash. Occasionally, we find the telltale skins of beans in ancient human feces, called coprolites. At other times, a few preserved beans may be found during excavations at an ancient dry cave site. In any case, most scholars agree that beans came to the Southwest by about 500 B.C.[12] Their addition was critical. Corn alone is a costly food to metabolize. Its proteins are incomplete and hard to synthesize. Beans contain large amounts of lysine, the amino acid missing from corn and squash.[13] In reasonable balance, corn, beans, and squash together provide complementary amino acids and form the basis of a nearly complete diet.[14] This diet lacks only the salt, fat, and mineral nutrients found in most meats to be healthy and complete.

By 500 B.C., nearly all the elements for accelerating cultural and economic changes were finally in place—a fairly complete diet that could, if rainfall cooperated, largely replace the traditional foraging one; several additional, modestly larger-cobbed varieties of corn that not only prospered under varying growing conditions but also provided a bigger harvest; a population large enough to invest the labor necessary to plant and harvest; nearly 10 centuries of increasing familiarity with cultigens; and enhanced food-processing and storage techniques. Lacking were compelling reasons to transform an Archaic society accustomed to earning a living with approximately 500 hours of labor a year into one willing to invest the 1,000 to 2,000 hours common to contemporary hand-tool horticulturalists.[15]

Nature then stepped in with one persuasive, if not compelling, reason for people to make the shift. Beginning around 500 B.C., episodes of dramatically unstable precipitation repeatedly put excruciating food pressures on the inhabitants of the San Juan basin. Casual, supplemental harvesting of domesticated crops, even teamed with small-scale food storage, simply was insufficient to see people through these recurring dry spells. Previously, the varieties of corn in use had been morphologically fairly consistent from place to place.[16] So far as archaeologists can tell, Archaic people had made no concerted effort to increase cob size and yield or to tinker with the genetic attributes of corn. When the droughts came, this changed.

Prodded by climatic circumstances, late Archaic people responded. Larger-cobbed, genetically different types of corn spread more widely, and additional varieties of squash and beans were introduced during the last several centuries B.C. Campsites became even larger, and some of them became somewhat more permanent, judging from the increased numbers of small pit dwellings in the uplands and well-floored brush shelters constructed in the valleys and basins. In these camp-sites people dug more and larger bell-shaped storage pits in which to store their harvests for times of need.

Precipitation and, perhaps more importantly, water tables did not generally rise again until just before A.D. 1.[17] Higher water tables meant that beginning around that time, streams, sinks, and springs became more plentiful. Groundwater was near enough to the surface in intermittent streambeds to support small-scale agriculture in more lower-elevation settings than previously. Small-scale agriculture, though more work, was an enormous advantage in the environment of the Four Corners.

The region is characterized by many species of edible wild plants. Some, such as piñon nuts, are high in calories and even fat. But the Southwest's semiarid, highly variable climate creates what ecologists call a "patchy" environment. Stands of desirable plants usually are small and scattered, forcing gatherers to keep on the move. Creating a garden plot with even 50 corn stalks, especially where squash and beans could be mixed in, created a more dependable supply of food *in one place*. This must have been quite seductive to people who frequently went hungry for short periods.[18]

In the first several centuries A.D., Southwestern foragers and farmers in a few localities began to farm more intensively. This made their food supplies more reliable, and so they stored more of it. As a consequence, we now find more scattered pit houses in those areas, and even some settlements of three to five dwellings. The bow and arrow had arrived and enhanced hunting capabilities,[19] but pottery had not yet come to the Four Corners. Clearly, not all hunter-and-gatherer bands adopted agriculture. In some areas, it wasn't productive. In others, those who pursued agriculture and stayed closer to their small farm plots during the fall harvesting season did not compete for the same wild resources, which made it easier for others to go on hunting and gathering just as they had always done.[20]

Archaeologists have long argued over these dynamics. One camp argues that people adopted agriculture because it was a benefit.[21] Others assertively maintain that it was adopted out of necessity.[22] I think both sides have failed to recognize that what was a benefit for some was a necessity for others in the same social group.

In the first several centuries A.D., economic behavior began to vary more dramatically from family to family than at any time before.

Some families drifted back toward more traditional hunting and gathering as their neighbors learned how to squeeze more food from less space through small-scale agriculture. That space was precious to those hunters who preferred the old ways. These families worked fewer hours, were more mobile, and had fewer children. Since they tended to hunt more—a high-status activity in virtually every traditional society—perhaps they enjoyed somewhat more prestige as well.

In contrast, families who farmed worked more, probably had lower status, were less mobile during planting and harvesting times, and, because they moved around less and their food supply was more reliable, had more children. These people became our Anasazi farmers during this time, while their hunter-and-gatherer cousins gradually faded into the past. Because the early farmers produced more children, they left more descendants. In the next five centuries, the hunters and gatherers were generally swallowed up or absorbed by the burgeoning agricultural population.

There are always ironies in these transformations. The more traditional foragers benefited most at the outset. They had a bit easier time of it, so they clung to traditional ways in order to pass them on to their children and children's children. It worked for a time. Then those who, of necessity, needed to work harder continued to experiment with farming and had more children. In the process of merely securing daily sustenance for their growing families, they inadvertently created a new world in which traditional foragers became seriously outnumbered.

Basketmaker:
The Transformation to Small Villages

That new world was based on more work, more stored food, an increasing birth rate, greater sedentariness, and accelerated changes in technology. Archaeologists refer to this new world as that of the "Basketmakers," a name coined by cowboy artifact hunter Richard Wetherill in the late 1880s from finds made in caves and overhangs in Grand Gulch, Utah.[23] There he found small settlements, storage caches, and burials tucked into the cliff faces. Dry and protected from the rain, many of these sites were remarkably well preserved. Huge quantities of beautifully woven baskets, bags, sandals, and cordage were found, but no pottery—hence, "Basketmaker." Depending on the place and the characteristics of the artifacts found, archaeologists have assigned many different labels, usually in the form of one or another "phases," to the Basketmakers' myriad local variations. Overall, it was an age of great experimentation. If we keep that in mind, we can simply refer to the early Basketmaker period (approximately A.D. 1-400) and the late Basketmaker period (approximately A.D. 400-750).

The early Basketmaker period was characterized by a noticeable degree of cultural and economic experimentation. On one hand, foraging and hunting continued to dominate in some seasons and locales. On the other, small-scale agriculture rapidly became more important—and more efficient, in the sense that output per unit of work rose. As a consequence, it began to support small settlements of two to five dwellings each. These have been found in the Navajo Reservoir district,[24] in the Nambe Falls area,[25] and on Albuquerque's west mesa.[26] All of these places are in upland margins surrounding the San Juan basin.

While a few scattered brush houses and shallow pit structures are known from the late Archaic, these newer sites were larger and more complex and their architecture more formalized. At Valentine village in the Navajo Reservoir district,[27] archaeologists found roughly a half dozen very early pit houses. They were circular in plan, and several also had a circular antechamber, forming a rough figure eight. Floor areas averaged about 300 to 400 square feet (or 30 to 40 square meters), and the dwellings were scooped out of sand or clay soils to a depth of about one-half meter.

One variety of these shallow dugout houses at Valentine village was carefully ringed with an apron of fist-sized to football-sized stream cobbles from the adjacent Pine River. The interiors were built up of cribbed logs that were plastered with mud on the inside. Floors were typically of semipolished clay. A number of storage areas were found—some were simple subfloor pits, but others were built up of coiled clay and resembled domelike beehives. Most of these houses also contained hearths or fire pits.

The second variety of shallow dugout house at Valentine village was less elaborate and had no apron of cobbles but was inhabited at the same time as the others. Such settlements were obviously still in an experimental phase. Fully standardized architecture and building techniques had not yet become the tradition. No pottery is found at these early pit houses, so archaeologists infer that stone boiling must have continued. Indeed, substantial quantities of fire-cracked and fire-reddened rock are present. These people had corn, beans, and squash, which they stored, but cooking techniques had made no major technological breakthrough since the Jay period—a span of some 5,000 years.

In contrast, hunting technology began to change dramatically. Because arrowheads, but not the earlier dart points, appear at Valentine and nearby Albino village, we can say that the bow and arrow reached the Four Corners from the northern Great Plains sometime between and A.D. 1 and 300. That was not true everywhere at this time. Less than 200 miles south, on Albuquerque's west mesa, Rio Rancho-phase sites of the same age had dart points and no arrowheads.[28] It must have been a bit like American life in 1910, when horse-drawn buggies and early automobiles first passed one another on country roads.

Even though these early Basketmaker pit-house settlements varied enormously in architecture and tool kits, they had some characteristics in common. Upland elevations overlooking lower ground and places near streams and intermittent washes were locations of choice. This makes sense if these settlers were farming corn in the small areas of richer soil and in the sandy washes nearby. Microscopic analysis of soil samples from such sites frequently reveals the presence of corn pollen. At virtually all sites, people continued to dig storage pits into open areas near their settlements—an echo of Archaic times. Gradually, however, the number and volume of storage areas inside the pit houses increased markedly. Were these folks becoming more protective of their surpluses? It seems so.

Major changes in the kinds of tools also tell a story. The earliest of Basketmaker dwellings contain a mix of basin metates and one-hand manos that look like elongated mortars and pestles. Slightly later dwellings tend to have more two-hand manos and trough metates with far larger grinding surfaces. Coarse choppers were slowly replaced by more elaborate stone axes, which were needed to cut pit-house timbers.

Burials are rarely unearthed in these pit houses, but some have been discovered a short distance away. At one, a burial in the Navajo Reservoir district, a middle-aged man had been carefully interred with a modest offering of polished stone flakes, then covered with clay before a cobble cairn was erected over him.[29] The later Anasazi practice of burying the dead in kitchen middens and in abandoned rooms among still-inhabited dwellings had not yet taken hold. This is perhaps not surprising, for hunters and gatherers the world over tend to avoid places of the dead. These burial data suggest that at least some groups of early Basketmakers still had a hunter-and-gatherer mindset even though they were experimenting heavily with an agricultural economy. Such clues also suggest that this period was one of more rapid transformation in economy and technology than in social behavior.

In contrast to the pit-house hamlets, there are many other, contemporaneous Basketmaker sites, typically in lower sand dune areas, that served as huge gathering and seed-processing camps. A few of these may have had shedlike brush-and-pole shelters, called *ramadas*, but no real pit houses. At such sites, dozens to hundreds of one-hand manos, small basin metates, and cooking stones are found. The last were used as griddles on which to parch grass and other plant seeds. Large numbers of bell-shaped storage pits were often dug nearby. Clearly, in the first three centuries of the common era, early farmers were settling down in pit houses only seasonally—probably during late fall and winter. During the spring and summer collecting seasons they acted more like traditional foragers in lower elevations.

In sum, agriculture was increasing in importance. Several larger-cobbed (but still not large-cobbed) varieties of corn supplemented chapalote, and beans and squash were frequently grown, too. Experimental pit-house villages appear to have been inhabited only seasonally but had increasingly extensive and elaborate storage facilities. Bows and arrows were beginning to replace the atlatl, and corn-grinding implements were refined to create larger and more efficient grinding surfaces. Changes in burial practices and other social behaviors lagged behind the more rapid changes in daily economy and technology. Growth was accomplished through numerous, clever, incremental efficiencies.

The Later Basketmakers: Potters and Farmers

Pottery first came to the Four Corners between A.D. 300 and 400.[30] The earliest kind is called Sambrito Brownware. Named for an archaeological site in southern Colorado, these thick, brown bowls and water jars were made locally. The knowledge to produce pottery was introduced from the south, where villagers in the Mogollon Mountains apparently had learned how to manufacture it several centuries earlier from agriculturists in what is now northern Mexico. Though pottery did not immediately replace basketry and woven goods, it really did make a difference—it dramatically revolutionized cooking.

Now, porridge and stews could be put to boil in a pot set directly into a central fire pit. The amount of heat lost and fuel used in the old cooking process—an endless cycle of collecting, heating, transferring, removing, and replacing hot stones just to boil a few quarts of water—had always been enormous. By comparison, cooking with pots became quick, easy, and far more efficient. In a world more densely populated, firewood had to be gathered from greater distances. Now, less of it was needed. And there was a newer fuel to supplement it—dried corncobs.

As corn grew in cob size after A.D. 400 and even more new varieties were bred or introduced, upland pit houses became both deeper and more standardized. Many sheaves of corn, dried on the cob, were undoubtedly hung in the rafters of these more complex pit structures. The corners of these dwellings were typically rounded and walled off to create good-sized storage niches adjacent to the entry.[31]

Through the harvest season, people ate corn fresh-roasted. Quantities of it were dried and hung. In winter, the dried kernels were stripped from the cob—which then became fuel—and were ground into meal on open-ended metates with even larger grinding surfaces than those on earlier Basketmaker ones. By spring, often only the most carefully selected kernels of seed corn would be left over. It was needed to plant anew.

Beans, squash, wild plants (yucca, prickly pear, acorns, piñon nuts), rabbits, rodents, and an occasional deer or elk rounded out the usual fare. At all times, wild plants and animals made up a large and regular part of the diet. Turkeys, domesticated by the Mogollon villagers three or four days' walk to the south,[32] were kept in pens either inside or adjacent to the pit houses. The turkeys were efficient, too, foraging on stubble in the harvested garden plots. Valuable for their feathers and eggs, they were rarely eaten. Artisans used their feathers, along with yucca fibers and strips of rabbit fur, to make open-weave "thermal blankets" — an extraordinarily clever blending of plant and animal by-products. These blankets were a comfort during the cold winters of the Four Corners. Similar blankets continued to be used by the Basketmakers, by the Chaco Anasazi descended from them, and by their Pueblo descendants in turn for another 1,500 years — right into the 1800s. An example can be seen today at the little museum adjacent to the great ruin of Guisewa at Jemez Pueblo.

There were other important changes. The number of pit houses in settlements increased while their size decreased. Most archaeologists consider this a clue to the accelerating formation of young, nuclear families rather than the larger extended families thought to have been housed in the earlier, larger pit houses. The later pit houses were often oval, then D-shaped or rectangular. As the next few centuries piled up, pit houses became far more standardized in size, construction techniques, and interior layout. By the A.D. 600 and 700s, they had finally become "traditional."

At a number of late Basketmaker villages, as many as 10 to 20 pit houses might be found. The largest settlements still lay in the uplands, where families not only stayed longer but also returned to harvest year after year. In the slightly lower, more open basins, too, the number of pit-house hamlets increased in the 600 and 700s — a good example is Shabik'eshee village in Chaco Canyon. But fewer of these appear to have had quite the same permanence as the larger upland settlements.[33] This increase in the number of open basin pit-house sites is a good indicator of continued population growth.

As the year 800 approached, people simply had fewer opportunities to return to foraging, so they settled in. At both upland and basin settlements, a new type of building emerged — the community house. These were typically two or three times larger than the average pit house, more carefully and lavishly constructed, and nearly always encircled by a bench, or *banco* in local usage, along the wall. Most had stylized fire pits and a stone or adobe wind deflector between the fire pit and the drafty antechamber. Some also had a "foot drum" hollowed out of the clay floor and planked over to create a sounding board. Dancers' footsteps created a rhythmic, pounding beat for chants and rituals.

Some archaeologists emphasize that community organization, as evidenced by the community house, grew more elaborate as families became smaller and more numerous. New forms of social "glue" were being developed to hold the community together. Other archaeologists point out that these large pit structures were the earliest form of *kiva,* the sacred, subterranean religious houses later used by the Chaco Anasazi and still in use in each of today's Pueblo villages. Whether formal religion or formal social organization was becoming more complex is moot. As villages grew and became somewhat more settled, people's social and religious imaginations combined to lend more complexity and texture to daily life.

By these late Basketmaker times (roughly A.D. 600-750), there are other indications that ideas and religion were changing. Burial places had moved closer to habitations—into the kitchen middens adjacent to houses or into abandoned pit houses and storage pits.[34] More grave offerings accompanied the dead: pottery, shell beads and other ornaments, or, less commonly, a few everyday implements. The grave items most often included pottery bowls or ollas (large jars). The fancier bowls were decorated with black-on-white designs, and some of the gray "everyday" jars were now intricately corrugated around their elongated necks.

Clearly, local pottery had become much more elaborate and therefore more costly to make. In some 400 years—less time than it had once taken to generate a single detectable change in dart tip shape or flaking technique during the Paleo-Indian period—dozens of new pottery shapes and decorative styles had been created. Finely made and decorated bowls changed more rapidly than did the gray utility wares. Time had speeded up for the Basketmaker Anasazi. In pottery manufacture, "doing things as they had always been done" now meant as they had been done for 50 or 100 years, not 500 or even 5,000.

Late Basketmaker villagers were not nearly so isolated from broader communities in the greater Southwest as Archaic and Paleo-Indian people had once been. Archaeologists have always been impressed that some of New Mexico's Paleo-Indian hunting bands trekked as far as west Texas, 200 to 300 miles away, to get the prized Alibates flint they used in lance points. Even more impressively, some late Basketmaker graves contain beads and ornaments made of shell from the Gulf of California and from the Gulf coast of Texas. These prized commodities had been traded into the Four Corners from a distance of some 750 miles in either direction.

Decorated bowls also began to travel over longer distances. The late Basketmakers traded some pottery with Hohokam people of central and southern Arizona. Trade in pottery also connected them to Mogollon villagers in southern New Mexico. Since the bowls made in one place were just as functional as those made in another, much of this trade had to have been based in desire for another's designs, rather than in basic necessity. Acquiring items for their own sake, though not exclusive to expanding societies, is certainly one hallmark of those who can "afford" some niceties. Mind you, these niceties were still few and far between. That, too, would change in the next few centuries.

The bones of these Basketmakers tell us other things. Daily life remained hard. Most people died in their twenties, thirties, or forties; few lived into their fifties or sixties. They all knew hard work. When strenuous, repetitive work is prolonged over a span of years, muscle insertions (the points where the muscles are attached to the supporting bone) become stressed enough to groove the bone deeply at the site of attachment. Most adult skeletons of the period show this evidence of overwork from long periods spent stooping over a stone hoe while tending garden plots (in the case of men) or grinding corn for countless hours while kneeling (in the case of women). Manos and metates had become far more efficient, but by contemporary standards, grinding corn and farming were grueling work.

Occasionally, later Basketmaker pit houses contained several mealing bins—stone catchments for cornmeal—set in a row. Manos and metates were placed inside these bins, and several women in the family could keep each other company as they worked. Grinding dried corn into meal on sandstone implements created another medical problem sometimes seen in skeletons—sandstone grit got mixed in with the cornmeal and ground healthy teeth down until truly appalling dental abscesses and jaw infections resulted. This was one price of a diet rich in ground corn. Another price was paid as the incidence of osteoporosis increased.[35]

Osteoporosis, rare among hunters and gatherers and still uncommon at A.D. 700, is a disease of the bone we associate with old age. It is commonly called "widow's disease," but it affects millions of modern American men and women, especially young female athletes. Genetics, diet, and intense physical activity may all play a role in its etiology. However, osteoporosis often develops when there is insufficient calcium in the diet. It can also be induced when people rely heavily on food such as corn, without getting enough complementary amino acids from other plants or meat. In such cases, the disease can begin as early as the late teens to twenties. The body, in its attempt to fully metabolize the nutrients in corn, actually draws essential calcium from the bones to get the job done. This leaves the bones brittle, weakened, and porous.

A few late Basketmaker burials show the extreme of this condition—skulls that are porous and eroded because calcium was shunted away for metabolic purposes.[36] This malnutrition also invited life-threatening infections, but more commonly at this time, local dietary imbalances simply made bones abnormally brittle. Once broken in falls or suffering stress fractures from heavy work, such bones did not heal perfectly. By the A.D. 700s, maladies typical of small-scale agriculturists were beginning to appear.

Still, there had been much change and progress. Axes were now more finely made and hafted, making timber cutting easier. The large two-hand manos and trough metates served as far more effective grinding tools than had the earlier basin metates and one-hand manos. People still made baskets, but these had become less elaborate as pottery replaced them for cooking and storage. Farm implements improved. In some locales the fire-hardened planting stick lengthened, reducing farmers' need to stoop. This tool was used to punch a hole in the soil so that a half dozen corn kernels could be inserted, in the hope that at least one in each hole would germinate. Composite stone and wood hoes began to replace simple wooden scoops, and small rows of cobbles were set where they might slow summer rainfall as it ran down washes and arroyos. This kept the thin soil from eroding, and the slowed water soaked the soil more deeply. Large ollas made it easier to carry water to the fields—hand watering was necessary during frequent dry spells.

Most families continued to rely on a mix of agriculture and some hunting and foraging. Several varieties of corn were available, each prospering under slightly different conditions. One variety, Pima-Papago, could be planted deep to make good use of soils moistened by winter snows.[37] But agriculture was a risky proposition in the uplands and canyons of northwestern New Mexico. Precipitation was "winter dominant" at this time, falling mostly in the form of snow. This meant that the corn crop often got off to a decent start in the spring, only to fail when summer rains did not come. Growing seasons were short in the uplands, where cool nighttime temperatures and last freeze dates in May are common now and likely were then. These risks made the combination of foraging and agriculture a happy marriage, so long as enough space was available to do both. Yet the poor nutrition evidenced by occasional cases of osteoporosis tells us that space was getting scarcer as the 700s progressed.

The marriage of foraging and agriculture also made the uplands prime territory for founding villages. By locating their pit houses on upland promontories where one or two watercourses joined, Anasazi villagers could exploit small areas of alluvial soils below their site and also have access to the forested mesas above them for hunting and plant foraging. Places where watercourses joined were also typically areas where great diversity in plant and animal life prevailed. Such locations are often on *ecotones,* an ecological term that connotes the border where two distinct plant communities abut. Many of the upland Basketmaker villages were situated where stands of both piñon and ponderosa grew nearby. The ponderosa made good roof timbers, and the piñon produced huge quantities of nutritious pine nuts when rainfall and temperature conditions were just right.

It was a system more than adequate to support growth—in quantities of corn harvested and then stored, in numbers of settlements founded, and in population sustained. As the population grew, favored upland localities filled up. Of necessity, more people moved into lower, basin elevations, building pit-house dwellings that dated not much earlier than A.D. 600 or 700. Some of these later villages were good-sized, but they were still more likely to be inhabited seasonally than year-round.

Just how much did the number of Basketmaker settlements grow in the span of five centuries? Ninefold! In 1980, participants in a symposium at the School of American Research, an anthropology think-tank in Santa Fe, compiled a list of all known sites ever recorded by archaeologists in the San Juan basin.[38] At that time, there were 102 recorded early Basketmaker sites and 934 later Basketmaker ones.[39]

And what did the Basketmaker Anasazi learn in the course of these five centuries? First, they learned that incremental efficiencies coupled with more work allowed them to support growing communities. Such increases in efficiency are evident in the size of corn, in the surface areas of grinding implements, and in changes in axe design. Second, they learned that pottery reduced the quantity of cooking fuel needed and greatly enhanced the security of stored grains from invading rats and mice, so they adopted and then elaborated it. Third, they adopted the bow and arrow, particularly since it was efficient and easy to master in comparison with the atlatl. This was important for men who spent more time in the fields and whose hunting skills had suffered. Fourth, some experimental farming techniques worked better than others; these were pursued. Fifth, new ways of doing things—building pit houses and burying the dead, for example—that initially had been experimental later became traditional. Precise styles of burial or building became more standardized as the centuries rolled on. And finally, the Anasazi learned that the world was larger and fuller than their ancestors had ever imagined and that connections with other agricultural communities were both exciting and of great practical value. Trade increased significantly, both in quantity and in geographic reach. During poor crop years, people in afflicted villages probably made many lovely bowls and traded them for seed corn to neighboring communities where summer rains had blessed the tasseling cornfields.

It must have been an exciting time. In only some 25 generations, these folks had transformed themselves from foragers and hunters with a small economic sideline in corn, beans, and squash into semisedentary villagers who farmed and kept up their foraging to fill in the economic gaps. The winter pit-house settlement, rather than a foraging territory, came to be home. Families spent much less time on trek and more in fully exploiting the potential of just a few localities. The increased number of burials found in the settlements lends credit to the claim that these were home places. If hunters and gatherers in the past typically avoided places of the dead as they have in historic times, then these burials imply that the Anasazi were emphasizing their differences from remaining hunters and gatherers while also making their new settlements uncomfortable for those "outsiders" to enter.

Communities also expanded. As the number of pit houses increased at the most favored locations, family size declined, and community social and religious houses—"proto-kivas"—filled new needs. Twenty-five generations before, extended family foraging bands had roamed incessantly, fearing places of the dead. Now, smaller families might roam part of the year but returned regularly to the winter pit-house communities where their dead had been buried. Social and ideological changes accompanied these new developments.

As foragers, the earliest Basketmakers had been obsessed with space in which to wander. Space is the coin of the realm in hunter-and-gatherer society. But later Basketmakers were farmers, and farmers the world over are obsessed with time — the time to plant, the time until the rains come, the time until harvest, the time until stored supplies run dry. "Time, time, time." One can almost hear its urgent rhythms pounded out on the footdrums in community houses of the 700s. Societies that march to the drum of time are very different from those that march into vast, nearly empty space under an endless turquoise sky.

Past and Present

More change took place in the 500 or 600 years of the Anasazi Basketmaker era than in all of the 10,000 years preceding it. True, the earliest of these people started with a population base small by modern standards. Growth from a small base, when successful, is usually easier and more dramatic than growth from a huge one, as any stock trader who purchases new, small technology companies will tell you.

Bill Gates, founder of Microsoft, parlayed this principle into many-fold gains in growth and wealth for his investors. So did Andy Grove with Intel. From 1988 to 1997, Intel's revenue increased ninefold,[40] and Microsoft's a stunning twentyfold.[41] But 20 years earlier, these corporations had been just dreams and ideas in the minds of visionaries or, if you prefer, eccentrics. What is forgotten is that a significant percentage of all new ventures fail. In ordinary times, no one remembers the failures, but they are legion. In 1995 for example, 168,153 new businesses were launched in the United States, but 71,194 businesses failed — a failure rate of nearly 43 percent.[42] We measure business and housing "starts" as an indicator of a huge national economy's health but take little notice of the failures in times of growth. An immense and powerful economy can both support more experiments and survive more failures than can a small one.

To illustrate this point, consider California, where one business was launched for every 1,350 inhabitants in 1995.[43] In that year, California's ratio of failures to starts was nearly 68 percent. Think of it: 24,091 businesses were founded, but 16,330 failed. In contrast, Mississippi launched only one new business venture per 2,636 inhabitants that year — half of California's rate.[44] But Mississippi's business failures came in at just under 23 percent — 1,024 starts to 230 failures. Putting it another way, California's economy tolerated one business failure per 1,947 inhabitants, whereas Mississippi's tolerated one failure per 11,739 inhabitants.

What is so different between California and Mississippi? Raw size and economic power. California's population was nearly 12 times larger than Mississippi's in 1995 (31.8 million versus 2.7 million),[45] but the relative *power* of its economy, measured as per capita income ($24,091 versus $16,690) multiplied by population,[46] was nearly 18 times greater. In other words, the power of California's economy to reward its workers in dollars was 50 percent greater per hour than that of Mississippi's. Notice that Mississippi's smaller, poorer economy is much more risk-averse than California's larger and more powerful one, but Mississippi's fewer economic experiments are, on average, much more likely to succeed. A fragile economy is no friend to the careless, so people living in one tend to experiment less and to be far more cautious when they do.

Anasazi Basketmakers undoubtedly failed often as they experimented with new crop varieties and agricultural technologies. Possessing a small economy, they paid a dear price for each failure. Early on, with open land still available, failure likely meant a return to hunting and gathering, so they may have experimented more freely then. Later, as the number of pit-house villages grew in the late 700s and unused land became scarcer, failure probably meant episodes of malnutrition and higher infant mortality, and perhaps the need to relocate villages to other areas requiring different agricultural techniques. In protracted sequences of bad years, it probably also meant occasional times of outright starvation for those who risked too much or worked too little. These factors seem to have slowed down the overall rate of growth in late Basketmaker society as A.D. 800 approached.

Still, the ninefold increase in pit-house villages in just half a millennium holds up well against modern comparisons. In 1890, the United States had about 12 million households. A century later, in 1990, there were 94 million households—an eightfold increase.[47] These data sound fairly impressive until one notes that the rate of creation of new households in the United States has slowed perceptibly since the late 1980s.[48] Clearly, we are not continuing to grow at the same rate we did early in the twentieth century. We are slowing down. This is strikingly similar to the Basketmakers' situation in the 700s—their ninefold growth in households was not to be matched for another 200 years.

The growth in numbers of households does not tell us everything; it is just one parallel between modern houses and ancient pit dwellings. The American period of 1890 to 1990 was also one of dramatic changes in economy (from agricultural to industrial), technology, quality of life, religion, and social fabric. I argue that the half millennium from A.D. 200 to 700 was similarly a time of change for the Anasazi—but archaeology provides only hints, not a perfect narrative.

One hint is the decline in the size of the Anasazi pit house over these five centuries, which archaeologists interpret as a shift to smaller, nuclear families. We see the same phenomenon in the American data, too. In 1890, the average American household comprised 4.93 persons, and houses of the 1890s, the Gilded Age, were large by contemporary standards. In eastern cities, many grand houses of this period have since been converted into apartments, even funeral parlors. Why? Because

American households averaged only 2.63 persons in 1990—a nearly 50-percent decrease in household size in one century.[49] I argue that the smaller Anasazi pit houses of A.D. 700 reflect much the same phenomenon.

Not unlike a new high-technology company, Basketmakers experimented, took risks, and grew impressively. Their culture changed dramatically in five centuries. They hit something of a plateau in growth after A.D. 700, and like Microsoft or Intel at times, they needed to reassess and reorganize. Incremental efficiencies provided fewer and fewer avenues to new growth as raw size increased. Every automotive engineer who has spent a lifetime trying to squeeze another mile per gallon from the gasoline engine, a technological legacy of the 1890s, will tell you it is time to find huge new oil fields—or explore new technologies. By A.D. 750 or 800, the far more risk-averse Anasazi were in much the same situation.

CHAPTER FOUR

The Rise of the Chaco Anasazi

A
S POPULATION INCREASED AND VAST OPEN LANDS BECAME SCARCER, the Basketmakers' strategy of combining agriculture with foraging during the off seasons began to lose its edge. Agricultural experiments that had come easily and at little economic risk when fewer people crowded the land now carried the much graver consequence of regional famine. This forced the late Basketmakers to pause and regroup.

As the creation of new settlements slowed and economic risks increased, these hunters and gatherers began to act more conservatively, like Mississippians, and less like Californians. They launched new experiments, but for a time these appear to have been cautious ones. Judging from increased consistency in pit-house architecture (neat storage areas; standardized placement of support posts and hearths), some practices that had begun as experiments now became more rigidly traditional. The number and characteristics of villages built during the Pueblo I period, to which archaeologists usually assign the dates A.D. 700 to 900, are unusually revealing.

An Uneasy Pause: Pueblo I

According to data from a survey made in 1979, between A.D. 700 and 900 the 934 sites known from the Basketmaker period increased only to 1,174 succeeding Pueblo I sites.[1] Had this rate of growth prevailed for the next 200 years, the second half-millennium of Anasazi development would have shown only a doubling in growth, not the ninefold increase of the first 500 years. But the 1979 data also show that by the early 1100s, the San Juan basin held a stunning 3,200 known Anasazi sites.[2] By now, thousands more have been discovered. These numbers tell us that growth slowed down, then sped up again dramatically.

Why? What does this mean? The great evolutionary biologist Stephen Jay Gould has taught the modern world that evolution works in fits and starts—by "punctuated equilibria," in his terms.[3] That appears to be the case here, so let us dissect the dynamics.

Pueblo I sites expanded geographically throughout the Four Corners and seemed to be moving into the uplands. These new communities were strikingly larger than those of the Basketmakers. At Alkali Ridge in southeastern Utah, for example, archaeologists found 130 squarish surface rooms, 16 pit houses, and 2 kivas.[4] Other sites of similar size or even larger have been found in the Navajo Reservoir district,[5] in the Mesa Verde area,[6] and along the eastern face of the Chuska Mountains at Skunk Springs.[7] Across the Four Corners country, Pueblo I settlements of 20 to 30 pit houses—in contrast to the 5 or 10 typical of late Basketmaker villages—became the norm.

Why were these sites so big? Why were people settling in the uplands? Was population again growing rapidly? No, this time the answer probably lies elsewhere. Now people were withdrawing from the lower elevations in order to find moisture. In the late A.D. 700s, climatic conditions were changing—precipitation year-to-year had both declined and become far more erratic.[8] The uplands were attractive because they received more winter snow and summer rain, so people moved uphill, changing the late Basketmaker strategy of hill-country farming and seasonal foraging at lower elevations.

They were also banding together in larger settlements to seek safety. One telltale sign is that along the eastern edge of the San Juan basin, small upland settlements of this period, called the Piedra phase, were often palisaded for defense.[9] The inhabitants of many small Piedra-phase settlements in the Gallina highlands of New Mexico have been found "buried" where they fell as enemies breached the wooden palisades and protective stone walls, then torched the settlement. This suggests that climate changes disrupted food supplies severely enough that nasty conflicts sometimes ensued. An isolated hamlet of perhaps a half dozen pit houses, each guarding modest quantities of stored corn to last the winter, was not a safe place in the mid-to-late-700s. Such settlements, once peaceful, became targets for the desperate. Banding together in larger settlements solved the security problem. Most Pueblo I villages postdating the unfortunate Piedra hamlets sat on easily defended ridges and promontories.

These larger settlements were much more architecturally uniform than earlier ones. Archaeologists have long known that house forms the world over generally evolve from oval to circular to rectangular and then squarish as societies grow and become more complex. Pueblo I pit houses were often roughly rectangular, and for the first time, rooms were built adjacent to them above ground. These Pueblo I changes, then, hint at greater complexity in community organization. Eighty years ago, archaeologists noticed the resemblance of the above-ground rooms to the dwellings of living Pueblo peoples. Concluding that sites from this time period forward were directly connected to modern pueblos, they named the period Pueblo I.

Like the pit houses, the early above-ground rooms were square to rectangular. They typically were constructed in rows, or arcs, two rooms deep. The first above-ground rooms were small and probably used for storage. Such rooms soon became larger and more standardized. Excavation of the front tier of rooms usually reveals fire pits and lots of household artifacts—manos, metates, pottery, bone awls (for weaving baskets and yucca-fiber sandals and mats), digging sticks, throwing sticks, and more—suggesting that these rooms were residences. The small rear rooms rarely had hearths and contained far fewer remains of household objects.[10] This is how we know they were storerooms.

In uncertain times, these communities offered a functional solution. Housing as many as 600 people, they were more easily defended. More labor was available in them to expand and tend garden plots, and storage facilities to secure the harvest expanded exponentially.[11] There was now nearly as much storage space as living room. Much of the harvest could now be stored in large pottery ollas with stone lids, all set in above-ground rooms lined with upright stone slabs along the foundations. This kept occasional roof leakage (a particular problem in winter as snow melted on pit-house roofs) from ruining seed corn, as it might have done when corn was stored in pits below the floors. The new storage method also made it harder for rodents to get at the supplies, particularly when flat sandstone or slate slabs were used to seal the floor. As time went on, stone floors became more common.

The style of wall construction in the surface rooms was often *jacal,* or mud-plastered upright poles, with a roof of saplings over rafters, covered with more clay. The coarse clay for walls usually came from the pit houses excavated in front of these rooms. The surface rooms and the pit houses in front were obviously built at the same time. The combination of mud-plastered, shedlike rooms and pit houses was a logical extension of older settlement patterns. The pit houses had long been winter quarters. Now the summer-season ramadas, once found near the huge seed-collecting sites in the lower dunes, were simply beefed up and built adjacent to the winter pit house in a higher-elevation setting. Yet it was not a perfect solution.

Most of these early Pueblo sites, though large, were occupied for only some 30 to 40 years and then were more or less abandoned.[12] The short growing season in the uplands surely played a part in this pattern. Cool night-time temperatures, long winters, and shorter growing seasons must have combined to make agriculture an unpredictable proposition in many places. A short-term solution to this lack of predictability seems to have been a dramatic surge in trade between communities. Much of that trade was in decorated pottery bowls. About the size and shape of contemporary serving bowls, they became far more common and far more elaborately decorated than pots in earlier Basketmaker times. Although similar black-on-white designs were painted inside the bowls, every locality seemed to specialize in its own minor variations.

Archaeologists are thankful for these variations. They enable us to trace the origins of the pots, and so we know that pottery exchange tended to be not with neighbors close by but with communities farther away, in slightly different ecological settings. The first Anasazi pueblo builders had begun to create the rudimentary equivalent of a "risk pool"—sharing risks of failed harvests with trading partners perceived as more likely to enjoy better rainfall elsewhere. Nowadays, we share risks by joining a credit union, buying mutual funds instead of just one or two stocks, or trying to qualify for the largest health maintenance organization we can. The times are different and the commodities traded have changed (dollars for labor instead of corn for bowls), but the principle is precisely the same.

Not surprisingly, the late eighth century was also a time of experimentation with new types of corn and cross-bred variants. Farmers needed to increase cob size, build in drought resistance, and produce crops in a relatively short growing season. A number of paleoclimatologists believe the late A.D. 700s to have been comparatively dry and hot (others disagree). A hot, dry period might actually have lengthened the growing season in some upland areas. This seems to have been the case at about A.D. 760 in the Durango, Colorado, area,[13] but consistently bringing in a large crop would still have been dicey. Perhaps this is another reason why so many Pueblo I villages were inhabited for only a generation or two.

What did the Pueblo I villagers learn during this complex transitional period? They learned that there was an advantage to congregating in larger villages and putting more labor into farming *if* they were in the right place at the right time. When they weren't, it was necessary to move, forage, or engage in trade. Apparently, they couldn't follow the Mississippi economic model forever—cautious or not, they absolutely had to create new options or see their families starve. Eventually, the climate would settle down, but they simply couldn't wait for that. They needed to take short-term action to enhance trade and social connections with other villagers living in different settings. And they needed to regain access to ancestral foraging territories partially abandoned during their experiment with aggregation—territory still used by remaining hunters and gatherers.

The Consequence of Mixed Signals:
A.D. 760–860

Pueblo I responses to changing climate do not tell the whole story of this era of uncertainty and reorganization. Unpredictable rainfall pressed some to gather in larger villages and expand agricultural production, but it left others hanging. After all, if larger villages had solved everyone's problems, there would have been no episodes of local conflict.

Hot, dry conditions enhanced by spotty, localized rainfall—a never-ending feature of the Four Corners—and followed unpredictably by cooler, wetter intervals were confusing to those simply trying to sustain their families. Think of this situation as similar to the fear and uncertainty that always follow rumors of impending "downsizing" and plant closings in large, modern corporations. Some employees go into psychological denial and carry on as if nothing will change. Others, unable to tolerate uncertainty, act impulsively and jump to another job, even a bad one. But most reduce their spending and hang on, trying to squeeze the last drops of security from their employer in the hope that they will survive the cuts.

The last Basketmakers and their hamlets did not just disappear instantaneously in the late 700s to accommodate these "new" Pueblo farmers, many of whom were actually their children, grandchildren, or great-grandchildren. Not all Basketmaker-style sites were abandoned by A.D. 800. Some of those in prime upland settings were renovated and expanded into large Pueblo I villages. In other, more out-of-the-way upland areas, such as the Gallina district, where archaeologists have found "Rosa-phase" pit houses,[14] small and medium-sized villages constructed in late Basketmaker styles continued to be inhabited largely unchanged for another hundred years—even after the geographic center of Anasazi society shifted to the lower elevations during the late 800s.

But at A.D. 800, most of the lowlands were simply not yet the place to be. Lowland Basketmaker sites similar to Shabik'eschee village in Chaco Canyon were abandoned altogether, and no Pueblo I sites were built on top. Many of the lower-elevation Basketmaker sites are believed to have been used only intermittently or seasonally, when intervals of cooler, wetter climate favored temporary gardening there. Three notable exceptions lie in Chaco Canyon itself, where Pueblo I-style settlements built just after 800 are considered the oldest core units at the eventual "great-house" sites of Pueblo Bonito, Peñasco Blanco, and Una Vida.[15] Each had an unusual number of multistory rear storage rooms behind the residences and pit houses.[16] Why should Chaco Canyon have been an exception? And why, apart from the University of Arizona's R. Gwinn Vivian, do so few archaeologists make anything of it?

First, most archaeologists hedge the dates of this period because some Basketmaker-and Pueblo-style villages coexisted in time, even though textbooks tend to emphasize the succession of distinct archaeological periods. Late Basketmaker is supposed to date from roughly A.D. 400 to 700, and Pueblo I is supposed to date from roughly 700 to 900. The next Puebloan period, however, called Pueblo II, had begun by about 830 or 840 with the first construction of small blocks of masonry surface rooms on the margins of the open valleys.[17]

Think of it: from about 840 to 860, settlements in the style of late Basketmaker, Pueblo I, and early Pueblo II all coexisted at one moment in time. Looking back, we might characterize the Basketmakers as in something akin to denial, like workers facing layoffs, and quickly becoming quaint, back-country dwellers. But even some among those in denial usually survive the consequences—then and now. If the Basketmakers were in denial, the tentative Pueblo II settlements remind us of the employees who jump ship too quickly. Predictably, the vast majority of Anasazi farmers between 840 and 860 were still in the Pueblo I villages, hanging on to see what happened next.

The reason these archaeological periods seem to overlap is that the three kinds of settlements were each in a slightly different geographic and ecological setting. The late Basketmakers were scattered in high, cool locations. Their villages tended to have unusually deep pit houses, just like the Rosa-phase pit houses of the Navajo Reservoir district.[18] Stands of ponderosa pine usually grew nearby. The large Pueblo I settlements, except for those in Chaco Canyon, were also in the uplands but at slightly lower, warmer localities that commanded an immediate view over the valleys below. These locations were often at the upper margins of the mixed piñon and juniper vegetation zone. The earliest aboveground Pueblo II sites were typically located along elevated edges of the valleys themselves, where the lower margins of the mixed piñon and juniper life zone abutted good farmland.

These moderate differences in village size, location, and mix of farming and foraging, along with the specific agricultural techniques that were most productive at each, were simply responses to mixed environmental signals. But the differences again provided grist for the mill of evolution, which was beginning to turn at a more urgent pace.

The Storm: Pueblo II

Between the mid-A.D. 800s and 1000, Anasazi farmers in and around the San Juan basin responded forcefully to climatic uncertainty, which is normal in the Southwest but far more important to farmers than to foragers. How much precipitation fell and when it came had never before mattered quite so much. Their response—to found new pueblos, expand everywhere, and move often—is reminiscent of the California business start model. An impressive wave of agricultural experimentation ensued.

Archaeologists have always been impressed by the dramatic expansion of farming hamlets during this period. In 150 years, at least 10,000 farmsteads were established, and agriculture reached its greatest geographical limits, never to be exceeded in the region during prehistoric times. As the Southwestern expert Linda Cordell has pointed out, Pueblo II settlements occupied nearly every farmable spot, "avoiding only flood plains during times when they were being buried by streams depositing quantities of sediment on them."[19] Risks be damned—these farmers were experiencing intense population pressure and simply had to find out what worked. They had no real alternative.

It was probably young families who took most of the risks. Remember, the earliest Pueblo II sites in the mid-800s were tiny dwellings of just a few sandstone masonry rooms built on the very edges of the open basins and floodplains. Presumably, the parents and grandparents of the pioneers were still living in older settlements of Pueblo I style or even in Basketmaker pit houses. Young families were moving away from home to make a living in a new location. This undoubtedly wasn't the first time such a thing had happened in human history, and we all know it wasn't to be the last. But why just then?

Again, climate tells the story. The aggregated settlements of the Pueblo I period simply could not rely on precipitation. The only villages that could be sustained were a few situated where reliable groundwater (seeps, springs, or marshes) could support agriculture. By the late 800s, there simply weren't enough of these little Gardens of Eden to go around. The only other practical solution was to spread out in smaller groups and hope that enough of the scattered farm fields would be hit by some rainfall each year—particularly the late June to August rainfall necessary to nourish the corn when the plants reached the critical tasseling stage. Archaeologists traditionally emphasize the cultural attributes of the Pueblo II period, such as pottery, tools, and architecture, but at its heart it was a classic logistical response based on practical statistics.

To be successful, this logistical response required consistency in the total quantity of crops produced, as well as some effective way to move surplus corn, beans, and even squash seeds around the San Juan basin, transferring them from those who had prospered to those who had not. Happily, the trade networks and more elaborate pottery styles worked out during the Pueblo I period provided the necessary method and currency.

How did the late Pueblo I sites at Chaco Canyon, with their enormous storage capacity, fit in? From at least the late 700s onward there were two distinct rainfall patterns in different parts of the Southwest. From Chaco Canyon west into Arizona and north into Colorado, "bimodal" precipitation prevailed. That is, most precipitation fell as either winter rain and snow or as summer rain. To the east and southeast, the bulk of precipitation came in the middle to late summer, just as it still does in New Mexico.[20] Chaco Canyon sat atop the boundary between these two rainfall regimes. Agricultural techniques and crop yields in the bimodal rainfall country to the north and west would have differed from techniques and crop yields at sites to the southeast in the same year. Trade across this boundary would have served as yet another type of risk management. In some years, the bulk of corn in those multistory Pueblo I granaries probably came from farmsteads to the northwest of Chaco Canyon. In other years, more of it came from the southeast. If pottery was the medium of exchange, then Chaco Canyon would not have had to make its own—and we know that it didn't. Apparently, by Pueblo I times Chaco Canyon had already begun to play the brokerage role that it was to enact for another three centuries.

Throughout this period there was considerable experimentation with and selection for larger-cobbed varieties of corn, all aimed at increasing crop yields. Some newer varieties came to the Four Corners from Mexico—probably Sonora—and southwestern Arizona. Among them were *oñaveno,* or *maíz blando.* Others were hybrids developed locally.[21]

Once the Anasazi had dispersed in the A.D. 900s, fewer people depended directly on the diminished produce of each small farmstead, so large-scale starvation was less a risk. Problems could be borne and contained locally. Why wasn't security the same problem it had been a century earlier? It appears that the movement of farmers to the basins forced any remaining hunters and gatherers out of the district altogether, or else drove them finally to take up farming as their foraging lands were squeezed by agricultural expansion into areas where once only wild plants had been harvested.

An enormous secondary benefit to farming "in virtually every conceivable spot,"[22] therefore, came in the form of renewed access to the rich stands of seasonal wild plants found in dune areas or other nearby spots that were not converted into fields. What was diminished was immediate access to prime hunting territory in the uplands—the fat, protein, and mineral nutrients in meat remained very important. Still, as long as grandparents and other closely connected kin controlled the remaining upland sites, all would be well. If the rains came at the right time, the larger-cobbed corn would create a small surplus to exchange for meat from uplanders as well as bowls from others in the basin lands.

By the early to mid-900s, Pueblo II sites had become rather standardized in plan. Typically, they consisted of linear blocks of small, paired (front and rear), fairly evenly sized rooms. Few sites were large. Six to twelve rooms was a common size, and, as a rough average, there was one pit structure in front of the room block for every six rooms.[23] The most common pattern was 12 rooms in 2 double rows of six and 2 pit structures in front.

The rear surface rooms rarely contained hearths or other architectural features suggesting living space. Like the rear rooms in Pueblo I sites, they were primarily for storage. When there are pairs of pit structures, one often shows clearer evidence of domestic use — bell-shaped storage pits below the floor, a mealing bin, a hearth, and many household implements — while the other is arranged more like a community house or early kiva.

This contrast is particularly clear at a small Pueblo II settlement just north of the magnificent Fajada Butte, which juts up across the canyon from the visitor's center at Chaco Culture National Historic Park. There, at site 29SJ1360 (in the Smithsonian Institution's numbering system, this code means New Mexico [29], San Juan County [SJ], site number 1360), which was founded about A.D. 850 and saw maximum occupancy between 950 and 1030, two deep pit structures were excavated.[24] They were about the same size, but structure "A" was designated a kiva because it was about two meters deep, contained no defined storage or work space, and had the encircling bench, or *banco*, along the inner wall that became so typical of Chacoan kivas a century later. Pit structure "B" was clearly a winter house, and its story is important.

The skeletal remains of two adult women and three infants were found unburied on the floor of pithouse B, where they are believed to have died of asphyxiation.[25] I will come back to this sad event in another chapter. Meanwhile, let us focus on the two women, one aged 39-45 and the other 35-39, both of whom had suffered episodes of severe malnutrition as infants.[26] This is evidenced by a number of interrupted growth lines on their long bones and by gray bands known to osteologists as *enamel hypoplasias* in their front teeth, both caused by near starvation. They died in about A.D. 1030, telling us clearly of episodic semistarvation in the 980s or 990s.[27] It seems likely that the pit house was purposefully burned immediately following the women's deaths, with household objects left in place.[28] This pit house contained a deep, slab-sided hearth and a large dugout ventilator shaft that provided air. The shaft connected to a chamber half-walled in adobe that took up nearly one-third of the floor area. This chamber, judging from the large plain pottery jars found there, was a storeroom.

Pottery in the other two-thirds of the house was smaller, and much more of it was decorated ware. In fact, two sets of decorated bowls, mugs, and other pottery forms were found. Had two women from the adjacent surface rooms withdrawn to the warmth of the deep pit house with three children to ride out a severe cold spell while the men were away hunting? It is possible. What is certain is that archaeologists unearthed the full range of household artifacts in this pit house, in addition to pottery. These objects included bone needles, awls, digging sticks, manos and metates, and a host of other small, practical implements, many of them fashioned from stone.[29]

Site 29SJ1360 is important for other reasons. Not only is it typical of many small, early Pueblo II farmsteads, but it was inhabited at the very same time that several of the great houses across the floor of Chaco Canyon—Pueblo Bonito, Una Vida, and others founded in the late ninth and tenth centuries—were being renovated on a grand scale.[30] This notable differentiation between "small-house" sites (ordinary farmsteads) and great-house sites (multistoried communal strongholds) began as early as the ninth century but typified the eleventh and twelfth centuries. Chaco Anasazi society had already begun to develop a social hierarchy in the tenth century, albeit with far more modest differences than it would display in later days.

The pace of growth and geographical expansion among the Pueblo II farmers continued with only a few short pauses until about A.D. 1000. Enormous changes took place in 150 to 200 years. A new style of farmstead construction became traditional. Archaeologists call these "unit pueblos": two rows of surface rooms, typically of sandstone and adobe, with a single pit structure-kiva or a pair of them built in the courtyard, all as one project.[31] Farming implements became a bit more sophisticated, as did pottery. More telling, the ratio of living space to storage space again declined. Grinding rooms (those containing mealing bins) now took up as much as 25 percent of all the space in some of these small pueblos in lush farming districts.[32] People would not have devoted so much space to grinding corn had there not been more of it to grind. The mealing bins were efficient in another way as well. Metates with different grinding surfaces—coarse, medium, and fine—could be lined up to speed the processing dramatically.

By A.D. 950, some farming districts, such as the Red Mesa Valley (which runs along Interstate 40 near Gallup, New Mexico), Skunk Springs, and the Chuska Valley to the west and southwest of Chaco were robust, densely packed communities sporting local variants of unit pueblos on every ridge and hillock. These three localities were clearly among the first real "breadbaskets" to fuel the rise of the Chaco Anasazi. The Red Mesa district was in the summer rainfall area, whereas Skunk Springs and the Chuska Valley were in bimodal territory.[33] Several varieties of large-cobbed corn were now widely available.

These early farming centers were the nearest outlying, surplus-producing farming clusters to Chaco Canyon in the early 900s. After 950, cultural changes in these districts and in Chaco Canyon itself began to take on a different character. Increasing complexity and grander architectural scale began to replace the raw growth in the number of small unit pueblos, set down in ever more localities as if stamped out by a giant cookie cutter, that had characterized the period from 850 to 950.

True, life wasn't perfect. Episodes of want, leaving their trace as osteoporotic bones, continued to intrude in one place or another, depending on where the rains had favored farm plots. The evidence from site 1360 at Chaco Canyon makes this clear. Many farmsteads were abandoned for a few years, then revitalized as families came and went, "following the rains," a phenomenon still talked about by Pueblo elders.[34] Daily life, by our standards, was very strenuous for these farmers. Broken bones, overwork, bad teeth, and seasonal hunger were common. Meat had become scarcer in the farming districts as population expanded. Large game was driven out by changing habitat, overhunting, or both.[35]

These early Pueblo II farmers all foraged for wild grasses and small game, but the better districts were densely populated, which restricted access to the great open foraging sites that had still existed in Pueblo I times. Most of these sites were overexploited or had already been converted to farm plots, reducing the quantities of wild foods to be harvested. I believe growth would have been aborted and the Pueblo II expansion turned into ceaseless local conflict had climatic conditions not changed at this crucial time.

Past and Present

Rapid expansion of economic production and increasing competition are the classic conditions that have led to episodes of economic collapse and financial panic in modern times. By A.D. 1000, these conditions certainly prevailed in the central San Juan basin.

Resources, especially wild ones, were undoubtedly spread thin. One analysis shows that between A.D. 800 and 900 in Chaco Canyon itself, game was already so scarce that it could provide not even 10 percent of the daily diet. Dried meat had to be imported.[36] One can easily imagine the increased risk of meat shortages a century later, even if corn was still available. In many areas, the related uplanders were dying out. In others, such as the Navajo Reservoir district to the north of Chaco Canyon, most of the Pueblo I settlements had long since been transformed into palisaded pit-house strongholds. The inhabitants turned their backs on the emerging Chacoans and did not engage in trade. No meat came from those highlands in the 900s.

The expansion of farming to nearly everywhere meant that a proportion of all farms would get rain. No one could tell just which plots would be blessed, or in which years, but if there were enough garden plots spread across the vast San Juan basin and enough tasseling cornstalks waiting with upturned leaves, some would receive the gift of water. What percentage of fields produced a crop? Was it as high as 57 percent—California's 1995 success rate in launching new businesses? Perhaps. We will never know precisely.

What we do know is that success came often enough to encourage continued expansion. It came often enough to require a significant increase in storage space, many more mealing bins, and significantly increased amounts of labor invested in the agricultural enterprise. In short, it came often enough to fuel an economic model, like California's, based on rapid growth and risk-taking—not one like Mississippi's more stagnant and cautious economy.

Except for increases in the size of corn cobs, the Anasazi had quit finding incremental efficiencies that would enable them to grow. As a society, each year they toiled to plant and nurture many more fields than would ever produce. This "waste" of labor, of energy, just to sustain a growing system is not efficient; it is precisely the opposite. A new growth dynamic, contrary to 8,000 years of experience, had been set into motion. The Chaco Anasazi had turned to *power*, to the economic principles that govern our own world—grow, spread the risks around, then grow again.

By separating into small farmsteads, most of these Anasazi farmers had made their families into small targets of risk in a vast landscape bound together by trade in pottery and other goods. And at Chaco Canyon, in several great houses, the advantages of trade between villagers of the two great rainfall regimes led to even further aggregation of people and surplus food. The local Chacoan version of the power model was even bolder than the general Pueblo II one. Paradoxically, sites in Chaco Canyon, which by A.D. 900 could not provide enough meat even to sustain the local population, had actually grown both larger and more complex by 1000.

This is less amazing than it first appears. New York City quit growing its own food supply a century and a half ago. Yet it has continued to grow during most of the time since then, supported not by farming but by trading—in food, money, commodities, and manufactured goods. The value of all these things changes, even if slightly, from place to place. Those changes in value create opportunity, if one is willing to take the risk. An American dollar is worth 8.95 Mexican pesos today.[37] Perhaps the dollar will buy 9 pesos tomorrow at the Bolsa in Mexico City. Russia needs wheat. Its rubles have lost value lately, so perhaps it can pay in oil, diamonds, and caviar.

Millions of us buy mutual funds, believing the risk is spread among many individual investors and a large "basket" of fund stocks. Millions divert a portion of each hard-earned paycheck to purchase such funds for retirement. "Get in! Get in!" hawk the TV ads. "The market is going up. Historically, it always goes up in the long haul. The average rate of return this century is 9 percent per year!"[38] Every one of us who does that is a Californian at heart, believing in growth, risk, *power*. It works—until an episode of too-rapid expansion in the market, combined with brutal business competition, threatens to undo it.

That is about what it was like, economically, at Chaco Canyon in the year 1000 — rapid agricultural expansion, no more land to be gotten, and deepening competition. Don't think of it as "romantic" or "primitive." Think of it as just like 1999 in the United States, when the Dow Jones Industrial Average hit 11,000 and 30 million investors held their breath to see what would happen next. In short, think of the emerging great houses in Chaco Canyon at A.D. 1000 as the first commodities exchange in ancient North America, and the floor of the canyon as the first trading floor. This is not, of course, the way the Chaco Anasazi likely thought of it themselves, since their society was couched in religion and suffused with spirituality, as is the society of their descendants, the modern Pueblo peoples.

But this is what first made Chaco Canyon someplace special. It is why Lieutenant Simpson found great houses clustered there as nowhere else. It is why these people became the Chaco Anasazi, instead of just small-time farmers scattered across 40,000 square miles of heartbreakingly beautiful but unpredictable landscape, now long forgotten.

But the Chaco Anasazi are not forgotten. They are legends from whom all Pueblo peoples proudly and rightly claim descent. Why? Because in only another century they had beaten the odds and managed to create a powerful regional society where nothing like it had ever prospered before.

How did they squeeze yet more from the reddish, metallic soils of the Four Corners? And why did they not fail at this critical juncture?

CHAPTER FIVE

The Chaco Phenomenon

I F IT IS TRUE THAT "THE GODS HELP THOSE WHO HELP THEMSELVES," THEN AT A.D. 1000 the Chaco Anasazi were overdue for such intervention. Collectively, they had invested incalculable toil, sweat, and care in first developing, then sustaining their agricultural enterprise under the limitations of a remarkably unpredictable rainfall regime.

Their solutions to this unpredictability were impressive—dispersal, trade, and planting more fields than would ever bear fruit in order to ensure a small harvest surplus across the region, rather than at any one locale. However effective this scheme was in the short run, it required that new agricultural fields be opened up faster than regional population grew. But new farmable land was running out by 1000, and population had grown through the 900s as young families built new farmsteads and had children. Had it not been for the Puebloan people's greatest cultural genius—an absolutely stunning tenacity—their fragile, emerging regional community might have come tumbling down as the 900s bore on.

Over the course of 8,000 years their ancestors had learned to sustain themselves on little when necessary. Those lessons carried them until the gods, perhaps seeing what they had done, helped by granting a solution from the heavens. In about the year 1000, the midsummer rains began to come much more predictably than was normal, and they continued this way with one interruption for nearly 130 years.[1] Mind you, the gods had not granted abundance, only predictability. Rainfall was, on average, not much greater than usual. It was merely more predictable.

This enhanced predictability was more than enough a gift. Across the Chaco Anasazi farming districts people pursued this opportunity with all the obsession of those absolutely certain good fortune will not last—but it did. In this fashion, simply by trying to make the most of one good crop year, then several, then a few more, they created once-impossible plenty from modestly more reliable summer rains.

As they saw their efforts begin to succeed, they worked even harder, stored yet more corn, and expanded farmsteads to new, previously unarable spots within the central San Juan basin. I think of this as the first great experiment with what is now called "in-fill" development in North America. With more reliable rainfall, they were able to farm virtually everywhere.

At first it was mostly dry farming. Even in the riskiest of places, new farmsteads sprang up. As unlikely as it seems in hindsight, they beat the odds often enough that their regional community again grew and was strengthened.

This favorable abnormality in the Southwest's rainfall lasted until about 1130. All this time the Chaco Anasazi continued to grow in numbers, social complexity, and power, behaving in ways inconceivable to any of their ancestors in the preceding 8,000 years. But we understand this behavior. In our age, it is normal and expected. They "grew their economy," increased their output, raised their productivity, invested in infrastructure, enhanced their "quality of life," and took their society "to a new level." John Maynard Keynes, the doyen of economic growth models, would have been pleased.

As masters of adversity, the Chaco Anasazi had neither known nor understood the complications of plenty. Now they were to discover them as they feverishly created the grandest and most complex society in all of prehistoric North America. We now call their creation the "Chaco phenomenon."[2]

The term *Chaco phenomenon* refers not just to the great-house ruins scattered across the San Juan basin but to the whole of this regional society during the years from about A.D. 1020 to 1130.[3] One, but only one, exemplar of it—great-house architecture—may still be admired by the visitor to Chaco Canyon. The true genius of Chacoan society, however, was that the whole was much greater than the sum of its parts. Chacoan society was based on clusters of far-flung farming communities interconnected by trade, sharing, and ritual. This stands in striking contrast to much of feudal Europe at A.D. 1000.[4]

The most impressive European feudal holdings of the same period usually consisted of a large town wrapped around the ankles of an imposing castle and surrounded by miles of farming districts. Loyalty to the local castle holder and landowner, often coerced, was the glue that held such districts together. Most of them, except at the great national ports, were distinct little islands of interesting but provincial local culture. Each was separate, and each had its own local social hierarchy. Eventually, kings rose from among the district magnates and demanded loyalty from local nobles, and with it, access to their estates' surpluses in the form of food and armed knights.

At A.D. 1000 in Europe, the church had only a secondary hold, after that of the landowners, over the affairs of (e)state, the souls of its congregations, or the labor of average farmers. Most local lords commanded only a handful of knights—not the hundreds seen in Hollywood movies. The castles of A.D. 1000 were typically stone-walled circles with a tower or two commanding the easiest approach. Inside the circle were thatched wooden huts, storerooms, the landlord's family, household servants, and, typically, four to six mounted and armed knights (the equivalent of contemporary lawyers on retainer).

Though the horses and armor might have dazzled them momentarily, no Chacoan would have been impressed by the size, scale, or quality of life of the average feudal European holding of the time. Beyond that, the idea of either an armed soldiery or land "owned" over the centuries by just a few families who inherited it would have made no sense. Chacoan society, with no romanticized Roman or Arthurian aristocracy as a specter from the past, was constructed from a pure "bottom-up" model—not the "top-down" European one. Chacoan society, the first complex society in the Four Corners, simply had nothing to live up to. It had no tradition of land ownership as we conceive of it. For 8,000 years land had been held when *used,* not *owned.*

But the Chacoan world did have the growing tradition of open, unfortified "communities" comprised of clustered farmsteads, and interconnected to other clusters by trade, sharing, and ritual across vast acreages. It was, after all, this practice of creating a regional community in the 800s and 900s that had allowed small farmers to survive and expand their way of life at the expense of foragers. Farming, storing, trading, sharing food and pottery with other farmers in other districts, and having more babies were the traditions that had finally separated them from the hunters and gatherers. And all these events were clearly recalled and retold through oral tradition. In essence, their whole identity as farmers must have been intimately interwoven with the idea of geographically expansive community. And they were religious. Kivas had been an integral part of local family life for centuries before the summer rains came more reliably.[5] It was farmers, not hereditary landlords, who first drove the creation of this more elaborate and complex regional Chacoan society after the year 1000.

The Development of Chacoan Society

The roots of distinctive Chacoan society extend backward into the late A.D. 800s, with construction of the first unusually large arc-shaped great houses and immense storage rooms at Pueblo Bonito, Peñasco Blanco, and Una Vida. But the true pinnacle of Chacoan society spanned the period from about A.D. 1020 to 1130.[6]

During this time, the entire San Juan basin and adjacent foothill country became interconnected into one remarkable and vibrant regional culture. New great houses were constructed both in Chaco Canyon and in the outlying, heavily settled farming districts. The most rapid growth and development first came to the southern San Juan basin, between Mount Taylor and present day Gallup, New Mexico.[7] This southern district depended on agricultural production from the many hundreds of farmsteads surrounding great houses in the central Red Mesa Valley, a few miles south of Crownpoint, and from old, established farmsteads in the western Red Mesa Valley, between Gallup and Fort Wingate.

The southern margins of the San Juan basin are magnificent countryside. Driving west on Interstate 40 from Albuquerque, one crosses wide, black lava flows at Grants after passing south of Mount Taylor and into the eastern tip of the Red Mesa Valley. As the highway turns northwest, it begins a steady rise as it nears the exit at Thoreau (locally pronounced "Thuhroo"). The hamlet actually lies about a mile north. Contemporary Thoreau is in Navajo country and lies nearly atop the Continental Divide. From any of the high ground west of the village, one can look west toward Gallup and down into the western end of the Red Mesa Valley.

That part of the valley runs east-west and was one of the first districts to see extensive early Pueblo II farming expansion in the A.D. 800s and 900s.[8] It is bordered on the south by the lovely, ponderosa-laden Zuni Mountains and on the north by the dramatic red cliffs of Red Mesa (properly it is Lobo Mesa) that jut up like a great garden wall from the valley floor. This magnificent red sandstone wall ends at Gallup, 25 miles to the west. Huge, rounded talus slopes of mixed sand, sandstone rubble, and soil appear to support the base of the wall. A thousand years of summer flash floods have carried a fair portion of this talus mixture down into the valley, filling in the low spots and covering hundreds of small farmsteads established between the 800s and 1000s. Yet on the piñon-studded hillocks and rocky outcrops that rise like frequent bumps from the valley floor, haphazard piles of rough-hewn sandstone still mark farmstead after farmstead.

Most of these, as we have already seen, consisted of 10 to 12 rooms fronted by shaded ramadas and 1 or 2 pit structures that, by these Chacoan times, had generally been renovated into true kivas.[9] But the once-great quantities of local Red Mesa Black-on-white pottery manufactured before the summer rains first became more stable were already declining when the first several great houses were built in the valley.[10] The western tongue of the Red Mesa Valley is some 2 to 5 miles wide and more than 20 miles long. From it, the intermittent Rio Puerco (colloquial Spanish for "dirty river") flows sluggishly out of the valley floor toward Arizona. At its muddy headwaters lies the great house at Coolidge.[11] Yet another great house was located farther west, near contemporary Fort Wingate.

The Fort Wingate great house lies so close to Interstate 40 that part of its immense kiva was actually destroyed in 1957 in the process of building the highway. This great house, or Chacoan "outlier," is situated on a low, isolated sandstone ridge that rises from the floor of the Red Mesa Valley just north of the Puerco's south fork.[12] It is a typical site location favored after the 900s—near water, with good visibility in all directions, and not wasteful of farmable bottomland. In the southern San Juan basin, formal Chacoan great houses were invariably established between 1020 and 1080, well after the farms were founded.[13]

The Fort Wingate site clearly reflects two distinct periods of construction. The first and easternmost "house mound," surveyed by archaeologists but not excavated, is of rough sandstone block construction, once mortared by adobe. This portion, designated house mound "B," contained an estimated 10 rooms.[14] (Not all room corners were exposed in the mound, but Michael Marshall and his colleagues on the survey in 1978 are among the most experienced field archaeologists in the American Southwest, so it makes sense to accept their observations.) As usual, the faint depressions from two paired kivas or pit structures were found. The predominant pottery types in this older portion of the site are those typical of Pueblo II, early Chacoan development, including Red Mesa Black-on-white and both plain and corrugated utility wares.[15]

Just to the west of house mound B lies a larger and more impressive ruin, house mound A. It once consisted of about 45 ground-floor rooms, a second story at the rear, and a great kiva built near the end of this community's life.[16] Only the great kiva was excavated during highway construction in 1957. It was in the generalized Chacoan style—benches, four square masonry pillars to support the roof, stone-lined floor drum, firepit and deflector.[17] We know the kiva was built a bit later than the house blocks because only very late Chacoan pottery, including black-on-red wares, was found in it.[18]

Other, more modest house mounds lie nearby. The nearest is only 500 feet to the east on another low knoll. Less than a half mile to the west are two more house mounds of 10 to 12 rooms each. Yet another lies a few hundred yards to the south. Virtually every knoll or low sandstone ridge lying above the floodplain was once home to the farmers who made this the first breadbasket of the Chaco Anasazi world.[19]

The outlines of the story are relatively clear. The Red Mesa district lies just south of the central San Juan basin in an area that I believe received the summer-dominant, single-season rainfall. The preponderance of midsummer rains must have made dry farming larger-cobbed corn easier there than in districts north of Chaco Canyon, even before the rains came predictably. So farmsteads expanded in the southern regions first.[20] Among the dense clusters of farmsteads a few hundred yards to a few miles apart, some great houses were constructed in the mid-1000s to serve local needs for trade, storage, and ritual. Indeed, the Chacoans' open communities nearly always consisted of a great kiva or great house surrounded by ordinary farmsteads. Regarding Fort Wingate, though no thorough excavation yet confirms it, most Southwestern archaeologists would accept the idea that house mound B was constructed in the mid-900s as part of ordinary, early Pueblo II farming expansion, whereas house mound A was likely built or expanded as the Chacoan world became more complex between 1020 and 1050[21] — a generation or two after the summer rains became more predictable.

Daily life in the farmsteads would have followed a seasonal calendar of planting, weeding, watering, collecting wild plants, occasionally hunting, and finally harvesting the crops in late fall. Both oral tradition and continuing Pueblo practices strongly suggest that a season of ritual events and gatherings followed the harvest. In spring, houses were replastered and the clay-and-beam roofs repaired. Then, when the sun priests announced that the time was right, seed was brought from the storage pits and the cycle started anew.[22]

At the Coolidge great-house community, farther east in the valley, similar house mounds have been surveyed with just one notable difference. There, unmistakable segments of an ancient roadway, carefully bermed with sandstone blocks, enter at one end of the main house block.[23] But this gets us ahead of our story, so let us return to the hamlet of Thoreau and continue our journey north to Crownpoint. There will be several great houses along the way. We'll visit some of the more interesting ones that best illustrate important stages in Chacoan development.

From Thoreau, State Road 57–371 winds its way east-northeast for about five miles along rolling hills studded with piñon and juniper. Navajo homesteads, called "outfits," are scattered along the way. A log *hogan*, a small modern house, and a trailer home are often all tucked together near the sheep pens and horse corrals so typical of a Navajo ranching family made up of two or three generations. Such scenes often feature a pickup truck or two in front of each cluster.

Then the road climbs and bends left in a long sweep where it turns due north. There, about a mile to the right of the road and below the mesa called Ojos Tecolotes ("owls eyes," named for several pairs of immense, shallow, circular rock caves carved from the sandstone and looking, at a distance, like the eyes of gigantic owls), rests the great house called Casamero, a sandstone stronghold constructed entirely after A.D. 1000.[24] This Chacoan outlier, at 6,920 feet in elevation, overlooks Casamero Draw and the floodplains adjacent to the wash — an eastern tongue of the Red Mesa Valley.[25] These ancient farmlands are dotted with piñon, juniper, prickly pear, and desert grasses. The soil is sandy and soft.

Like Coolidge and Fort Wingate, Casamero has a great kiva, a masonry house block of about 20 ground-floor rooms, and a second story of about 10 rooms,

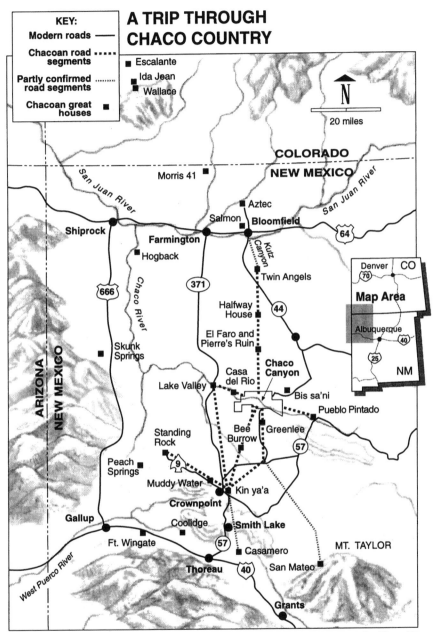

A TRIP THROUGH CHACO COUNTRY

KEY:
Modern roads ——
Chacoan road ·····
segments
Partly confirmed ··········
road segments
Chacoan great ■
houses

■ Escalante
■ Ida Jean
■ Wallace

N
20 miles

COLORADO
NEW MEXICO

Morris 41 ■

San Juan River

■ Aztec
Salmon
Bloomfield

Shiprock

Farmington

■ Hogback

San Juan River

64

Kutz Canyon

Denver CO
70

Map Area

666

371

Chaco River

■ Twin Angels

Halfway
House ■

44

Albuquerque
40

NM

25

Skunk
Springs ■

El Faro and
Pierre's Ruin ■

Chaco
Canyon

ARIZONA
NEW MEXICO

Casa
del Rio
Lake Valley

■ Bis sa'ni

Pueblo Pintado

Standing
Rock

Bee
Burrow

Greenlee

57

Peach
Springs

9

Muddy Water

Kin ya'a

Crownpoint

Coolidge

Smith Lake

MT. TAYLOR

Gallup

Ft. Wingate

57

■ Casamero

Thoreau

40

San Mateo

West Puerco River

Grants

Carol Cooperrider

all arranged in an L with an enclosed plaza to form a rectangle.[26] The back, or west, wall of the rectangle is fully 100 feet long. The great kiva is encircled by above-ground rooms in the extension of the L, which juts out to the east.[27] Within an area of about three-quarters of a square mile lie another 14 house mounds, most of them tucked along the base of the indented mesa bordering Casamero Draw.[28]

Unlike Coolidge and Fort Wingate, Casamero was constructed of rough stone-and-adobe-cored walls veneered with shaped sandstone blocks in a banded style.[29] In this type of masonry, rows of larger sandstone blocks alternate with rows of thousands of small sandstone spalls used as chinking. There are three or four variants of this banded masonry, but all of it dates to the Chaco phenomenon's apogee between 1020 and 1130.[30] Casamero was excavated in the 1960s, but only one incomplete roof beam was datable at the Laboratory of Tree Ring Research in Tucson, Arizona. It dated to A.D. 1041.[31]

The pottery found at Casamero yields a few more clues to the period when great houses were first built in this district. Red Mesa Black-on-white, a type that faded in importance during the early to mid-1000s, is quite scarce. The Gallup Black-on-white styles so typical of the peak Chacoan growth years after 1050 predominate.[32] Even some of the fabulous Dogoszhi-style ceramics first found during the 1896–1899 excavations at Pueblo Bonito, in the heart of Chaco Canyon, have been recovered.[33] For many years Dogoszhi-style cylinder jars and related forms were known only from Pueblo Bonito. In short, Casamero has "Chaco phenomenon" stamped all over it.

Archaeologists estimate the dates of the Casamero great house at A.D. 1020 to 1120, with most of the construction taking place between 1050 and 1090.[34] This guess is bolstered by the fact that a kiva is set into the above-ground block of rooms forming the L. This, too, is a classic Pueblo Bonito trait that became increasingly common after 1050, as did the T-shaped doorways also found at Casamero.[35]

What makes these sites so clearly Chacoan great houses, or outliers? It is a combination of multistoried sandstone masonry architecture, oversized or built-in kivas, pottery styles, and certain details of construction. Tree-ring dates help, but in all of the 10,000 years since the Southwest was first settled, this kind of banded sandstone masonry was used for only about 150 years.[36] To archaeologists, Casamero's large house mound and well-made banded masonry walls, nearly identical to those Lieutenant Simpson described as "intricate mosaics" when he first saw them at Chaco Canyon in 1849,[37] might as well be highway billboards saying "Stop! Visit! See the Ancient Chacoans!"

Not far north of Casamero, Route 57–371 passes the Smith Lake Navajo chapter house and the turnoff to Borrego ("desert sheep") Pass before it reaches its zenith crossing the Continental Divide at Satan Pass. The surrounding countryside is breathtaking: great sandstone cliff faces, unexpected twists and turns between imposing mesas, gray-green junipers nestled against dark green piñons, and every imaginable natural shade of orange, red, and brown juxtaposed in rock, sand, cliff, and soil.

After Satan Pass the road begins its descent into the Chacoan heartland, the central San Juan basin. There, rainwater, if it doesn't first sink into blistering soils, runs north toward the seasonal Chaco River, which flows right through the middle of Chaco Canyon itself. Modern Crownpoint lies a few highway miles north of Satan Pass. This town is home to the Eastern Navajo Agency, a grade school, the Indian Health Service hospital, a small airport, and the delightful Friday night Navajo rug auctions held monthly at the schoolhouse.

As the crow flies, Pueblo Bonito and Chaco Canyon are just over 30 miles to the northeast. Passing Crownpoint, the modern road forks into three branches. The left fork, Indian Route 9, goes west toward Standing Rock. The middle fork, State Road 371, only recently paved, pushes north to the Navajo settlement of Lake Valley at the west end of Chaco Canyon. The east fork, still Route 57, branches again. The left branch, 20-odd miles of graded clay and rock, runs almost due north into Chaco Canyon near Pueblo Bonito. The main paved road (Route 197) continues east to Pueblo Pintado, Lieutenant Simpson's first great house. In Chacoan times, the road layout was nearly identical.

A contemporary highway engineer or urban planner would simply point out that Crownpoint is strategically located and that topography dictated most of the modern routing possibilities, since people in surrounding districts must go to Crownpoint for necessities—groceries, gasoline, and medical facilities. The Chaco Anasazi already had this figured out by A.D. 1100. In those days, their strategic community consisted of the remarkable great house called Kin ya'a ("tall house" in Navajo) and its dozens of surrounding farmsteads.[38] Kin ya'a lies just southeast of Crownpoint at the edge of a small, tilting floodplain near the north face of Lobo Mesa, on the far side of the great natural wall of the Red Mesa Valley.

Unlike the other great houses we have visited, Kin ya'a was built in the early 1100s, and three of the great Chacoan roads branched from it. The west branch, known as the Great West Road, went to another great house, now called Muddy Water, on its way to Peach Springs in the southern Chuska Valley.[39] The middle branch is known as the Southwest Road; it went north to the great house constructed about 1100 at Lake Valley,[40] then on into the west end of Chaco Canyon. The east fork, known as the South Road, went northeast and then in a more northerly direction at Bee Burrow, past other great houses,[41] before entering Chaco Canyon a bit to the east of Pueblo Bonito—just as the graveled south road to the park still does. If anything, the Chacoan roads were once maintained to a higher standard than these contemporary county roads.

Kin ya'a itself is still impressive. It once contained some 26 good-sized ground-floor rooms. It was a terraced and tiered sandstone structure oriented to face the winter sun. The rear half rose in two stories and the back tier in three, for a total of at least 36 rooms in this tall but compact citadel.[42] From its third terrace rose a great tower kiva, another full story taller and once measuring nearly 40 feet above the foundations.[43]

The Chacoans did not build many of these four-story tower kivas, so massive were the foundations and lower walls, but those they did construct were all raised between roughly 1080 and 1110.[44] Several different Navajo origin myths and oral histories speak of Kin ya'a as the home of the Kin ya'ii', one of the original four Navajo clans, indicating that this imposing ruin was an important landmark for later Navajo people, whose descendants still live in the area.[45] The surrounding farming community must have been equally impressive in its day.

In the four square miles surrounding Kin ya'a's great house, an additional 104 ruins have been recorded. Most are 10- to 20-room pueblos, but several others were multistoried, having as many as 50 rooms.[46] Judging from the pottery, virtually all the other masonry house blocks were constructed between A.D. 950 and 1100.[47] The Kin ya'a great house was probably the last major project built in this locality. How do we know that it was Kin ya'a and not any of the other house blocks that was most closely connected to Chaco Canyon as the Chaco phenomenon approached its peak? The roads go right through it and not the others.[48] We don't know when Kin ya'a was abandoned, but judging from dated roof beams, its tower kiva was burned sometime in the early to mid-1100s.[49]

The modern road north from Kin ya'a, like the prehistoric one, still passes through the Lake Valley great house. In contrast to Kin ya'a, Lake Valley was built, if anything, a few years later and was not surrounded by established farmsteads as were the others.

Lake Valley (Kin Lini, or "many houses," to the Navajo) consists of three single-story house blocks without evidence of a kiva.[50] Its rooms, at 20 feet on a side,[51] are immense by prehistoric standards. The main house block's walls, like those of most Chacoan great houses, are of sandstone core-and-veneer masonry. Evenly banded rows of light sandstone block, painstakingly pecked smooth with rounded hammerstones, alternate with even rows of intricate spall chinking. Some of the ceramics found here actually postdate the heyday of Chacoan society in the Red Mesa Valley by a few decades.[52] This is significant because both the Southwest Road and the Great West Road cross at Kin Lini.[53] Do the late pottery styles at the great house mean that these roads, too, were constructed at the very end of the Chaco phenomenon? Or were the roads built first, before Kin Lini was created to provide a service base for them, much as isolated settlements sprang up in the 1940s to serve motorists on the Pennsylvania Turnpike?

Unanswered questions notwithstanding, our modern road tour is instructive. It takes us past ruins representative of different stages in the Chaco phenomenon's development. First, a few great houses appeared at Chaco Canyon in the 800s, apparently to store surpluses that could be redistributed between people living in each of the two great rainfall regimes. Then little more happened in Chaco Canyon itself until after the exhilarating explosion of farming in the southern San Juan basin and Red Mesa Valley. Probably the Red Mesa Valley prospered first, since it was in the district south of the canyon receiving the most summer rainfall.

Later, as the rains came more predictably after about 1000, the Red Mesa Valley prospered even more. And those rains enabled many others to establish new farms in places where farming had previously been unproductive. These less productive districts, such as that surrounding Casamero, had only sparse Basketmaker and Pueblo I populations but expanded dramatically after 1000 as farmers worked less desirable soils in the eastern Red Mesa country. In other areas, entirely new farming districts, like the one around Kin ya'a, sprang up in the early to mid-1000s, long after the predictable summer rains first came. Finally, outliers like Lake Valley were built in the late 1000s to early 1100s in areas where farming communities apparently never existed before.[54] Possibly such outliers acted as service sites for major prehistoric Chacoan roads. Obviously, Chacoan society grew in stages as farming conditions and techniques permitted expansion.

This is what a tour through a cross section of the southern San Juan basin tells us: the sequence starts with early growth, then further expansion in the oldest, most favorable farming districts such as the Red Mesa Valley (Coolidge and Fort Wingate), followed by growth and expansion at older but secondary locations (Casamero), followed finally by vibrant new farming communities (Kin ya'a) with no Pueblo I or Basketmaker roots. At each stage, infrastructure and architecture became a bit more complex. Finally, after A.D. 1050, formal roadways were constructed to the most architecturally complex great houses. If that is the view of Chacoan development from the south, what view can be gained from Chaco Canyon itself?

Chaco Canyon: The Heartland

Chaco Canyon lies at an elevation of roughly 5,900 feet (1,850 meters) above sea level.[55] It runs east to west for about 18 miles, sloping downhill, so its waters eventually drain to the northwest. The Chaco River empties into the San Juan River west of Farmington, near the contemporary community of Waterflow.

THE HEART OF CHACO

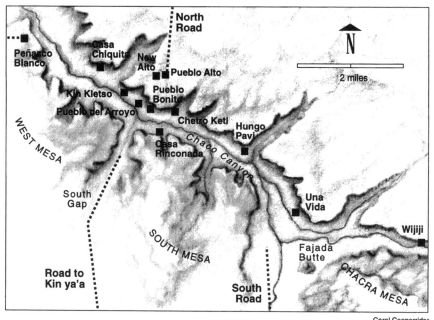

Carol Cooperrider

Contrary to many tourists' images of the place, it is not desolate by farmers' standards — only by those of modern city dwellers.

The canyon itself was cut deep into the sandstone of Chacra Mesa and its detached western extensions, now called South Mesa and West Mesa. The canyon's rock walls vary from about 30 feet to nearly 100 feet high. The Chaco River, really a seasonal wash, runs right down the middle. Now entrenched 10 to 15 feet deep, the wash once bisected the canyon floor far more gently. In Chacoan times it was a shallow stream running seasonally. By Lieutenant Simpson's time, it had become a narrower and deeper ditch entrenched about 3 feet (1 meter).[56]

When Richard Wetherill, the cowboy ruin hunter who named the Basketmaker finds in Grand Gulch, Utah, first came to Chaco Canyon in the early fall of 1895, he, like Simpson, was stunned by Pueblo Bonito and the other great houses that were still partially standing. Almost immediately he wrote to Talbot Hyde, the New York financial patron of his earlier Grand Gulch expedition, requesting funding for a new treasure hunt at Pueblo Bonito. In that letter, dated December 1, 1895, Wetherill described Chaco Canyon differently from the way we view it today: "grass and water is plenty — wood is scarce."[57] Sheep and cattle grazing in the canyon and its environs have taken their toll over the last century.

You already know that the earliest great houses in Chaco Canyon were Peñasco Blanco, situated on the far west end, Pueblo Bonito, in the center, and Una Vida, at the east end of the canyon. Peñasco Blanco and Una Vida were each spaced some 2.5 to 3 miles from Pueblo Bonito. All three were strategically located where gaps in the canyon walls permitted easy entrance.

What few people realize is that even as these great houses were founded, nearly 200 small Pueblo I pit-house sites were in use, too, either continually or intermittently.[58] Farming was clearly the daily occupation of families at most of these small house sites in the 900s, and it is quite likely that at least a portion of the surplus assumed to have been stored in the three early great houses was locally produced.[59] One might argue that the great houses, like early versions of savings-and-loan banks, safely stored all the local surpluses when part-time Pueblo I farmers drifted away for the winter. But the pottery found at these three great houses was rarely made in the canyon. Most of it came from the Red Mesa Valley, and much of the rest, from the Chuska Valley to the west[60] — where the Skunk Springs and Peach Springs Pueblo I communities were growing at the same time.

While some of the earlier Pueblo I settlements may have been seasonal, it is important to note that the dramatic transition to above-ground masonry "unit" pueblos of the 800s and 900s, so apparent in the Red Mesa Valley, did not come to farmsteads in Chaco Canyon until a bit later. The outlying farming districts seem to have been the driving force behind changes in domestic architecture, whereas Chaco Canyon clearly had an early lock on the great-house phenom-

enon. In short, the growth and spread of dense farming communities prior to
A.D. 1020 proceeded far more dramatically outside the canyon than in it. Roughly
80 years passed after the first great houses were built in the canyon before a new
wave of change took hold.[61]

Between 1020 and 1050, land use and settlement patterns changed rapidly and
dramatically in the canyon itself. New great-house construction exploded in
Chaco Canyon, and older sites like Pueblo Bonito were boldly expanded to a
scale huge by earlier standards. By 1100, there were nine great houses on the canyon floor (Peñasco Blanco, Casa Chiquita, Kin Kletso, Pueblo del Arroyo, Pueblo
Bonito, Chetro Ketl, Hungo Pavi, Una Vida, and Wijiji) and three on the mesa
above (Pueblo Alto, New Alto, and Tsinkletzin).[62]

The scale of construction was enormous by any standard. By 1120, more than
100,000 square meters of floor area sat under roof.[63] An estimated 215,000 ponderosa trees had been cut just to support the roofs of the canyon's great houses.[64]
There were no large stands of ponderosa near Chaco Canyon; those immense
logs, each up to 30 feet long, had to be cut with stone axes and carried 20 to 30
miles from outlying forests.[65] Archaeologists believe that many of those roof
beams were carried to Chaco on the shoulders of young men moving along the
formal roads constructed after 1050. The archaeologist Stephen Lekson estimated that it took 193,000 man-hours to construct just the west wing of Pueblo
Bonito.[66] From this figure, I extrapolate that well over 2 million man-hours of
labor went into the great houses in Chaco Canyon between A.D. 1020 and 1120.

No one knows how much labor and material was invested in the entire Chaco
phenomenon's architectural projects during this period. Yet it is clear that great-
house architecture and the storage, ritual, and redistribution functions that went
with it were being "exported" from the canyon to older, outlying farming districts throughout the southern San Juan basin. Kin ya'a, Muddy Water, and
Casamero, all south of the canyon, were built in the midst of existing communities during this wave of Chacoan growth.[67] Kin ya'a was again expanded later,
at about 1100.[68] Most archaeologists consider the date 1100 to mark the beginning of the Pueblo III (or "great pueblo") period and lump it with the heyday
of the Mesa Verdean cliff houses, which flourished in the 1200s. I differ, but I will
come back to this point in chapter 7.

In addition, at least two new great-house communities were established, one
at Hogback, in the northern basin near Farmington,[69] and the other at Standing Rock, where the left fork of the road through the Kin ya'a great house
branched northwest.[70] I believe that when the summer rains became more reliable after 1000, agricultural productivity increased markedly to the north and
west of Chaco Canyon under the bimodal rainfall regime. It had once been too
risky to farm that region profitably, except in old Pueblo I localities such as

Skunk Springs and Peach Springs, where local groundwater was plentiful. The folks in Chaco Canyon apparently wanted a piece of the new action, so after 1050 they began to spread into farming districts in the northern basin with few underlying Basketmaker and Pueblo I houses or none at all.[71] New great houses followed in rapid order. Then came roads. Nothing the Chacoans in the canyon did appears to have been haphazard.

Their new great houses were carefully planned and laid out. When the older great houses were expanded, it was done with an eye to the integrity of the earlier design. Pueblo Bonito is the classic example.

Construction Phases at Pueblo Bonito:
A.D. 1020–1120

Pueblo Bonito is a dramatic D-shaped apartment and ceremonial complex tucked up against the north wall of Chaco Canyon. It faces south.[72] Though founded in the 800s, it expanded in size just after the quiescent period in the canyon ended. At the time of its first significant expansion, other new great houses were also built — Pueblo Alto atop the mesa behind Pueblo Bonito and Chetro Ketl about a half mile to the east on the canyon floor.[73] Unlike Pueblo Bonito, these were not arclike rows of rooms fronted by a straight-walled plaza, in the Pueblo I style. Rather, they were linear roomblocks with a curved front plaza — as if someone had inverted the D-shaped Pueblo I site plan from front to back.[74]

Of the three original, curving Pueblo I great houses founded in the canyon, only Pueblo Bonito was expanded so extravagantly or so continually. The expansion of 1020 to 1040 added two stories of rear rooms and beefed up the immense curved rear wall adjacent the canyon.[75] Part of the older structure was already three stories tall, and the new additions, slightly uphill, stood level with the old roof line. Some of the oldest rooms on the west had already become partly buried by drifting sand in the century or so since they had been built.

Then, by 1050 or 1060, wing additions were added to the outer east and west ends of the growing D, and the front courtyard was partially rewalled. Chetro Ketl, 500 yards away, got wings at the same time.[76] After the wings had been added, Pueblo Bonito was enlarged again between 1060 and 1065 — this time vertically, as new stories of rooms were added.[77] Stephen Lekson argues that a disproportionate number of these new upper-story rooms were devoted to storage rather than living space.[78] Much the same thing was going on at Chetro Ketl next door. At about 1075, foundations were laid for a major new addition to Pueblo Bonito that was never completed.[79]

Finally, near the very end of Chacoan expansion, between 1090 and 1115, Pueblo Bonito was "finished." It looked much as it does today. Part of its tenth-century core was pulled down and rebuilt with larger rooms and 14 new kivas—most of them "blocked in" above ground and surrounded by large rectangular rooms. This work filled in a significant portion of the huge front courtyard, so that ritual structures dominated it. The courtyard itself, already nearly 200 years old, was then formally divided by a north-south wall.[80] As one's eye moved to the rear, the upper stories rose in four dramatic, terraced steps.

When completed, Pueblo Bonito had 33 kivas. Its great kiva measured 52 feet in diameter and nearly 12 feet deep.[81] The ponderosa posts used to support the kiva roof were so immense and carried so much weight that they had to be set into four sandstone collars the size of oxcart wheels just to keep them from being driven into the earth. The perimeter of Pueblo Bonito's outer walls stretched 1,300 feet. Bonito contained nearly 700 rooms, about half of them devoted to storage. The entire floor area covered about 18,530 square meters, or nearly 5 acres.[82] No other apartment block of this scale was built in North America until the 1880s—nearly 800 years later.

Pueblo Bonito, like most of the other great houses, had also been carefully laid out with an eye to cosmology. The great houses captured the essential movements of the sun and moon through architecture—for example, windows that focused the sun's rays at the summer solstice—and through complex geometric configurations of plazas, room blocks, and kivas. As such, they were much more than public buildings housing ritual, residential, and storage space; they were re-creations on earth of the rhythms of the seasons and therefore the rhythms of Chacoan society.[83] The deep religiousness evidenced in the construction of paired kivas at so many farmsteads after A.D. 900 had been absorbed into the expanding Chaco phenomenon, then monumentally amplified across the vast San Juan basin in both the architecture of great houses and the rituals performed in them.

As the Chaco phenomenon broadened its reach across the northern San Juan basin in the late eleventh and early twelfth centuries, new roads began to stretch toward the north. So let us now leave Chaco Canyon itself and head that way on a much more ancient road to discover the rest of the Chaco world.

The Northern San Juan Basin

By the early twelfth century, several impressive prehistoric roads flowed north from Chaco Canyon toward the San Juan River.[84] Archaeologists have debated for more than half a century whether the roads were economic or ceremonial in nature. It is clear that they were both. Chacoan people apparently made little distinction between sacred and secular. The seasons, the ancestors, and the ancestral gods were inseparable from everyday activity. It is we in contemporary society who so frequently compartmentalize religious life and secular life.

Even more importantly, religion and the earth itself were not separate, but one. Spirits and spirituality were tied to events and to places where those events occurred. Over a lunch, I once argued to Alfonso Ortiz, a distinguished Pueblo Indian anthropologist, that a portion of the Great North Road out of Chaco Canyon led "nowhere," because I could grasp no practical economic function for it. Alfonso smiled enigmatically and suggested that road went nowhere as defined by my world—not by his.

We now know that this portion of the Great North Road runs north from Chaco Canyon about 30 miles to the floor of Kutz Canyon, across desolate and never heavily populated country. Along the road are various elevated kivas and shrines, including the great kiva atop a pinnacle called El Faro, "the lighthouse." The roadway, about 30 feet wide, quite straight, and bermed in spots, ends in an ancient wooden staircase that leads down into Kutz Canyon.[85]

The archaeologist Michael Marshall believes that Kutz Canyon may be the mythic location of the *shipap*, the underworld place of origin for Pueblo people and the northern place to which all Pueblo souls return after death in order to complete their journey back to their own mothers and into the fourfold womb of the earth itself.[86] In historic Pueblo religions, the spirits of the dead are continually returning to the underworld, just as the spirits of unborn children continually emerge from it.[87]

In understanding the Chaco phenomenon it is necessary to recognize the likelihood that its ideological organizing principle was religious rather than economic. It is we who are driven by economic obsession. We explain almost everything, even religion, in terms of money and commerce. So it should come as no intellectual shock that though the Chaco phenomenon was first and foremost an extension of religious ideas, enormous practical and economic consequences were interwoven into its fabric.

One of those economic practicalities has to do with the efficiency of a road system in a society that had neither horses nor wheeled vehicles. Horses were inadvertently reintroduced into North America by expeditions such as Coronado's in 1540–1541 and by a succession of Spanish shipwrecks off the coast of Texas in the sixteenth and seventeenth centuries. What did people who traveled on foot, shod in yucca-fiber sandals, need with roads?

In 1977, E. Pierre Morenon, a young archaeologist working on the excavation of a Chacoan outlier called Salmon Ruin, carried out some practical experiments with a respirometer, which measures oxygen usage during exercise. He discovered that walking along the remnants of Chacoan roads between any two points reduced caloric expenditures by an average of 38 percent compared with walking on the natural desert floor a few feet outside the roadbed.[88] Even if some of the roads were constructed as ceremonial pathways and inspired by the need to communicate with the gods, those gods were efficient.

In the Chacoan world of 1050 to 1100, many hundreds of thousands of ponderosa beams and even more pottery bowls and seed-laden ollas were transported along the roads. The Chacoan roads seem to have fallen into two size categories—12 to 15 feet across and 20 to 30 feet across.[89] Nearly all road segments began at a great house. Except for the road to Kutz Canyon, most connected with other great houses.[90] All of the roads were carefully constructed in straight-line segments. Low places were filled in, arroyos were bridged when necessary, and high spots were cleared off. The rocky debris from construction was generally piled along the way, forming low, cobbled berms. Dozens of way stations and distinctive, horseshoe-shaped shrines, called *herraduras* by archaeologists, dot high points along the roads.[91] Where necessary, stairways were cut right into the rock to ascend the side of a mesa so that the road could proceed straight up, then across, and down by another set of steps before proceeding in its ordained direction across the basin floor.[92]

About 400 miles of roadway 12 to 30 feet wide have now been documented by a combination of high-technology imaging techniques and low-technology surveys on foot.[93] Most of the authentic Chaco roads have thin, intermittent scatters of broken prehistoric pottery along the edges—testament to everyday mishaps. Some roads in the area, when cross-sectioned and exposed through excavation, show evidence of distinctive, half-moon-shaped soil compressions in the sticky subsurface clay. These were made when either autos or horse-drawn Navajo wagons packed down the soil.[94] Roads displaying the compressed wheel traces are usually not Chacoan roads but date from later historic periods. Those with thin scatters of broken pottery and no compressed subsurface clays are usually the genuine article.

At the west end of Chaco Canyon, another wide road pushes northwest from Casa del Rio to Kin Lini, the great house at Lake Valley mentioned earlier. Further segments are still not completely verified on the ground but appear to lead north by northwest to the great house at Hogback near the San Juan River.[95] The Hogback community evinces both early and late construction. The south cluster of farmsteads near the Hogback great house has 23 house mounds scattered around a great kiva. Most of the ceramics in this cluster are earlier Pueblo II types.[96] It was there long before the great house was built and may have been abandoned before the later settlement was established.

The great house itself lies a few hundred yards to the north. It has a late, blocked-in kiva and is surrounded by a dozen farmstead mounds. Much of the pottery found near this great house is local, but some widely traded black-on-red wares typical of the 1100s are also in evidence.[97] Still other pottery fragments are in the later Mesa Verde style, typical of the late 1100s to 1200s, manufactured long after the Chaco phenomenon had collapsed. The combination of late trade wares and locally made pottery at Hogback is atypical for any great house. Why weren't typical Chaco-phenomenon trade wares found to be dominant there? Were they no longer being manufactured in the farmsteads to the south? Was the Hogback community isolated from Chaco Canyon in the 1100s? Was the Chaco system already fragmenting when the Hogback great house was built?

The answers lie in other late Chacoan great house sites along the San Juan River. One of the most magnificent is Salmon Ruin on the riverbank's north terrace at Bloomfield, New Mexico. It lies 50 miles due north of Chaco Canyon at a point that would be aligned with the Great North Road, one of the three roads running north from Chaco Canyon out of Pueblo Alto. One cannot reach it nowadays by driving a modern road adjacent to an ancient one; to reach the ruin one must now take New Mexico Route 44 northwest to its junction with U.S. Highway 64 at Bloomfield. On the left about two miles west of this junction is the lovely San Juan County Museum. The ruins lie below it, near the river.

Excavated by Cynthia Irwin-Williams in the 1970s, Salmon Ruin was mostly built as one massive project between A.D. 1088 and 1090.[98] The great house was constructed in the shape of a square C. Its back (north) wall is 450 feet long. The two arms of the C, each 200 feet long, reach south toward the Great North Road from Chaco. The great house once stood two to four stories tall, contained at least 175 rooms, and had a floor area of 90,000 square feet—nearly two acres.[99]

Salmon Ruin, like other great houses in this northern district, was built a generation or more after most of the great houses in the southern and central San Juan basin. Most importantly, it was built in the midst of the worst drought since the rains had become more favorable 90 years before.[100] Ninety above-average harvests had already fueled enormous growth. The Chacoan system had reached its maximum in size, power, and number of operating farmsteads by the time Salmon Ruin was constructed. Its population had undoubtedly grown significantly. Now a shortage of new farmland was again looming, for summer rainfall had begun to decline noticeably about 1080. By roughly 1090, this decline had turned into genuine summer droughts, a calamity that lasted for five or six years. The pairing of a large population with a drought-created shortage of new farmland in which to expand shook Chacoan society to its roots. Five or six years is an eternity to farmers. This was roughly the same length of time as the American Dust Bowl of the 1930s.

Salmon Ruin was obviously an effort by a large community of Chacoans to relieve pressure on the Chacoan core and provide better living conditions while agricultural production in the southern San Juan basin faltered.[101] There is important evidence that this worked for a time. The waters of the San Juan River compensated for the drought. Large game, scarce in the Chacoan core, was still available around Salmon Ruin. There were no dense clusters of nearby farmsteads to compete for the game, so abundant remains of deer and antelope are found in the early levels of the ruin. Corn, beans, and squash were grown, but huge quantities of wild plants that matured sequentially from spring to late fall were also harvested.[102] Clearly, both wild plant foods and game served regularly as important supplements to the diet at Salmon Ruin; they were not just remedies in seasons of want. This was more like the older Basketmaker III and Pueblo I diets than like the diet of large-cobbed corn and small game eaten in so many contemporaneous Chacoan sites to the south.

In contrast to Chaco Canyon, where pottery was imported, artisans made most of the pottery at Salmon Ruin locally. This pottery even included an inexact local copy of the late Gallup Black-on-white style so favored in the central basin at this time.[103] Why wasn't true Chacoan pottery in abundance at Salmon Ruin? After all, it lies at the terminus of the Great North Road.[104] Or does it? It was believed so in the 1970s and 1980s, and some knowledgeable archaeologists still assume that is the case,[105] but others insist that no road segment has yet been confirmed between Salmon Ruin and the sacred *shipap* at Kutz Canyon.[106]

If not, why not? Perhaps, as Michael Marshall argues, the Great North Road was intended to veer eastward a bit and end at Kutz Canyon. It could also be that the last segment running due north was never completed, interrupting the link that would have connected Salmon Ruin to Halfway House, Pierre's Ruin, and El Faro. This would make sense if the Chaco phenomenon was already running out of steam or was in serious social disarray by the early 1100s.

The evidence from Salmon Ruin is poignant and ambiguous. After an initial period of prosperity following the huge construction project, little further renovation took place. Eerily, its last roof beams were repaired and replaced at A.D. 1116, the same year repair and expansion stopped in most great houses within the canyon.[107]

Salmon's diet also changed as the repairs ended. The large-cobbed corn that was generally ground into flour became scarcer, and smaller-cobbed flint and popcorns, which stored well and were drought resistant, became more common. Large game became much scarcer, and rabbits, prairie dogs, and turkeys—long considered valuable for eggs and feathers—became the more common fare. By the early 1100s, corncobs themselves, not just the kernels, were sometimes eaten, too.

After this period of want, people drifted away from Salmon Ruin, either driven off or attracted to the huge new great-house complex constructed about

1115 near present-day Aztec, New Mexico.[108] This site is now a national monument. Salmon Ruin was then abandoned for more than half a century until it was again inhabited by Mesa Verdean people in the 1200s.[109]

The Big Picture

It is clear that farmers in the southern San Juan basin first drove the geographical expansion of ordinary farmsteads and the refinements in farming techniques, not long after those first three great houses went up at Chaco Canyon. Then, as the summer rains became more favorable, farming quickly spread into new locations in the central and west-central basin. Great-house architecture at Chaco Canyon expanded forcefully between 1020 and 1050 and again in at least two more huge but distinct waves of construction in the canyon. The second wave came between 1050 and 1075; the final wave, between about 1090 and 1116.

The second wave of construction in the canyon, if not the first, was accompanied by the creation of a road system in the southern basin and the spread of great house architecture to the old farming districts there. The third wave of construction seems to have been born of crisis—the drought of the 1090s—when new great houses were built in the northern basin. About this same time, multiple roads were also laid out to the north. In a number of cases there were no established farming communities in the more desolate northern localities, so the great houses there could not have served as the ritual and economic heart of a dense farming district like the older great houses in the south. What, then, was their function? To make work, like a modern road project? To service the roads? We do not yet have all the answers.

By A.D. 1100, most of the great houses in the southern basin were abandoned, even as new ones were being built in the north. These were short-lived. The last roof beam raised at Bis sa'ani, a late Chacoan stronghold 20 miles north of Chaco Canyon, was cut in 1139. Defensively sited on a great shale ridge, Bis sa'ani was inhabited for only about 20 years.[110] No later, unequivocally Chacoan roof beams have been found anywhere in the central San Juan basin. By 1140, the Chaco phenomenon had ended. Between the first drought about 1090 and the next in 1130, it fought back at nature, shrugged off enormous stresses and strains, built more kivas at Chaco Canyon, and sponsored more roads, rituals, and great houses.

Then, at some point along the way, the Chacoan elites must have lost control of production, trade, exchange, and, perhaps most cruelly of all, the perfect rituals once performed in Chaco Canyon's great houses and in the magnificent separate kiva now called Rinconada. From their perspective, those rituals had created a predictable and rhythmic world for agriculture and permitted eight generations to be born and live without conflict. It was, in the final analysis, ritual that regulated this immense regional community of 120-odd great houses, 10,000 to 20,000 farmsteads, and 400 miles of majestic roadway.

In the grand scheme of things, Chaco Canyon ceased to be the heart and soul of Anasazi dominions in the early 1100s. The heart, if not the soul, then shifted north toward the San Juan River, southwestern Colorado, and Mesa Verde. Great houses at Aztec in New Mexico, at Ida Jean and Wallace in Colorado, and at sites that the archaeologist Earl Morris called simply 40 and 41 on La Plata Creek near the Colorado–New Mexico border were all built *after* 1100.[111] By then, most of the great houses in the southern basin and in the Red Mesa Valley stood nearly empty. Still, this is not the entire story, but only half of it.

The other half lies in the humbler ruins of the "small houses," the ordinary farmsteads clustered around the older Chacoan great houses. It was these farmers who provided the corn, beans, squash, pottery, jewelry, and labor that fueled most of the Chaco phenomenon. We need to know how they lived and behaved. We need to understand their place in the Chaco phenomenon, and we need to understand why so many of their farmsteads in the southern basin lay empty by the early 1100s, when Aztec was built north of the San Juan River.

Past and Present

No great undertaking is ever accomplished without countless small steps. To create the Chaco phenomenon, ordinary farmers likely took most of those steps. If it required two million man-hours to build the dozen great houses in Chaco Canyon, how many millions did it take to build the other 100? Another 16 million? How many million more hours were needed to build an estimated 400 miles of road? At an average width of 20 feet, that would be more than 42 million square feet of rough basin floor either built up or cut down at least a foot.[112] And all this done with fire-hardened digging sticks and shallow cottonwood scoops! While someone worked on such a project, who brought him food and water? And from how far? In the early years, most great houses and the roads between them could have been logistically supported by the surrounding farming communities, but the late great houses and roads had no local base of support. Surely these expensive and complicated projects were subsidized in ways that are no longer obvious.

Beyond that, how much hand labor did it take every year to plant tens of thousands of acres of farm plots, many of which would never yield a crop? How about the simple acts of carrying the daily water, collecting the daily firewood, grinding corn, cooking, and making tools, clothes, fabulous pottery to trade, cotton cloaks, and rabbit-fur and turkey-feather blankets for the winter? What of the significant investment in the rituals and feasts necessary to sustain the rhythm of the seasons and of the rains? Put it all together and the Chaco phenomenon is, by contemporary standards, truly phenomenal. The Chacoans invested tens, if not hundreds, of millions of hours of back-breaking labor in creating it, and then sustaining it for another century. Why did they do it? Quite simply, because it worked.

Societies nearly always push on with ways of doing things that have an immediate and visible benefit, even after the benefit begins to erode. Overplanting, overbuilding, and overreaching were not quaint Chacoan folkways. They were surefire avenues to success—so long as the rains came and new farms could be planted at a more rapid pace than population increased. Until about 1090, the system worked with a vengeance. It was only then that the Chacoans' growth model failed and overreaching caught up with them.

Until then, they must have felt powerful indeed—they commanded the power of growth, the power of life, the power of their ideology, the power of permanence. It must have been every bit as reinforcing as the sense of power Americans have enjoyed since the 1930s. We, too, understand the power of growth, of overproduction, of our ideology. We worship our founding fathers because our system, through their principles, has made us powerful—and rich. Or is it more honest to say that some among us worship the founding fathers because those few have become rich and are in power, even as others curse those same principles, the rich and powerful, and their own luck while trying simply to feed their children and pay the doctor on minimum wage?

Why did the Chacoan system fail after two relatively short droughts that would scarcely have perturbed their Pueblo I forebears? We need to know this, not just out of curiosity but for our own sakes as well. If the Chaco phenomenon itself is evidence that these people were, for a time, seduced by growth and power but could not sustain their society no matter how hard they were willing to work, then we, too, should worry. It sounds so much like our own story.

Their growth, like ours, came in waves. The archaeological data are clear on that. Housing starts in Chacoan society exploded in the mid-900s and surged three more times during the years from 1020 to 1100. After 1100, growth came only in the form of new great houses or expansions of existing ones at Chaco Canyon and in the northern basin. Ordinary farmstead construction ceased. In sum, tree-ring dates suggest that waves of growth in the 1000s were followed by periods of more modest activity, each roughly 20 years apart. Is this just an accident of archaeological data recovery? Or is it eerily like our own business cycles and the rhythm of contemporary housing starts?

I think it is the latter. We moderns believe we can find a technological solution to any problem, but how is that different from the Chacoan frenzy of kiva building and accelerated ritual activity in the late 1000s and early 1100s? Isn't that reasonable evidence that they were convinced a solution would be found from more, and more perfect, ritual?

They overreached, and somehow Chacoan society became so fragile that events that would have sparked few consequences in the first 8,000 years of Southwestern prehistory—two droughts about 30 years apart—undid it completely. The real question is, How did the Chacoans become so vulnerable? Is there a lesson in it for us? The answers lie in the marked contrast between the daily lives of those who occupied the great houses and those who dwelled in the farmsteads.

Photo 11. The tall sandstone walls of Kin Kletso great house are in stark contrast to Chaco's farmsteads. Photo taken about 1935 looking southeast across the Chaco River toward the University of New Mexico field school building (now leveled) barely visible to the right of Pueblo del Arroyo (top left and east). (Courtesy NPS.)

Note: Site diagrams accompanying photographs are all from *Chaco Canyon* by Robert H. and Florence C. Lister, University of New Mexico Press, 1981.

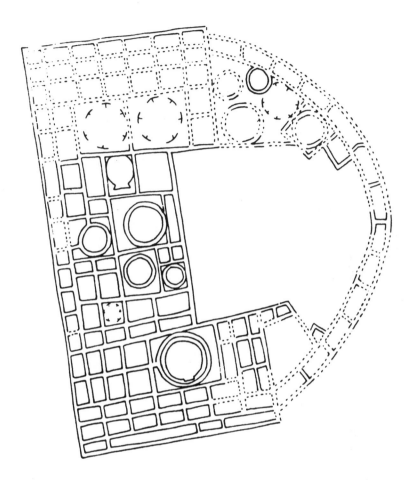

Photo 12 (*opposite*).   Aerial view of Pueblo del Arroyo, just east of Kin
Kletso, looking toward the north wall of Chaco Canyon (top). Chaco River in
foreground. Note the well-planned, C-shaped roomblock and kivas set into
square masonry surrounds typical of great houses begun in the A.D. 1000s.
The courtyard is to the east (right). A separate circular, triple-walled
structure was built later at the edge of the dry riverbed (left).
Photograph by Charles Lindbergh, 1929.
(Courtesy Museum of New Mexico.)

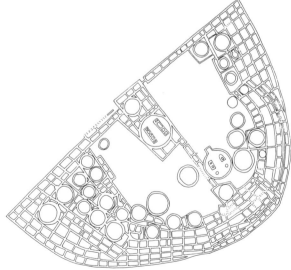

Photo 13 (*opposite*).   Pueblo Bonito, the jewel of Chaco Canyon's great houses. The canyon's south gap and the ancient road to Kin ya'a (top left) are behind modern National Park Service buildings, now razed. Note Bonito's multistory standing walls (left foreground), curving rear wall typical of the great houses founded during the Pueblo I period, and the courtyard with its immense kivas (center). The courtyard was not walled until the A.D. 1100s as conditions deteriorated. (Courtesy NPS.)

Photo 14.   Pueblo Bonito, view to the southeast, taken from right center of previous photo. Note the fine masonry of the rear wall, the numerous circular kivas with encircling benches, and the great kiva in the courtyard (top right). The narrow rooms (center left) are the oldest. The larger rear rooms (bottom left), kivas, and great kiva were built later in distinct construction stages. (Courtesy NPS.)

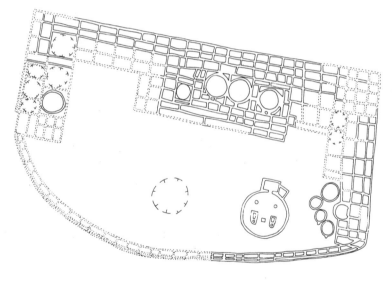

Photo 15.   Chetro Ketl and Talus Unit (top left), tucked against the north canyon wall, were contemporaneous. About half of Chetro Ketl is excavated in this view (looking northeast). The rectangular, multistory great house was built between A.D. 1000 and 1115. The great kiva in the courtyard and the circular kivas set within square roomblocks (center) are features shared with Pueblo Bonito, out of view to the left (west).
(Courtesy NPS.)

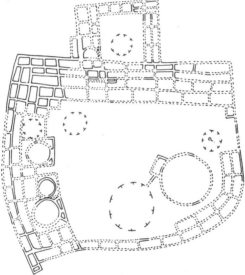

Photo 16.   Una Vida, another of the founding Pueblo I great houses (circa A.D. 800) in Chaco Canyon, lies about two miles east of Bonito, past Hungo Pavi (not pictured). Never completely excavated, it, like Bonito, began as a modest curving arc of storerooms with a pit house in the courtyard. Tucked up against the north cliff, Una Vida underwent expansions (including kiva, left foreground) between A.D. 930 and 960, yet it did not grow in the late 1000s like Bonito or other great houses in the central canyon. (Courtesy NPS.)

Photo 17.   Wijiji, with some 90 ground-floor rooms, protected the far east end of Chaco Canyon, about five miles upstream from Pueblo Bonito. It has never been formally excavated, but archaeologists believe it was one of the last multistory great houses constructed during the heyday of the Bonito period (1050-1120 A.D.). Its rectangular floor plan is mimicked in several "scion" communities built far to the north by presumed Chacoan refugees in the mid-1100s, after the Chaco phenomenon collapsed in disarray. (Courtesy NPS.)

Photo 18. Pueblo Pintado, about 13 miles southeast of Wijiji, was the first Anasazi great house that Lieutenant Simpson encountered in 1849. Probably built as one planned project in A.D. 1060-1061, it contains about 60 immense ground-floor rooms and several kivas. A Chacoan road was built to it at about the same time. I view it as a public works project akin to CCC and WPA projects initiated by the U.S. government in the 1930s to absorb idle labor and shore up a failing economy. Those same conditions prevailed in the Red Mesa Valley farming district south of Chaco Canyon at about 1050. (Courtesy NPS.)

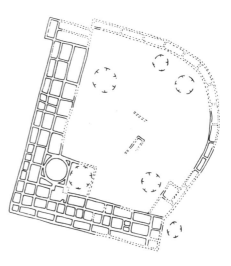

Photo 19.   Greenlee great house lies a few miles south of Chaco Canyon near Vicente Wash, which flows past spectacular Fajada Butte and Una Vida to empty into the Chaco River near Hungo Pavi. It was constructed adjacent to a prehistoric Chacoan roadway that once went south toward San Mateo. Like other roadside great houses at the edge of the Chacoan core area, it had no great kiva. Its dry-laid tabular sandstone walls are well made but not as lavish as the elaborately chinked and banded walls of larger great houses in Chaco Canyon. (Courtesy NPS.)

Photo 20.   Aerial view of Kin ya'a southwest of Chaco Canyon near modern Crownpoint, New Mexico. The distinct rectangle (lower center) is created by the U.S. government fence protecting the site. The whitish area near the bottom corner of the rectangle is the partially excavated site. The black dot to the left of the light area (arrow) is the shadow of the tower kiva shown in the next photograph. Both Chacoan and modern roadways intersect at the ruin. (Courtesy NPS.)

Photo 21.   Standing wall of the great four-story kiva at Kin ya'a. This part of
the wall is visible as the black dot in previous photo. The floor of the lower
kiva chamber is partly visible below the archaeologists' photo board. The
South Road from Pueblo Bonito in Chaco Canyon passed by Kin ya'a's
courtyard wall. (Courtesy NPS.)

Photo 22. Lithograph of "Jackson's stairway," cut into the cliff face behind Pueblo Bonito. It led to Pueblo Alto on the mesa top above, where the Great North Road to Kutz Canyon began. (Courtesy NPS.)

Photo 23 (*opposite, top*).   Bis sa'ani ("house atop clay" in Navajo) sits atop a dramatic clay and shale pinnacle about seven miles northeast of Chaco Canyon. Built in the A.D. 1130s, it contained the latest roof beam found in any Bonito-period site (A.D. 1139) and may have been built to protect the central canyon's great houses from unrest among Chaco's northern farming communities at that time. Virtually all of the dark rubble cascading down (right center) consists of tabular sandstone blocks once part of the citadel's walls. (Courtesy NPS.)

Photo 24 (*opposite, bottom*).   South House at Bis sa'ani. The pinnacle is so narrow that the Chacoans had to construct two house blocks separated by a knife-edged ridge. The sandstone was quarried one-half mile away. View is to the northeast across badlands drained by Escavada Wash. With spectacular views in every direction, this pinnacle would have been difficult to attack. (Courtesy NPS.)

Photo 25. El Faro ("the light house" in Spanish), looking west. The elevated kiva and signal tower were built next to the Great North Road in the early A.D. 1100s, when uneasy residents of Chaco's great houses walled their courtyards and built control gates where roadways passed village walls. Archaeologist Steve Lekson is on the pinnacle. (Courtesy NPS.)

Photo 26.   Kutz Canyon at the terminus of the Great North Road from Chaco. Nearby, an ancient wooden staircase descends to the canyon floor. Archaeologist Michael Marshall argues that this sacred place represented an entry into the Chacoan underworld where souls departed this earth to await eventual rebirth. Tabular sandstone blocks, remains of a roadside shrine or way station, clutter the hillock (center). The archaeologist in right foreground is unidentified. (Courtesy NPS.)

Photo 27 (*opposite, top*).   The great house at Aztec National Monument on the Animas River, with its immense keyhole-shaped kiva, was inhabited well after the Chaco Canyon collapse. Some scholars believe the Great North Road ended here and not at Kutz Canyon. Note the C-shaped room block similar to those at Pueblo del Arroyo and Wijiji. Some Chacoans sought less crowded conditions along the Animas and the San Juan about A.D. 1100. (Courtesy NPS.)

Photo 28 (*opposite, bottom*).   Salmon Ruin great house on the banks of the San Juan River (out of view, right) about seven miles southwest of Aztec. Note the same C-shaped room block (left) with kiva in courtyard. Founded just before 1100, Salmon was a Chacoan refuge until a number of its women and children were burned in the tower kiva that once arose from the main block (left center). Modern buildings in the far lower left are from a field school held at Salmon in the 1970s. (Courtesy NPS.)

Photo 29 (*above*).   Sandstone block tower atop the mesa at Manuelito Canyon, southwest of Gallup, New Mexico. Manuelito endured into the upland period following Chaco's collapse because, like other Chacoan upland refuges on the perimeter of the San Juan basin in the 1100s, it enjoyed plentiful water, firewood, wild plants, and game to supplement its harvests. By that time, all of these were scarce at Chaco itself. (Courtesy NPS.)

Photo 30.   Two unidentified archaeologists inspect a small cliff-face site
built into the wall of Manuelito Canyon below the tower in the previous
photograph. Such sites were a harbinger of the upland period that succeeded
Chacoan society in the late 1100s and 1200s. (Courtesy NPS.)

CHAPTER SIX

The Fall of Chacoan Society

IN CHACOAN TIMES, DAILY LIFE IN THE GREAT HOUSES CONTRASTED DRA-matically with the quotidian realm of the farmsteads. Though most of the great houses were modeled on farmstead architecture, and the rhythms of the seasons were the same for both, the differences far outweighed the similarities.

The great houses, recall, originated in Chaco Canyon. It was at least a century before they were exported to the outlying farming districts, where a frenzy of farmstead founding had preceded their arrival. It must have been at times much like the situation in small towns in America during the 1960s, as each one eagerly awaited the arrival of the first McDonalds—proof from afar that this was a community to be noticed and reckoned with. Validation is validation, and all human communities seek it.

To the populace of Chaco Canyon, this expansion would have seemed logical, even natural. Great houses, after all, were *their* invention. Combining ritual space, immense storage capacity, and some residences, the great houses were key to maintaining contacts and trade among the expansive, open farming communities throughout the basin. Even though most present-day Pueblo descendants and many "new age" admirers of Anasazi society favor a nearly pure religious explanation for the great houses, archaeologists continue to reflect on the fact that the ratio of residential to storage space in the farmsteads was about equal for all of the Chacoan periods from the A.D. 900s to the 1100s.[1] In contrast, the proportion of space devoted to residential use clearly diminished over time in the great houses as storage space and more ritual space (kivas) was added in the huge expansion projects of the mid- to late 1000s. In general, less that one-third, and often only one-fourth, of all space in the great houses was devoted to daily living.[2]

This means that as the Chaco phenomenon grew in size, extent, and complexity, the amount of food stored in the ordinary farmsteads did not increase, but the amount stored in the great houses grew exponentially. This is indirect but persuasive evidence that after the rains became stable, the increased harvests of those many farmsteads got scooped up and stored at the great houses.

It is also important to recall that the first formalized kivas are found at the great houses.[3] True Chacoan kivas are usually masonry lined and have far fewer floor features—hearths, subfloor storage pits, mealing bins, partitioned storage nooks, and so forth[4]—than do pit structures. Great houses and kivas—that is, storage and ritual—were Chaco Canyon's specialties. Since virtually every farmstead had its own storerooms and kivalike pit structure, it is clear that the storage and ritual exported by Chaco Canyon functioned at an organizational and social level above that of the farmsteads. This provides us evidence for at least a two-tiered socioeconomic hierarchy by the A.D. 1020s.

But both great houses and great kivas were far larger and more densely clustered at Chaco Canyon than they were anywhere else.[5] In addition, all Chacoan roads connected to the canyon.[6] That is rather like the "all roads lead to Rome" dictum of classical European historians. Just as that saying implies that Rome was the organizational center of its universe—and we know from copious written records that it was—the Chacoan roads imply that Chaco Canyon was the Anasazi world's nerve center and its sacred "Center Place". This yields us at least a three-tiered Chacoan hierarchy by about 1050—farmstead, district great house, and Chaco Canyon great house. If these three functioned as a true hierarchy, we would expect more wealth, goods, and reflections of power at each tier as we compare the archaeological remains of daily life found in them. To save suspense: though there are troubling gaps in the excavation data, this is exactly what archaeologists have found.

The "small-house" farmsteads at Chaco Canyon provide crystalline contrasts with their associated great houses, often only a few hundred yards away. This is partly because "progress" in farmstead development proceeded more slowly inside Chaco Canyon than in the rich farming districts to the south. It is almost as if Chaco Canyon learned how to squeeze some early advantage from trading across the two rainfall regimes and founded those first three great houses, but simply could not muster the energy and resources to raise daily life in its own farmsteads to a higher level. That higher level came first to farmsteads in the Red Mesa and southern Chuska valleys, where masonry replaced poured adobe and small kivas replaced pit houses well before those innovations came to farmsteads in Chaco Canyon.[7] In contrast to Chaco Canyon, well-built farmsteads were the rule rather than the exception elsewhere in the early 1000s. Perhaps Chaco Canyon really wasn't so superb an agricultural environment after all—its great-house residents' real forte may have been connecting one open farming community to another.

The Small Houses

What do archaeologists find in the ordinary farmsteads? Abundant evidence of a daily regime based on hard work and few luxuries. Most Chaco-period farmsteads ranged in size from about 8 rooms to 18—half of them devoted to storage.[8] Simple sandstone masonry was a common medium of wall construction, but varying combinations of poured adobe, post-and-clay jacal, and some slab lining (echoes of the Pueblo I period) are also observed. In some sites, such as 29SJ627 at Chaco Canyon, all of these construction methods contributed to cycles of growth and renovation.[9] When "unit pueblos" were founded as single, neatly constructed projects, it was most always after the rains had stabilized and farming had expanded into new areas during the early 1000s.

Site 29SJ627 (or Site 627, for short) is a wonderful but relatively rare example of a farmstead with a long, unbroken history. Located in a side canyon called Marcia's Rincon, the site faces east toward Una Vida, its rooms once lit by the rising sun. The original farmstead was positioned to take advantage of summer runoff from the sandstone cliffs of South Mesa and an adjacent area of old sand dunes. The dunes were a prime place for dry-farming corn, much as the Hopi still do.[10]

Site 627 started modestly enough about A.D. 780 as a Pueblo I settlement of one pit house and an adjacent block of five small storerooms. The pit house was dug out, and the native soil walls were plastered over with adobe mud. The nearby storerooms were also scooped into the gently sloping hillside so that their floors lay below the original ground surface. Walls were both built up and plastered with puddled adobe that had been fortified with sandstone spalls.[11] Compared with the careful masonry and ponderosa-beam construction of Una Vida across the canyon—built just after 800 as one of the three earliest Chacoan great houses—this type of construction seems crude, but these modest storerooms remained intact and in use for nearly 350 years.

In front of the storerooms was a ramada divided by low adobe walls, reminiscent of a duplex's divided front porch in older American cities. Later it was divided even more permanently when the low adobe walls that had once partially enclosed the twin areas under the ramada were built up in a combination of sandstone blocks and more adobe until the rough outline of a larger roomblock was created. This expansion came between 950 and 1000,[12] the same time as the proliferation of Red Mesa farmsteads 60 miles to the south. Two more rear storerooms were added to the original five at this time, and a poured adobe floor filled in the entire ramada area. The finishing touches to the early Pueblo II version of this site included the addition of another pit structure.[13]

The third major construction project at Site 627 included a new poured adobe floor over an even larger area and construction of simple, sandstone-block walls to create another 12 rooms, for a total of 19. The two pit houses were renovated into kivas, and daily domestic life moved into the above-ground rooms. All of this took place between 1000 and 1050,[14] the period during which great-house architecture both expanded in Chaco Canyon and was exported to the old farming settlements to the south.

Not surprisingly, great quantities of Red Mesa Black-on-white pottery were found in portions of the site.[15] Una Vida and the farms near it probably had strong connections to farmers in the Red Mesa Valley to the south. Finally, a third masonry-lined kiva was added, perhaps about 1050, and was used more or less continuously until the early 1100s. This later kiva contained no Red Mesa pottery. Rather, its pottery came primarily from the districts north and west of Chaco Canyon,[16] where great houses and roads were built in the late 1000s and early 1100s. By then the Red Mesa Valley was no longer important to the canyon's dwellers.

This farmstead is believed to have been inhabited first by a family of 5 to 7 persons in the A.D. 780s. Later it sheltered some 20 to 25 people, probably related in an extended family. Generations of their descendants then lived at Site 627 from the 900s until the early 1100s, when the site was abandoned.[17]

Before they left, its inhabitants farmed several varieties of corn and squash and gathered many wild plant foods found locally. They ate deer and pronghorn antelope, occasional turkey eggs, and, as time went on, more and more small game—jackrabbits, prairie dogs, kangaroo rats, and the like. They had mealing rooms in which to grind their own corn, made yucca-fiber sandals and sleeping mats, and kept smallish dogs.[18]

Burials at this site indicate health conditions typical of traditional Anasazi farmers of the 1000s and early 1100s. Infants are overrepresented; adult males are underrepresented. Grave goods are modest—a decorated bowl or two, a yucca twill mat, perhaps a potter's polishing stone or an arrowhead or two. Evidence of episodic malnutrition is abundant.[19]

Another farmstead just a mile away, 29SJ1360, was introduced in chapter 4 as an example of a small-house site founded in Chaco Canyon before the Chaco phenomenon took on its full form. Built around 850—some 70 years after Site 627—this farmstead comprised ten surface rooms and two pit structures in the larger of its two house blocks, and six rooms in the smaller house block. The two house blocks were connected by an open ramada. Like most farmsteads, Site 1360 did not sit in the canyon's floodplain. Rather, it was situated atop a prominent ridge that protrudes north from Fajada Butte. In early Chacoan times, the larger house block was still in full use, as was one pit house. This room block was probably inhabited more or less continuously from about 900 to 1030.[20] It yielded skeletal evidence of famine in the 980s, before the rains stabilized.[21]

Site 1360 was smaller, less prosperous, and shorter-lived than Site 627. Still, in the course of 130 years, its inhabitants used and discarded surprising quantities of artifacts. Archaeologists unearthed more than 2,000 pottery vessels there. In the portions of the site that predated the Chaco phenomenon, four or five kinds of pottery were found—a typical number for a small farmstead—including some lovely black-on-white bowls and jars. The later portion of the site, like pit house B first mentioned in chapter 4, is considered "remarkable for its variety of ceramics": 12 distinctive types of pottery characteristic of the period from 1000 to 1030.[22]

How did the inhabitants of Site 1360 acquire this unusual variety of pottery? We cannot be certain, but two factors might account for some of it. Pit house B had burned and its timber roof had fallen, crushing some items but preserving an otherwise intact and complete inventory of household goods right where they had been used or stored at about A.D. 1030. The site's excavators found clear evidence that strands of shale beads, or *heishe,* were being manufactured there.[23] Heishe, a common adornment, was usually made of either soft stone or shell. Pit house B had been home to an artisan who might well have been able to trade the strands of prized, charcoal-colored beads over a fairly wide area in exchange for desirable pottery. Though the bulk of the pottery at this site was Red Mesa Black-on-white (the traded pottery that connected most of the farmsteads in the Una Vida canyon community to early Pueblo II farmers in the Red Mesa Valley), much of the more exotic ware had come from areas to the north, near the San Juan River.[24] That is likely where some of the raw shale for beads originated, too. It is easy to imagine that the family artisan or another kinsman traded finished beads for both raw material and San Juan pottery, either directly or through a connection in one of the canyon's great houses—even Una Vida—where such pottery styles are far more commonly found.

There is the possibility of one other unusual economic activity at Site 1360— raising dogs. In all, excavators found the remains of more than two dozen small dogs there, a mix of puppies and adults.[25] Perhaps these farmers, like many farmers the world over, had several nice little sidelines going for them—craft and kennel—as increased agricultural productivity and expansion of the Chaco phenomenon fueled people's appetites for jewelry and useful pets. Dogs eat rats, warn of attack, chase predators away from turkeys, and curl up to sleep against you on cold winter nights.

That is what one of the household puppies had done on a singular night in about the year 1030, when five members of pit house B's household, two women and three children, died together.[26] Afterward, the pit house was torched with the bodies and all the household goods still in it.[27] As it burned, the roof fell and sealed this tragic vignette for archaeologists to uncover more than 900 years later.

Mystery still surrounds this event. The archaeologists who excavated and reported on the site concluded that the five had died of asphyxiation. J. Stanley Rhine, a noted forensic anthropologist at the University of New Mexico whom they consulted, concurred.[28] The oval-shaped pit house was entered by climbing down a ladder from a smoke hole centered in the timber, bark, and clay roof. The slab-lined fire pit sat directly below the smoke hole, near the base of the ladder. Fresh oxygen was supplied by a ventilator shaft whose mouth opened into a connecting storage chamber just above the floor. The other end opened outside at ground surface just beyond the domed roof.

On that luckless night, a woman between 35 and 39 years old, 5 feet 1 inch in stature, lay on her side asleep. Her feet were but inches from the warm fire pit. Her head, pointed west, lay on a stone headrest near the plastered earthen bench that encircled the pit room. A lovely necklace of nearly 4,000 shale heishe beads draped down from her neck. Tucked up against her knees was the puppy that died with her. A 12-month-old baby sleeping on a small yucca-fiber mat, its head resting on a miniature version of her stone headrest, died about a yard away.[29] Some six feet to the south of the woman, just beyond an adobe wing-wall that separated the ventilator hole and storage areas from the living room, the skeleton of another adult female was found.[30]

This second woman was between 39 and 45 and stood nearly 5 feet 3 inches tall. She had apparently been squatting while holding an infant of about two years above her to get air from the ventilator shaft. But it seems that no air got there that night, and she fainted, then fell backward, pinning the child's legs and one arm behind her head and shoulders as both expired. A small adult dog died several feet away from the two of them.[31] Finally, the skeleton of another infant, one to two years of age, lay in an earlier ventilator shaft that had been abandoned and filled in.[32]

It would certainly have been possible, on a still winter's night with a temperature inversion and a dying fire in the fire pit, for so little fresh air to have circulated in the pit house that fatal concentrations of carbon dioxide and monoxide accidentally collected. Other pit-house accidents of this kind have been found, and sadly, it still happens every winter in the contemporary United States, usually when improperly vented gas furnaces in trailer homes strike down an entire family. But the woman lying near the fire had died with two stone arrow tips in her—one in her chest and another in her abdomen. She also had a circular hole punched through her right ulna, as if she had raised her arm to fend off, unsuccessfully, yet another arrow.[33]

When 29SJ1360 was excavated, these findings initially caused some researchers to speculate that the woman had died after being hit by arrows shot down the smoke hole that night—evidence of conflict at Chaco Canyon in the 1030s. Although this is plausible, it is important to note that the shaft hole in her right arm had already begun to heal when she died.[34] It is far more likely that she had been attacked several weeks earlier and was still recuperating on the night she died. Since the ventilator shaft was found blocked—though it could have been filled by falling debris as the roof collapsed—my bet is that either the ventilator shaft was stealthily plugged on purpose (one flat sandstone slab would have done the job) or, more likely, a quiet snowfall accidentally plugged it during the night. Why? The puppy asleep at her knees. Had enemies approached the smoke hole, both dogs would have been up and barking, especially an excitable puppy. On balance, I think these deaths were probably accidental and the uninjured woman stirred too late to save the group. They suffocated, and the pit house was then burned, likely by grieving kinsmen who walked away, never to use it again.

Though Site 1360 presents us a compelling scene of ancient tragedy, it raises other important but as yet unasked questions. Where were the men of the household that night? Were they off hunting, at a ritual in Una Vida across the canyon, or away working on an early road project (the South Road to the Red Mesa Valley entered the canyon nearby)? For that matter, were the women young enough to have borne these babies? Surely, at 35 to 45 years old, these two were the grandmothers. Remember, these are the skeletons discussed in chapter 4 whose severe infant malnutrition fairly screamed across the ages, "Food shortages in the 980s or 990s."

Site 1360 denies us answers to these tantalizing questions. But its preserved household utensils, material goods, and human bones give us an illuminating picture of farming life. They tell us that even in the household of an artisan and farmer prosperous enough to have a dozen kinds of pottery instead of four or five, the women and children, if not everyone, suffered from anemia and an irregular food supply. They tell us that women in their late thirties and early forties suffered from severe dental caries and from spinal arthritic conditions typical of those who frequently carry loads too heavy or who stoop to do labor that is too hard.[35]

Do burials elsewhere tell a similar story? Yes. Hundreds of additional burials excavated from dozens of small farmsteads scattered throughout the Four Corners at this time confirm a similar and consistent picture of the farmer's lot. At farmsteads throughout the Chacoan world in the A.D. 1000s, infants too often died in their first few years of life from anemia, malnutrition, parasites, or diarrhea.[36] Underweight mothers often cannot produce enough milk, and corn gruel, the pabulum of the day, is too low in protein, fat, and vitamins to fortify an infant against the diseases typical of crowded conditions, unpurified water, and constant animal contact.

At "prosperous" Chaco Canyon, children younger than five years made up nearly 26 percent of all burials—and this was the lowest percentage in the region.[37] In outlying districts, the figure rose to about 45 percent.[38] Over time, it got even worse as the Chaco phenomenon faltered in the early 1100s. One study estimated that mortality prior to age 18 was 50 percent in the Gallup area at A.D. 1100.[39] Can you imagine the agony of coping with the deaths of half the children born into a community? That study tells us that women had to average four births apiece just to sustain the Gallup district's population, and after A.D. 1000, the farming population in the Gallup and Red Mesa districts was actually in decline owing to excess infant mortality.[40] These are appalling statistics. In the contemporary United States, only about 2 percent of all burials each year are of children under five.[41]

Adults also tended to die young by our standards. Although these burial populations do contain mature adults in their forties to sixties, young adults, particularly females, often died in their late teens and twenties. Indeed, the same burial study in the Gallup area that documented such appalling infant mortality also tells us that 60 percent of all young adults who reached age 18 had died by the age of 35. A disproportionate percentage of those were females in their child-bearing years. Men lived an average of seven years longer than women, the precise reverse of modern conditions.[42] Most adults (about 80 percent) evidenced some hypoplasia lines in their teeth. Most also suffered from severe dental caries, tooth erosion from sandstone grit in the cornmeal, and periodontal disease. Broken and poorly mended bones were common, as were advanced arthritic diseases and osteoporosis. Together these maladies are the hallmark of poor diet and intense physical activity.[43]

Severe iron-deficiency anemia, which dramatically increases susceptibility to infectious diseases, dysentery, and respiratory disorders,[44] afflicted 83 percent of children under the age of 10 at Chaco Canyon in the eleventh century.[45] This is in striking contrast to a 16-percent rate in the Navajo Reservoir district two to four centuries earlier.[46] The earlier Basketmaker-style diet of corn, beans, and squash supplemented by significant quantities of wild game and plant foods was a better diet, but such an economy worked only when population densities were low, foraging space was plentiful, and people moved camp frequently.

In comparison with late Basketmaker and Pueblo I times, the Chacoan world by the late 1000s had grown large, complex, and crowded. Firewood, clean water, game, and wild plant foods had all become scarce in the established farming districts. Perhaps this is why Salmon Ruin was founded in the 1080s.[47] Perhaps it also accounts for the outright abandonment of many farmsteads in the old farming communities of the southern San Juan basin by the same decade, even *before* the drought of 1090.

The Great Houses

The elites in Chaco Canyon's great houses fared much better. Studies of burial populations indicate that both great-house males and females were on average 1.8 inches (4.6 cm) taller than their small-house cousins living as close as 500 to

1,000 yards away.[48] We also know that mortality among children five years or younger was only 9.5 percent at Pueblo Bonito.[49] A child's statistical chances of living to age five were therefore a sobering three times better in a great house than in a farmstead within sight of it.

By our modern standards, the great-house residents themselves suffered high rates of osteoporosis, anemia, trauma, and early death. Nonetheless, great houses were the places to be in the late A.D. 1000s and early 1100s. Many more bones of large game animals such as deer and antelope are found in these sites than in the farmsteads.[50] Great-house burials often contain many lovely bowls and porringers,[51] not just one bowl or the single corrugated potsherd often given as an infant's burial offering in the farmsteads. And in the great houses, grave bowls typically contained food offerings for the dead.[52] In the farmsteads, food was apparently too precious to be frequently bestowed as a gift at death. There are other contrasts, too. For example, great-house burials are nearly always found inside buildings, but half of all farmhouse burials are outside, in the midden.

Other burials and burial offerings in the great houses were simply stunning. At Pueblo Bonito, Neil Judd's excavations in the 1920s uncovered a middle-aged warrior who had been buried with his quiver of 16 stone-tipped arrows beneath him. Between his knees, an additional 28 arrow points were arranged in a triangular pattern.[53] In another room at Pueblo Bonito, Colonel D. K. B. Sellers found the mummified body of a woman along with a large quantity of turquoise beads and two delicate, carved turquoise birds.[54] Indeed, 25 percent of all great-house burials at Chaco contained turquoise beads, whereas they have been found in only a single farmhouse burial there.[55]

In room 38 at Pueblo Bonito, excavators under the direction of George Pepper in the late 1890s discovered 14 buried macaw skeletons[56] — evidence that these prized birds from Mexico were kept for feathers and ceremony. In room 33, they uncovered a marvelous cylindrical basket completely covered in turquoise mosaic.[57] In yet other rooms, they found carved flutes, dozens of elaborate ceremonial sticks, copper bells from Mexico, intricate turquoise beads, carved pendants, and hoards of the fabulous Dogoszhi-style cylindrical jars.[58] By 1899, Pepper had shipped more than 70,000 high-status items dug from fewer than 40 rooms at Pueblo Bonito to the American Museum of Natural History in New York.[59]

In short, great houses such as Pueblo Bonito contained huge quantities of fine pottery, turquoise, ceremonial objects, and high-quality household goods. Not only did the great-house elites wield local economic clout, but their reach stretched far beyond the Four Corners to acquire macaws from either Veracruz on the Caribbean or Sinaloa on the Pacific coast of Mexico; spiny oyster shells from the great bays north of Guaymas, Mexico; copper bells from Zacatecas; pottery from Arizona's Hohokam people; Mimbres Black-on-white pottery from southern New Mexico; banded pipestone from southern Alberta and the Dakotas; and other shells used to make heishe from the coasts of both California and Texas.

In the outlying great houses spread across the central and southern San Juan basin are found many of these same types of fine pottery, turquoise, and macaws. These seem to have been "signature" status items of the Chacoan elite at the older great houses.[60] In contrast, great houses in the northern basin constructed after about 1100, such as Salmon Ruin, appear to have been more isolated and to have had fewer exotic goods.[61] This hints that the Chacoan elite's economic grip was faltering at some great houses in Chaco's eleventh hour. This brings us back to the customary explanations for the rise and fall of Chacoan society with which the last chapter ended.

One View of the Chaco Phenomenon

The differences in daily life and economic circumstances between small farmers and great-house occupants, both in Chaco Canyon and in the hinterlands, paint a clear and vibrant portrait of the Chaco phenomenon's rise and fall.

I believe that Chaco Canyon first gained its strategic advantage in Pueblo I times by trading the food and seed corn stored at its three great houses for pottery, meat, cotton, and other valuables that came from late Basketmaker and Pueblo I hamlets on the western and southern margins of the San Juan basin. Remember, from Pueblo I times onward, only trifling quantities of the pottery found in either Chaco's great houses or its farmsteads was manufactured there. Most was imported.

The western margins of the basin, including the Chuska Valley, were located in the bimodal rainfall regime, and people there had already developed a distinctive pottery style known to archaeologists as the Chuska series.[62] The Chuska farmers had ready access to meat and wild plants from the Chuska and southern Lukachukai mountains, which separate Arizona from New Mexico.

The southern margins, including the Red Mesa Valley and its side canyons, were surrounded by Lobo Mesa and Mount Taylor on the north and east and Cebolleta Mesa and the Zuni Mountains on the south. These "southerners," too, had access to meat and wild plant foods. They traded with the Mimbres people to the south, who made fine pottery, grew more cotton, and were closer to the sources of shell and other exotic items, such as macaws, obtained from old trade routes into northern Mexico. They, too, had a distinctive pottery tradition, with roots deep in the Basketmaker period, which had given rise to the Red Mesa styles traded into Chaco Canyon. Most importantly, these southern Anasazi farmers lived in the summer-season rainfall district. In that climatic regime, rainfall was concentrated in the critical months of July and August, when corn tasseled.[63]

The amount of water received in spring during germination and in summer during tasseling largely determine the annual yield of corn. In the period before the midsummer rains stabilized, farmers in these southern districts would ordinarily have been able to produce larger crops than the farmers who manufactured Chuska ceramics to the northwest. And sure enough, until the early 1000s, after the rains came, Red Mesa pottery was far more abundant than Chuska wares at Chaco Canyon.[64] The Red Mesa Valley's surpluses likely drove early Pueblo II development in Chaco Canyon.

When the rains finally did stabilize about A.D. 1000, farmers in the northwest would have gained a proportionally greater crop yield because they lived in a district where sparse rainfall had once been divided between winter and the summer tasseling season. This had always limited their crop yields more severely than yields in the south, and those who had been most limited also benefited the most when summer rainfall became more reliable. At Chaco Canyon, accordingly, Chuska series ceramics began to overtake Red Mesa wares in the 1030s to 1050s. By the late 1000s, few ceramics were still being imported from the Red Mesa district.[65] Although ceramics from the southern district waned, the change to more reliable midsummer rainfall probably benefited agriculture there. The better summer rains apparently enabled some hard-pressed farmers to expand into less favored locations in the southern districts and in the Chacoan core, temporarily easing crowding while the northwestern farmers were still playing catch-up.

If small farmers at the margins of the San Juan basin provided both the surplus corn stored at Chaco and the pottery used there, what did those farmers get in return? Remember, even though regional rainfall became more reliable, it usually fell in a spotty pattern. I believe local districts that got little rain one year would have desperately needed food for the winter and new seed corn in the spring. That corn, I suggest, came from the proliferating storage rooms at Chaco Canyon. I also suggest that formal canyon ritual was associated with the corn. To this day the Zuni people, who number descendants of the Chacoans among their clans, celebrate the Shalako ceremony, usually in early December.[66]

Shalako is a feast and series of ancient ritual dances designed to bless the earth and all humankind and to share a portion of the Zuni harvest with visitors, whether long known or strangers. I view Shalako as the kind of important community ritual and sharing event that once likely made possible the open farming communities of the Chaco Anasazi. Further, I surmise that the earliest true masonry great kivas appeared at Chaco Canyon precisely because this type of ritual, which connected one community to another, was intimately interwoven with the storage, trade, and redistributive activities at the great houses.

The greatest invention of those who participated in the Chaco phenomenon were those open communities and the trade and ritual that interconnected them in order to defeat the effects of spotty and unpredictable rainfall across the Four Corners. Think of it: in a time when one could travel safely in few parts of the world, and in which power was so often obtained and held through force of arms, not a single early Chacoan great house was walled off from its neighbors in the surrounding farmsteads. Farmsteads, too, were unfortified. Even the cluster of great houses in Chaco Canyon itself was a remarkably open cluster, without an architecturally defined central core. As powerful as the canyon must have been in its heyday, no evidence of a large, armed warrior class has been found. The "warrior" burials at Pueblo Bonito seem to date to roughly A.D. 1100,[67] about which more will be said.

Meanwhile, the open Pueblo II farming communities in the Red Mesa district carried within their success the seeds of their own destruction. Having quickly expanded into virtually every farmable location after 1000, they were the first to run out of new farmland in which to expand. Unable to plant new farms more quickly than population had grown during the 900s, they benefited briefly when the summer rains became more reliable, then found themselves hemmed in on all sides as new farming districts expanded elsewhere. Some of the farmers undoubtedly devoted more time to making pottery. That would explain why such huge quantities of the later styles of Red Mesa Black-on-white are found at both Chacoan great houses and farmsteads until about 1030. Others probably left their family farms, drawn to the great houses in their own valleys and to those in Chaco Canyon.

By the early 1000s, the Red Mesa Valley's dramatic population growth of the mid- to late 900s had become a liability rather than an asset. Crowded farmsteads clustered close together, like those in the Coolidge and Wingate communities, eroded diet and health. The Zuni Mountains were overhunted, and other communities now competed to trade pottery. Instead of the exhilarating expansion of a century before, by the mid-1000s daily life had become a fearful struggle. Infants died at horrific rates. Mothers died in childbirth, and most adults had both anemia and those telltale gray lines in their teeth from near starvation as children. How many toddlers cried themselves to sleep, hungry in spite of a bloated belly, we will never know. And not all the hungry children had the energy to cry. It was the quiet ones who slipped away in the night, staring blankly with open eyes, unresponsive to the world around them. As these agonies piled up, farms were abandoned in the central Red Mesa Valley. Some were empty by 1050, and many more before the drought of 1090 hit the region.[68]

These early dislocations from ancestral farms apparently threw excess labor into the larger Chacoan economy. If there were few new places to farm, just what could the displaced do? I suspect that some of the men became the laborers who built great houses and roads far from the farms where so many of their children and their young wives or daughters-in-law had been lovingly wrapped in their yucca-fiber sleeping mats and then buried with a cherished bowl.

Archaeologists have long been aware of a growth spurt at Chaco between 1050 and 1075, when road building and the far-flung export of great houses accelerated.[69] Establishing new communities both in the Chacoan core area and in the near northwestern districts between 1050 and 1080 must have eased problems in the older districts somewhat by opening up new farmland and relocating some population. During this second wind at Chaco, substantial expansion projects were implemented at the canyon's great houses themselves—adding yet more storage space and ritual kivas.

The added storage space makes sense as an economic stratagem while new open communities, albeit in poorer farmlands, were being founded in the northern and northwestern San Juan basin. But why more ritual space? As I commented in the last chapter, ritual and religion were *the* organizing principles of Chacoan society. Ritual was power, and the proof of its power was that the great-house rituals at Chaco Canyon, perhaps specifically those at Pueblo Bonito, had brought seed corn to starving farmers in the 900s, then summer rains to the entire Anasazi world at 1000. The drums and chants had called to the gods before, and the ancestral gods had answered with seed, then rain. That the rains came each July as they had never done before was not just the hint of an answer from the gods, a dreamlike possibility. It was a thunderous answer that all could see, hear, smell, and taste for themselves every July thereafter.

That is, every July until A.D. 1090, when something went horribly wrong. In that year, the traditional prayers must have gone up to the heavens as they had for each of the 90 years before. This time they went unanswered.

True, there had been warning signs—the sheer quantity of those July and August rains had been tapering off for nearly a decade.[70] But both the small farmers and the great-house elites knew how to deal with that. The farmers planted even more fields that might not produce, and the elites built roads north to the San Juan River and founded new great houses like Hogback and Salmon. Some farmers, already displaced from communities too densely packed and soil grown tired after 200 plantings, likely joined the work crews on these projects. Archaeologists have long noted that some room corners don't quite match up,[71] as if different work crews, using different units of measurement, had been assigned construction in adjacent portions of the newer (and otherwise beautifully planned) great houses, such as Pueblo Pintado, the first one Lieutenant Simpson saw in August 1849.

But this year, 1090, was different. There was no answer at all from the heavens. Nor was there an answer the next year. Nor for four more after that. By the third year, if not the second, the huge storerooms at Chaco lay empty. It must have seemed to some Chacoans as if their entire "social contract" had been torn asunder. First, no rains, then no seed corn.

This had to have been particularly hard on those who farmed in the people-saturated open communities on Chaco's southern margin, where life had been daunting for at least half a century. Recall that the burial study done in the Gallup area tells us that at this time women had to bear at least four children just to replace the population. That means two of every four children died in infancy, and yet others died before reproducing. Not surprisingly, the burial study tells us that population was in decline in the western Red Mesa district by 1100 because poorly nourished women were unable to reproduce often enough to sustain their community.

I believe it was the drought of the 1090s that ripped apart the very fabric of the Chaco phenomenon. This was the event that forced small farmers to go it alone and walk away from their farms in droves. Their participation in ritual and the cost of supporting it no longer brought them enough rain or seed corn. Those who had strong kin or trading connections in the great houses apparently tried to get into them. There were residential expansions in old communities such as Manuelito Canyon southwest of Gallup and the San Mateo (Mount Taylor) district,[72] as well as in the northern great houses. Some residential expansion also took place at sites like Pueblo Alto and New Alto at Chaco Canyon itself.[73]

It must have been a troubling time. As the hardest-pressed small farmers walked away, probably with the same combination of anger and defeat that Tom Joad felt in *The Grapes of Wrath*,[74] the Chacoan elites seemed temporarily immobilized. True, they took in some of the displaced farming clans. It was, after all, their ritual that had failed. But they simply could not accommodate everyone. Their own supplies were short. Then, at the height of the drought, they launched their greatest building projects, adding to great houses and leveling new roads. Ironically, new great houses, including Casamero, went up in the old Red Mesa district between 1080 and 1100 in an apparent attempt to stabilize the local farming population. Still, farmers left in droves. Another great house, Village of the Great Kivas, 17 miles northeast of Zuni, extended the Chacoan reach to an area, like that of Salmon Ruin to the north, where good water, uncrowded conditions, and upland game were available.[75]

Then the rains came again, apparently adding to the elites' power and reinforcing their formulaic response (roads, rituals, and great houses). The number and sizes of kivas built at this point reached truly astounding proportions. This was the time when tower kivas were added at Kin ya'a.[76] The front courtyard at Pueblo Bonito was walled and divided, and new kivas were added during the same period. By the early 1100s, the outer great-house walls that Lieutenant Simpson saw at Chaco Canyon had all been built.

New great houses were established at Aztec (A.D. 1111-1116, expanded in the 1200s),[77] Escalante (1125-1129),[78] Ida Jean (about 1125),[79] and Wallace (about

1125),[80] all north of the San Juan River. Others were built in higher elevations bordering the old Red Mesa farming district. One, the San Mateo great house on the lower slopes of Mount Taylor, may have been intended to hold what was left of the desperate farming population in that district.[81] Others, at higher elevations of about 6,500 feet, were expanded or built at this time around the perimeters of the Chacoan core area.[82] Clearly, some of the Chaco great-house residents were again maneuvering for new locations where water, firewood, and upland game were available outside the heartland.

Meanwhile, other interesting architectural changes took place in the Chacoan core during this last period of building and expansion. Most construction in the canyon itself stopped between 1116 and 1120,[83] and some older great houses such as Chetro Ketl were actually being abandoned.[84] But at others, as at Pueblo Bonito, new walls and room blocks were built to close off old courtyards and limit access. More tower kivas, such as El Faro on the Great North Road,[85] were built and appear to have been used as watchtowers as well as in religious ceremonies.

The rooms at Pueblo Bonito where "warriors" were found buried with their arrows are near other late habitation rooms where people who were killed violently have been found in group burials.[86] All of this evidence of violence dates to the 1100s. But the core of Chacoan great-house society had already been irreparably shattered by the time towers and citadels were constructed to contain the violence and reduce chaos. The greatest society in ancient North America had come undone, a victim of the drought of the 1090s. In a stunning but final building frenzy, the Chacoan elites then erected their grandest buildings in an effort to "pump up the economy." Apparently they failed to realize that without the small farmers to produce corn, they were already finished. That point was cruelly, forcefully, and finally driven home by a second drought beginning in 1130 — the coup de grace.[87]

To me, the citadel of Bis sa'ani on the Great North Road says it all. That fortified house, atop its formidable shale ridge, was clearly built for defense. Erected during the 1130s, it contains the latest roof beam datable to the great-house elites in the Chaco heartland — A.D. 1139.[88] It was the last gasp of the Chaco phenomenon, probably built to protect the northern approaches to the canyon when the second drought hit in 1130.

Past and Present

If ever there was archaeological evidence for the short-term power but ultimate futility of psychological denial and social myopia, it can be found in the late-eleventh-century great houses of Chaco Canyon.

Parts of Chacoan society were already in deep trouble after A.D. 1050 as health and living conditions progressively eroded in the southern districts' open farming communities. The small farmers in the south had first created reliable surpluses to be stored in the great houses. Ultimately, it was the increasingly terrible living conditions of those farmers, the people who grew the corn, that had made Chacoan society so fatally vulnerable. They simply got too little back from their efforts to carry on.

We should worry about this. Did you know that in 1998 there were 300,000 fewer farmers in the United States than there were in 1979?[89] Did you know that 94 percent of American farms are still small, family farms, but family farmers receive only 41 percent of all farm income?[90] Our farmers are walking away, too. Why? They aren't getting enough to carry on, either. Is urban America any more aware of this than were the village elites in Chaco's great houses? Many of us are not.

Still, the great-house dwellers didn't merely sit on their hands. As some farms failed, they used farm labor to expand roads, rituals, and great houses. This prehistoric version of a Keynesian growth model apparently alleviated enough of the stresses and strains to sustain growth through the 1070s. Then came the waning rainfall of the 1080s, followed by drought in the 1090s.

Circumstances in the farming communities worsened quickly and dramatically with this drought; the very survival of many was at stake. The great-house elites at Chaco Canyon apparently responded with even more roads, rituals, and great houses. This was actually a period of great-house and road infrastructure "in-fill," both in and near established open communities. In a few years, the rains returned. This could not help but powerfully reinforce the elites' now well-established, formulaic response to problems.

But roads, rituals, and great houses simply did not do enough for the hungry farmers who produced corn and pottery. As the eleventh century drew to a close, even though the rains had come again, they walked away, further eroding the surpluses that had fueled the system. Imagine it: the elites must have believed the situation was saved, even as more farmers gave up in despair. Inexplicably, they never "exported" the modest irrigation system that had caught and diverted midsummer runoff from the mesa tops at Chaco Canyon and made local fields more productive. Instead, once again the elites responded with the sacred formula—more roads, more rituals, more great houses.

Nonetheless, by the 1100s the roads, like the West Virginia turnpike—a "make-work" project that was the butt of jokes 40 years ago—began to go "nowhere." Other roads (like the one to Salmon) were never completed, and though some great houses were clearly built to move some of the elites out of an increasingly tense and impoverished core area, others were just erected in the middle of nowhere at the end of a new road, then never continuously used.[91] This is all rather like the wave of unneeded savings-and loan towers so scandalously built in America by deregulated bankers in the 1980s and ultimately paid for by the taxpayers.

The unbelievable explosion in kivas about A.D. 1100 points to a ritual life that had stopped nurturing open communities and had grown increasingly demanding and obsessive. We can see this phenomenon at work in American society today in what the news magazines have termed our "culture wars." In our modern version of this behavior, a narrow sector of society designates itself the "chosen one" and attempts to regulate the values, morals, even politics of the rest. The explanation for every problem that besets us—recessions, crime, drug trafficking, teen pregnancies, and many more—becomes our nation's declining moral values and secularization. In the end, this type of behavior blames the victim: one is poor in America because one is morally and ethically defective. No matter what you, the reader, think about such behavior—whether you embrace it or reject it—either way, it feeds no babies, makes no young mother strong, and sends no child to school. The same was true of the Chacoan elites' rituals: however base or pure their motives at the time, ritual alone did not feed the babies or create new food-producing enterprises to sustain farming families over the longer haul. Failure to address this problem destroyed Chacoan society.

I also find it ironic that the greatest Chacoan building projects were, like many of the CCC and WPA projects of our own Great Depression, the desperate economic reactions of a frightened and fragile society. In fact, most such projects support displaced people only in the short-term, rather than address the production and distribution of basic necessities. Nonetheless, their projects, like ours, tend to be viewed as grand achievements, reflecting the pinnacles of power. We are as myopic as they were, because such projects are often proof of a hollow shell. In Chacoan times, that hollow shell may have hidden the misery and hopelessness of the small farmers just as our make-work projects of the 1930s did. The great houses may even now hide those facts from the many tourists who visit Chaco Canyon and go away as impressed as Lieutenant Simpson was in 1849. But grandiosity cannot hide the essential facts from the field archaeologists who have excavated countless small houses in the last 25 years.

At the bitter end of the Chacoan era, many elites remained in their great houses, probably trying to hold onto the past, rather like Scarlett O'Hara trying to hold onto Tara in *Gone with the Wind*.[92] But the farmers who had brought in the corn harvests were long departed, like the black slaves who had supported Tara before the Civil War. Chacoan society collapsed, the farming pillar of its once great productivity shattered. The beleaguered Chacoan farmers had buried their babies one last time. Then they abandoned Chaco Canyon and most of its outlying great houses.

Most archaeologists know what happened to the elites who survived in the great houses. Some stayed. Others moved on to the high country at Mesa Verde, the Chuskas, and, eventually, the Pajarito Plateau surrounding Bandelier National Monument, northwest of Santa Fe.[93] What happened to the farmers? That story is the subject of the next chapter.

And what did the Chaco Anasazi learn from all this? That investment in infrastructure which produces no food is not the way to fend off starvation. That in a stratified society there can be no cooperation between the "haves" and "have nots" if the daily needs of the humble producers are not sustained. That the larger and more complex a society, the less capable it is of carrying on after losing even a moderate percentage of its critical resources. This recalls the Arab oil embargo of the 1970s. The United States lost 5 percent of its total petroleum supply and went into economic gridlock.[94]

And finally, the Chacoans learned that at the end of the day, formal religion and the religious values that go with it, no matter how powerful and integrating, can withstand only a finite number of deserted farms, broken dreams, and haunting memories. How many lonely young men who worked on the last of the road crews do you suppose carried the burden of having prepared a child's fresh grave, followed by another for his young bride, as the final memory of an abandoned farm? One more yucca mat and one more bowl.

This is a novelist's view of the end. The economist's view would be that it had taken both constant expansion in farmed land—the contribution of the farmers—and constant trade and redistribution—the contribution of the great-house elites—to make the open communities work. As resources of all kinds declined, the two groups' interests no longer converged, so each went its own way in a massive logistical and social "disconnect" that spelled the end of Chacoan society.

At least the Chacoans had an excuse: they had never in 8,000 years dealt with a society so large, so complex, or so fragile. Their greatest invention was not the roads, the great houses, or the rituals. It was the expansive, open farming communities that had once traded with one another. But in spite of its ecological elegance, that invention died because the society's obsessive, formulaic response—roads, rituals, and great houses—was of no practical use to the farmers after the drought of 1090. The Chacoans simply could no longer keep their farmers on the land—a labor problem of defining moment.

We moderns have seen some of these same things in the United States, and we have read history. Most of our forebears washed up on these shores after similar failures in other lands. Most of us are the direct descendants of people who once walked away from societies that could not or would not sustain them. We do know how it works. But have we yet learned the lesson?

CHAPTER SEVEN

The Upland Period

T HE FAR-FLUNG TRADE NETWORK THAT HAD CHARACTERIZED THE CHACO
phenomenon for more than a century vanished quickly. As infant mortality and
abandonments destroyed their open communities, farmers stopped making pottery to trade. The vast expanses of the Four Corners were no longer connected
as a functioning economic machine.

Those elites who hung on in a half dozen of the more stable great houses after
A.D. 1130 lost access to nearly all the signature trade goods that had marked their
status.[1] More importantly, they lost access to the surpluses of corn, dried meat,
and other foods that had once made them taller and their babies three times
more likely to survive than a farmer's child.

Archaeologists refer to a number of these late great houses as "scion" communities because they are believed to have been founded when groups of elites
left the earlier great houses in the Chacoan core and attempted to carry on in
new places.[2] They were smaller, lacked great kivas, and were located in arable
spots on the margins of the San Juan basin. Lacking great kivas, the scion communities provide us with superb evidence that Chaco's ritual and its regional
economy were interdependent. Apparently, the disintegration of Chaco's regional trade network equaled no great kivas in the 1120s to 1140s. Meanwhile, as
some Chacoan elites clung to a pathetic facsimile of their old order, surviving
farmers were busy laying the foundations of a new one.

The first farmers to walk away from the Chacoan world benefited the most.
They returned to places of ancestral Basketmaker and early Pueblo I hamlets in
the uplands even before violence overtook the Chacoan core in the 1100s. A return to the uplands was utterly logical. Many upland districts, such as Mesa
Verde, had lost most of their population during the two centuries of Chacoan

expansion.[3] Those first returning faced little competition for the wild roots, berries, and large game to be found in the cool piñon and ponderosa vegetation zones. In the Southwest, more rain and snow fall as one moves higher in elevation. The region's mountains literally force rain from moisture-laden clouds as they rise and cool while being pushed over the pinnacles by prevailing winds. It is a wonderful and rich environment—provided that population densities are as low as they were in early Basketmaker times.

But there was also a downside. Cool nighttime temperatures and the resulting shorter growing season restricted the size, quantity, and varieties of corn that could be grown.[4] This is why the late Basketmaker people and their even more numerous early Pueblo descendants had left the uplands nearly three centuries before for the vast, lower basins. This great shift in settlement pattern had made the Chaco phenomenon possible in the first place. Now it was working in reverse.

Few archaeologists have commented on this "back to the uplands" movement by farmers. The upland sites are hard to see and identify because the farmers no longer built large masonry, or masonry and adobe, farmsteads. Instead, they returned to an ancestral architectural style—the pit house.[5] Why? Pit houses are efficient. They can easily be built by two to four persons, and they provide excellent thermal buffering. This reduces the need for firewood in winter and provides a cool haven in summer.[6]

In July, the Southwest's hottest month, the floor temperature of a pit house would have been only about 63°F. Sleeping on a yucca mat laid over a cool floor of thick clay poured over insulating sand would have been quite comfortable. In January, the Southwest's coldest month, the floor temperature would still have been 60°F.[7] In moderate upland elevations of 6,500 feet, pit-house hearths in a site with a southern exposure would have been useful for cooking but not really necessary for comfort.

Few pit houses of the early 1100s have been excavated. Those that have tell us that these farmers made both crude copies of earlier Chacoan-style pottery and new varieties of simple black-on-white bowls. Neither type seems to have been widely traded.[8] The corn found in these sites is usually described as "retrograde," "stunted," or "atypical."[9] Some of this small-cobbed corn was small probably because it was stunted by cool nighttime temperatures and the shortness of the growing season. It is equally likely that hard-kerneled, cold-resistant varieties of chapalote-like corn, which fell into disuse during the Chaco era, were being planted experimentally, another upland adaptation. Genetic evidence to support either possibility, however, is currently lacking.

Sites of this period usually consist of a single pit house, or sometimes two or three. Most of the sites are tucked away unobtrusively in mountain coves.[10] Few luxury goods of any kind have been found in the early pit houses.[11] The overall picture is one of studied isolation and self-sufficiency combined with better access to a healthier diet based on hunting and gathering supplemented by agriculture. Regrettably, the earliest farmers to leave the failing Chacoan society got to enjoy these advantages for not much more than a generation.

After the drought of A.D. 1130, tens of thousands of farmers and others displaced from shrinking great houses also fled to the uplands. Chacoan society was dispersing as if flung outward by centrifugal force. This wave of migrants flowed into every upland area surrounding the San Juan basin—the Chuska and Lukachukai mountains on the west, the Mesa Verde and San Juan ranges on the north, the Gallina highlands on the east, the foothills of Albuquerque's Sandia and Manzano mountains on the southeast, and Cebolleta Mesa, the El Morro district, and the Zuni Mountains on the south.[12]

No large resident populations met the Chaco emigrants in those uplands except in the Taos, New Mexico, district and in the Gallina highlands flanking the west side of the immense Jemez Caldera.[13] The people already living in those two areas were descendants of late pit-house dwellers who had turned their backs on the emerging Chacoan world about A.D. 800 by refusing to trade. They had maintained a distinct society in the uplands for hundreds of years. Their cool climate had never allowed them to grow large surpluses, and now their land was wanted by refugees from the huge lowland society they had disdained. The picture soon grew ugly.

Gallina sites such as LA 11843, excavated in 1976 by the Museum of New Mexico's Timothy Seaman, were compact, fortified, pit-house communities. In the early 1100s, LA 11843 was laboriously stockaded. Some of the post holes for the stockade had actually been gouged out of the sandstone mesa top. No Chacoan-style ceramics are found at such sites. Instead, excavation turns up distinctive local gray utility wares and Gallina Black-on-white bowls,[14] along with small-cobbed, small-kerneled corn, wild plant foods, and remains of deer, elk, and antelope.[15] Invariably, the stockades have been breached and the sites burned.[16]

The condition of the human remains tells us the rest. The late Herbert W. Dick, first famous for his excavations at Bat Cave, spent many of his last years surveying and excavating Gallina pit-house sites in the Santa Fe National Forest.[17] In the 1970s, Dick reported that of the dozens of burials in his entire site sequence, *none* was 100-percent intact. Many of his excavated sites included remains of dismembered bodies, both children and adults. That they had been purposely dismembered is certain—flint knives had left deep striations on long bones where limbs were separated from the torso.[18] Many had had their skulls crushed, probably by stone axes and mauls. Others had been decapitated—even children.

Because no long, sharp-bladed tools were known by or available to the Anasazi in that era, the process of decapitation was surely slow and brutal when compared with the swifter, more clinical stroke of the headsman's ax or great-sword used in Europe at the same time. Put simply, these were not ritual or "le-gal" killings. They were the desperate conclusions of hand-to-hand fights among people struggling either to acquire land and foraging territory before they starved (in the case of the Chacoans) or to hold onto it (in the case of the indig-enous residents) merely to support their own families.[19] An estimated 60 percent of adults and 38 percent of children died violently in the Gallina highlands af-ter the collapse of Chacoan society.[20]

Similar findings have been published for the Taos area,[21] where burned and vandalized pit houses have also attracted archaeologists' attention. And it was much the same nearly 150 miles southwest of Chaco Canyon in the Apache Creek district on the northern frontier of classic Mogollon society.[22]

In 1983, Robin Farwell, at the Museum of New Mexico, and I published a comprehensive paper on these findings, assigning a mean date of A.D. 1154 to all similar upland pit-house settlements then known.[23] It was fascinating to us that traces of late Red Mesa Black-on-white pottery had been found at a number of these pit-house sites in upland districts both north and south of Chaco Canyon, though not in the Gallina district.[24] Were former residents of the Red Mesa Valley or, perhaps, their children living in these sites? Had some of them carefully car-ried away prized heirloom bowls as they left their farms near Casamero, Win-gate, and Coolidge some 30 years before? We liked to think so. Collectively, these upland pit-house sites were most common in the period from about 1100 to 1190.[25] Farwell's and my estimate was that the fighting peaked in the 1130s to 1150s and began to abate in the 1170s. It was an awful time, characterized by isolation, chaos, hunger, brutality, and massive population decline.

It may surprise readers of Southwestern archaeology that the collapse of Chacoan society was followed first by a wave of old-fashioned but efficient pit-house settlements in the uplands. These sites are difficult to find and date be-cause pit-house depressions are usually subtle and the pottery is meager. These sites simply are not very impressive, so the story contained in them is often over-looked. Moreover, out of habit, most published works focus on the years from 1100 to 1300 as the Pueblo III, or "great pueblo," period. And indeed, a few large pueblos were built as Chacoan society fragmented.

In chapter 6 I mentioned the sites of Ida Jean, Wallace, and Escalante Ruin. These were all built in the Mesa Verde region to the northwest of Chaco Canyon during the 1120s. They were clear attempts to maintain some aspects of the Chacoan great-house lifestyle.[26] But unlike the pit houses, few of these Chacoan "scion" communities were situated in the higher uplands. Instead, most of them, including Ida Jean and Wallace near McElmo Creek in southwestern Colorado's Montezuma Valley, sat at about 6,200 feet in elevation.[27] Their environment was much more like Chaco Canyon's than like the cooler, wooded uplands where the stockaded pit houses are found.

Some archaeologists have argued that these great houses and others farther north were founded by groups of male colonists, the religious elites, who migrated out of Chaco Canyon in the 1120s.[28] The argument has been made that these elites then mostly married local women and built these compact great houses to resemble structures at Chaco, especially Wijiji.[29] They were built, Chacoan style, in a C shape with paired kivas in the courtyards.

This scenario is certainly possible, for some powerful religious leaders presumably retained followers even as the Chaco phenomenon collapsed. Nonetheless, the scion communities were soon separated from their Chacoan roots and became distinctive little islands of Chacoan refugee society surrounded by a sea of upland farming and foraging people. DNA analysis of human bones from these displaced scion communities and from Chaco Canyon might either establish or refute this scenario, but no such research has yet been done.

In any case, the residents of these scion communities manufactured McElmo-style pottery, the precursor of later, full-blown Mesa Verde Black-on-white.[30] They grew somewhat larger-cobbed corn than that found in the pit houses, and they ate a wide range of wild plants and upland game. These people also ate their turkeys. This suggests hard times, because in more prosperous seasons they would have kept them for eggs and feathers.[31]

Escalante Ruin, which has been only partially excavated, is another possible scion community in southwestern Colorado.[32] Unlike sites in the Montezuma Valley, it was built at an elevation of 7,200 feet. Construction of a compact rectangle surrounding one large kiva took place in the 1120s and again in the 1130s.[33] As with the other great houses of this time period, no Chacoan roads led to Escalante; it was built after the road projects ceased. Escalante was occupied until sometime in the 1140s. Its pottery was manufactured in the surrounding local districts and did not include Chacoan trade wares.[34] I think it is important that no Red Mesa Black-on-white pottery has been found at these northern scion communities. That pottery was the favorite of the first farmers who walked away from the Red Mesa Valley in the late 1000s and carried heirloom pieces to many places in the uplands. It has been found only at the upland pit houses and some modest pueblos built near them. This reinforces the notion that farmers founded the pit houses and elites founded the scion communities.

Because the Escalante great house was situated at a high elevation, its residents' diet featured more variety. Remains of cottontail rabbits dominate the animal bones from the site, followed by deer and turkey. But even at Escalante, rock squirrels, pocket gophers, wood rats, prairie dogs, and deer mice went into the soup pot.[35] Corn grown here was generally smaller-cobbed than that grown at the Ida Jean and Wallace great houses a thousand feet lower in elevation.[36] It does seem plausible that these sites represent the last echo of Chacoan great-house society. Nonetheless, their distinctive ways were soon swallowed up, and the last vestiges of the Chaco phenomenon faded away as upland populations burgeoned in the mid- to late 1100s.

By the A.D. 1170s, Chacoan society was but a memory. A new, very different regional society was forming, and it linked one ponderosa-studded upland to another. The open Chacoan communities in the basins were dead and gone, followed by three generations of isolation and warfare. Then new trade networks again began to tie the hundreds of small, isolated mountain settlements to a broader world. This trade was almost exclusively in well-made black-on-red pottery bowls.[37] The earliest of these pottery styles is called St. Johns Black-on-red, after the contemporary town of St. Johns, Arizona, about 40 miles southwest of Zuni.[38] Later versions added a wavy, ghostly white line to the outside of the brick-red and black bowls, making it a three-color, or polychrome, pottery. The growing trade in St. Johns Polychrome bowls in the late 1170s coincided with significant changes in architecture and settlement patterns.

Though pit houses were still being dug and used, people in some districts returned to building small, above-ground, masonry pueblos. Most encompassed 10 to 16 rooms and lay at elevations of 6,500 to 7,200 feet,[39] somewhat lower than the pit houses, which had been hidden away at 6,900 to 7,900 feet.[40] Many of the small pueblos founded in the 1170s were located far from the Chacoan core, in areas that had missed the first land rush to ancestral places after the Chacoan economy failed. Interestingly, none appears to have been fortified or tucked away in a hidden mountain cove. Apparently, upland farmers felt more secure in the 1170s than they had 20 years earlier, during the era of palisades.

The Pajarito ("little bird") Plateau, near Los Alamos, New Mexico, came to be heavily settled at this time. The Pajarito is now home to Bandelier National Monument and Los Alamos National Laboratories, of atomic bomb development fame. Its ponderosa- and piñon-dotted mesas are liberally sprinkled with medium-size house blocks of quite evenly sized rooms built between the 1170s and 1190s. Most are made of rough-cut sandstone or dense volcanic tuff. Few have kivas or pit structures. Obviously, patterns of family religious practice were again undergoing rapid change.[41]

Corn grown at these sites was still small by Chacoan standards but not as small cobbed and thin shanked as the highest-elevation pit-house varieties.[42] New styles of well-made black-on-white pottery were now painted with carbon-based paint (from burnt plant material) rather than Chacoan-style mineral-based paint (from crushed iron ore). On the Pajarito Plateau, the local pottery is called Santa Fe Black-on-white.[43] Its color scheme is actually described more accurately as a light gray background with dark, charcoal gray designs. The carbon-painted designs sink into the clay before it is fired, lending a ghostly quality to the simple but well-designed decorations.[44]

Carbon-based paints replaced the earlier mineral paint technique throughout the eastern Anasazi area. Most books on the subject point out that the carbon paint technique traveled from the Kayenta Anasazi in northern Arizona to Mesa Verde and then to the Pajarito.[45] I prefer to point out that the carbon paint technique had been known and used in most of the uplands since at least late Basketmaker times. Small quantities of carbon-painted wares had occasionally been traded into Chacoan great houses during the Chaco phenomenon's heyday,[46] but it is easy to overlook their modest presence among the truly staggering quantities of mineral-painted, Chacoan-district trade wares found in those early great houses.

The Cliff Palaces

As the year 1200 drew near, the uplands came into their own, and after a hiatus of nearly 80 years large pueblo sites, architecturally distinct but comparable to Chacoan great houses, again began to be constructed. No other sites in the Southwest have attracted more popular attention or been featured on the covers of so many books than these so-called cliff palaces. The first sight of Cliff Palace or Mug House at Mesa Verde provokes a deeply emotional response. Perhaps these ruins stimulate our memories of ancient cave dwellings. The neatly angular masonry constructions contrast pleasingly with the natural rock overhangs that frame them. Similar sites are found at Bandelier National Monument, in the Gallina highlands, in the Chuska Mountains, at Montezuma Castle and Navajo National Monument in Arizona, and at Gila Cliff Dwellings in the Mogollon country.

The primary construction at each one took place between the 1190s and 1260s. That's it. Just 70 years.[47] All those books and photographs would have you believe that nearly all the cliff palaces endured for centuries, but most were inhabited for less than a hundred years. They were also scarce when compared with the numerous small farmsteads built in the surrounding mesa country. Though archaeologists have lumped them with Chacoan great houses as "great pueblo architecture," the trademark of the Pueblo III period, the two kinds of settlements are not really alike at all.

The Chacoans had built their great houses with open courtyards, and the roads that passed those courtyard walls extended outward like open arms to embrace a vast world—a world controlled by the rhythms of their ritual and the dictates of their trade. In short, it was a world that understood the Chacoans' power and did not challenge it.

The cliff palaces were nearly the opposite. They were much more like closed citadels, as were European castles of the same period. But instead of resembling a European town nestled under the walls of a great castle, cliff palaces were compact, angular villages tucked under the warm, protective breast of a great sandstone mesa. They were elegant solutions to the need for defense in a time when harvest surpluses still drew envious and unwanted attention. Unlike Chacoan great houses, they do not radiate power.

The cliff palaces are quiet, almost mysterious places. Perhaps visitors find them mysterious partly because they exude efficiency. Efficiency is something we talk about and say we want, but we do not really understand it, for we are the children of humankind's greatest age of power. In contrast, cliff dwellers in the Four Corners were acculturated to the idea of efficiency as a way to create a society able to succeed the ruined Chacoan one.

In what ways were the cliff houses efficient? First and foremost, nearly all of them faced south, southeast, or southwest.[48] They acted as immense solar collectors that caught the low winter sun each day as it crossed the southern sky. In summer, most of the village, tucked under the overhanging rock, enjoyed cool shadow while the sun passed high overhead. Since virtually all the cliffs overlooked canyons, the bottomlands below and the talus slopes adjacent to the village could be farmed. The warm winter sun actually lengthened the growing season at farm plots located on the rock-warmed side of the canyon, facing south. Generally, no one lived on the slopes of the north-facing canyon wall because they stayed cold and snow-covered in winter.

Even if the far canyon wall was beyond the reach of an arrow shot from a 25- to 30-pound bow, the basic need for defense from surprise attack had already been met. Any arrows that might reach the stone walls of the outer towers from an unusually strong bow would glance off before clattering harmlessly down the slope below the village. Unless the enemy had wings or could draw a bow while hanging upside down, batlike, over the lip of the protecting rock overhang, it took only one or two sentries with dogs posted on the mesa above the site to protect the occupants from sneak attack. To mount a successful attack required skill and bravery enough to negotiate an unfamiliar, often sheer cliff face in the dead of night without arousing the dogs.

The villagers pecked handholds and footholds into the rock face so that sentries and farmers could scale the cliffs. There were farm plots on top, both adjacent to the cliff house and scattered along the mesa near the small, unprotected, 10- to 30-room farmsteads nearly always found above the cliff house.[49] It is likely that the cliff houses held the greatest concentration of occupants in times of war and raiding or in winter, when those mesa-top farmsteads were vacated until the next planting season.

Interlude in the Basins

The reemergence of long-distance trade in the early 1200s signaled an increasingly successful adaptation to the cool uplands and their short growing season, as well as new ties to the lower-elevation basins. As I mentioned earlier, this trade is most evident in the movement of the distinctive St. Johns Polychrome bowls made near Zuni.[50] Highly prized, these bowls were evidently traded for the local black-on-white bowls made in increasingly formal styles in each upland district. In addition, the Taos district's black-on-white pottery was exchanged for both the prized polychrome and other upland styles of pottery. The Santa Fe district's black-on-white went both north, near Taos, and south, into the Albuquerque district. Lovely Tularosa Black-on-white pottery, with its bold "lightning" designs, was traded out of the area south of Zuni to a number of other upland districts.[51]

We do not know whether the traded bowls contained anything of value, such as seed corn. But we do know that the net effect was to connect one highland district to another and a few highland districts to adjacent, lower-elevation basin lands. The need to reconnect to basin lands is easily illustrated by the geographical distribution of Mesa Verde pottery. Mesa Verde Black-on-white found its way back into the San Juan basin in the early to mid-1200s.[52] At a time when several of the abandoned great houses in Chaco Canyon itself were renovated and used briefly by highlanders farming the warmer basins, there seems to have been a renewed but temporary emphasis on access to the lower elevations in other areas as well. This was the same time period during which highlanders from the Pajarito Plateau founded LA1, Pindi Pueblo, near Santa Fe. Just as the Mesa Verdeans reoccupied the Chacoan great houses only briefly, Pindi was used for just 20 to 30 years before the population again withdrew to higher elevations.[53]

What caused some upland people to move temporarily back to the basins after the tragedies suffered there only a century earlier? Archaeologists circulate many complex theories, but my own view is simple. Farmers do not like to move, but when they do relocate, they typically go to places where they can continue to farm. The Chacoan core area must have become more farmable again in the early 1200s. To me that means that it must have begun to get more precipitation than it had been receiving in 1130, when the Chacoan farmers left. And would farmers have moved out of the uplands at this time unless conditions there absolutely dictated such a move? I believe they would not have unless the uplands somehow became less farmable or population expansion forced some to seek new land. How can we know which of these scenarios is most likely?

We can provide an answer by focusing again on one kind of archaeological site that is often overlooked when summaries of the Pueblo III period are written—the scarce but important pit house. Beginning about 1200, deep pit houses again began to appear throughout the highlands of the Southwest in elevations somewhat lower than those of the mid-1100s. They are found in eastern Arizona, at Taos, in the Santa Fe district, at Apache Creek, on Cebolleta Mesa, and in the Sierra Blanca near Ruidoso, New Mexico. The mean date of these pit houses is A.D. 1223.

Unlike the earlier, conflict-period pit-house sites, these sites average six dugouts per settlement. Upon excavation, the structures yield an average of more than a dozen kinds of pottery that were traded across the uplands.[54] Why would comparatively prosperous farmers of the early 1200s leave their small mesa-top farmsteads, move to nearby downslope localities, and dig deep pit houses? Probably because it got very cold in the uplands at this time. In Europe, the early 1200s are known as the Little Ice Age. Although I do not argue that climate was identical in northern Europe and the American Southwest from about 1200 to 1230, the creation of thermally efficient pit houses by some people at the same time others moved into the warmer basins tells us what we need to know—it probably got colder and wetter for a time.

More pit houses of this period need to be found and excavated. Most that have been excavated lie underneath the genuine Pueblo III mesa-top pueblos that were soon to be built. I will come back to that shortly.

Meanwhile, the interlude in the basins during the early 1200s is interesting in several respects. For one thing, the renovation and new construction at Chacoan great houses was quite shoddy by earlier standards. Instead of fine, banded masonry walls, the Mesa Verdeans erected walls coarsely fashioned from big, rough-cut sandstone blocks.[55] The earlier Chacoan rooms were so large that the Pueblo III renovators often divided them right down the middle by adding a rough wall, creating two small apartments out of one.[56] Similarly, many grand American homes built during the prosperous 1890s later got cut up into apartments or made into rooming houses. One sees the same phenomenon in Glasgow, Edinburgh, London, Paris, and other great cities where economic cycles have created waves of renovation, alteration, and new uses for old structures.

Even though the Mesa Verdeans came back to Chaco, there is no real evidence that they attempted to re-create Chacoan society. Some archaeologists insist that a few Chacoans remained in the canyon all along.[57] This is possible, but if so, both they and the newcomers were simply too few to re-create much of what had existed before. Hundreds of the old rooms in the canyon's great houses remained untouched. A few of the kivas were replastered, but others never saw use again. Few new buildings were constructed, apart from a compact, triple-walled tower structure and surrounding rooms at Pueblo del Arroyo.[58]

At approximately the same time, other Mesa Verdean sites began to dot the San Juan basin. Most of them are remarkable for their locations atop formidable, isolated buttes and rock outcrops. One of these, CGP-54–1, was recorded by the University of New Mexico's Office of Contract Archeology in 1974.[59] It took climbing gear to get to the site, which perched atop an isolated butte with sheer walls about 80 feet (25 meters) high. The site consisted of 10 to 12 habitation rooms and storerooms and either 2 or 3 kivas. It had been constructed of coursed sandstone blocks, and it covered the entire top of the butte. The pottery was pure Mesa Verdean in style, suggesting use between 1220 and 1260.

Another, similar site, CGP-56 (Coal Gasification Project, number 56) lay near it on another sheer sandstone pinnacle.[60] It was even larger, with nearly 20 rooms. Why on earth would habitation sites have been built on such pinnacles in Mesa Verdean times? Clearly the answer is fear. A dangerous world surrounded the Mesa Verdeans who huddled together for protection on these small mesas. But who were they afraid of? After the fall of Chaco, conflict had quickly shifted to the uplands, and very few people remained behind in Chaco Canyon. Those remaining, if any, were so few that the Mesa Verdeans who returned to the basins had the run of Chaco Canyon without incident shortly after A.D. 1200.

Navajo oral tradition may help us learn something about the enemies of the Mesa Verdeans. One series of ancient and remarkable Navajo tales tells of a poor beggar woman and her son who went from Chacoan great house to great house seeking food.[61] Several great houses such as Pueblo Bonito, Wijiji, and Aztec are referred to by name, and the kinds of food and specific events at each (such as plucking turquoise offerings from the cliff behind Pueblo Bonito) are recounted. In the tale, Keet Seel, White House at Canyon de Chelly, and another cliff house (probably Jacquet) near Farmington are mentioned. All these sites contain Mesa Verde Black-on-white pottery, so we know they were inhabited during the 1200s, in Mesa Verdean times.

Although this tale is not absolute proof that Navajos roamed Chaco Canyon while some of the great houses were still in use, it is strongly suggestive. Just as the broad outlines of many stories in the Old Testament of the Christian Bible have subsequently been confirmed by archaeologists, I expect these Navajo stories to one day be independently confirmed as well. The Navajo, of course, are not waiting for confirmation from us. They hold these tales to be true, and obviously so. After all, how else would their ancestors have known who lived at the great houses and what food they offered or refused the beggar woman and her son?

Of course, these tales do not tell us whether the old woman asked the original Chacoans or the later Mesa Verdean reoccupants for food, so the time when the recounted events happened could have been anywhere from about A.D. 1050 to about 1260. Some recent archaeological research strongly suggests that Navajo interaction with the canyon's Mesa Verdean (perhaps mixed with Chacoan) population is more likely. Dental remains typical of Navajo (Athabascan) people were uncovered a few years ago at Trinidad Lake, Colorado, and laboratory dated to approximately 1175. If these data are confirmed by additional finds, it could suggest that Navajos moved into their final homeland just after the Chaco Anasazi world spilled out of the San Juan basin in the mid-1100s.[62]

Until recently, most textbooks maintained that the Navajo came to the Southwest from the north only between the 1400s and 1500s. But several recent compilations of excavation data suggest that at least a few Navajo houses, or hogans, may date to the 1300s.[63] That leaves the archaeological gap between Mesa Verdean reoccupation at Chacoan great houses and Navajo settlement in the Four Corners at just a century, not the four or five that most textbooks report. When powerful societies collapse, they often leave a vacuum and are sometimes replaced by more efficient and modest ones—often hunters and gatherers. When the great Maya city-states in lowland Yucatán collapsed in the A.D. 900s, the jungle reclaimed them, and then nomadic hunters and slash-and-burn horticulturists claimed the land. The Navajo were nomadic hunters and gatherers upon their arrival in the *dinetah* (the Navajo homeland), which ultimately encompassed the San Juan basin. They eventually learned agriculture from Puebloan people or their Anasazi ancestors.

Navajos or no Navajos, why was the period of Anasazi reuse of the basins so brief? The Mesa Verdeans had, after all, been able to grow larger corn at Chaco Canyon than in the uplands in the 1200s. No one is certain, but it is likely that the small farming villages in these lowland settings were simply unable to hold onto their harvests and fend off raiders, whether Navajos or other Anasazi. The pinnacle locations of the CGP sites testify eloquently to the general nature of the problem. So does the destruction and abandonment of the reoccupied great house called Salmon Ruin on the San Juan River. It was apparently attacked, and more than 30 women and children who had sought refuge in its impressive tower kiva died horribly in the fire set to destroy the town. Even the margins of the San Juan basin offered danger.

So post-Chacoan society returned to the highlands in the mid-1200s. Expansion at some of the cliff houses continued, but resettlement of the basins came to an end. Between roughly 1230 and 1260, large new pueblos such as Bayo Canyon Ruin near Los Alamos, New Mexico, were constructed on hundreds of mesa tops throughout the Southwest. Many of these really do fit everyone's idea of "great pueblos," as archaeologists once defined the architecture of the 1100s to 1300s. Traditionally, this period, usually called Pueblo III, lumped the last great building projects at Chaco (A.D. 1050-1140) with the great cliff palaces built in the uplands during the 1200s. In fact, the cliff houses were separated from Pueblo III buildings at Chaco Canyon by more than 100 years of elapsed time and by nearly 1,000 feet in elevation. An era of stunning conflicts, followed by a massive die-off of population in the late 1100s, also separated Chaco's great houses from the newer upland sites. But some were as big as, or even bigger than, Chacoan great houses had been.

Taking these differences into account, I think it makes little sense to call both the Chacoan great houses and these late upland sites Pueblo III, since they were created by such different times and events. My concern isn't over the name "Pueblo III" itself. Rather it is that the decline of Chacoan society in the basins and the painful rise of a successor in the uplands is obscured by using a scheme that lumps the largest and most prosperous sites of the two distinct periods together. The decline of Chacoan society was *the* defining event for Puebloan farmers. Its consequences affect them to this day.

The Mesa-Top Sites

However archaeologists label these large mesa-top sites, Anasazi society regrouped and aggregated into them in the 1230s. For this reason, such sites are called "Coalition period" sites in the northern Rio Grande,[64] where many of them have been found, typically at 6,600 to 7,300 feet in elevation.[65]

Many of these villages were quite large. One of the largest, overlooking Guaje Canyon near Los Alamos, is known as LA 12700.[66] At about 7,000 feet above sea level on a sloping mesa north of Bandelier National Monument, it consists of at least three immense room blocks, each fully enclosing an interior plaza. There are five deep kivas divided between the two room blocks built at the east end of the mesa.[67] Just beyond, the mesa ends, narrowing into a shape rather like the prow of an immense ship. The site was well protected on three sides by steep cliffs. The kivas had been pecked by hand, right into the mesa's soft volcanic bedrock. Dozens of small, clustered "cavate" rooms had also been gouged deep into the south-facing volcanic tuff cliff, right below the room blocks. These served as warm, sunlit refuges from the upland's cold winters.

The three primary room blocks above the cave rooms contained at least 400 ground-floor rooms.[68] A hundred yards to the west of and slightly above the main house blocks, on the mesa's gentle uphill slope, lies an impressive reservoir once walled with clay-faced sandstone.[69] It trapped rainwater and snowmelt as they flowed down the mesa toward the village. Several tiny, unexcavated structures, possibly sentry houses, lie to the west of the boomerang-shaped reservoir, and remnants of masonry hint at either low check dams or defensive walls. This village was clearly designed to be self-sufficient and to withstand siege.

So were most other large villages of the same period. Nearly 130 miles southwest of Guaje Canyon lies Mariana Mesa in the southern Zuni highlands. There, at the back of the gritty floor of Horse Camp Canyon, partially hidden by a hump-backed ridge of volcanic rubble, rests Site 616 at 7,300 feet in elevation. Like other mesa sites of this period, it was built on top of the upland-period pit houses that preceded it. By A.D. 1230, the village's outer walls enclosed a rectangle measuring 800 feet long by 650 feet wide, an area of about 11 acres. Room blocks completely surrounded a central plaza so large that a football field could easily fit inside.[70]

Site 616 was constructed like a huge fort. No windows, doors, or gates opened to the exterior. Unlike the walls of Chaco's great houses, its walls were composed of cobble-and-adobe masonry. That type of wall construction simply could not carry as much weight as the Chacoan banded type, so Site 616 stood only one story in height. Nonetheless, 500 rooms faced its plaza.[71] Many of the rooms could be entered only by ladder from the roof above. In one corner of the plaza there was a huge D-shaped kiva, rather like some kivas still found in the Rio Grande pueblos. In another area of the plaza, a deep circular well had been dug. Its winding spiral steps led down to a bedrock bottom. Like Guaje Canyon, Site 616 was designed to withstand a siege.[72]

Nothing was wasted when the well was dug. The coarse clay near the top served as adobe to mortar the angular, cobbled walls. As the excavation went deeper, kaolin-rich clays replaced the coarser overburden. These went into fashioning much of the site's everyday cooking pottery.[73] Evidence that corn was grown here is scarce, but enormous quantities of locally abundant wild plants, seeds, and roots were harvested and stored. Both large and small game animals were regularly harvested and eaten.[74]

In spite of its fortified design, Site 616's story is tragic. The village came to a violent end sometime between 1260 and 1270 when it was successfully raided. Apparently the marauders breached its walls and came in across the rooftops, felling several inhabitants with their arrows.[75] A young girl was caught on the rooftop and killed with an ax blow to her forehead. Her right arm was severed at the elbow as she lay dying. The room below, perhaps her family's, was then put to the torch. She fell with the burning roof as it caved in, the remains of a delicate necklace of fine jet beads still at her throat.

The general looting that might have been expected during such a raid never came. The goal was apparently either to kill or to drive off Site 616's residents—a goal that the raiders achieved. The inhabitants did abandon the site after this event. Although we cannot be certain that they departed immediately, they left behind nearly all of their possessions, which suggests a hurried exit.

Abandoning household effects was rare. In most of the sites of this period, every functional tool and piece of pottery was used and reused until nothing salvageable remained. Most of these sites call to mind depression-era households in the United States, where socks were darned, shirt collars turned, and Christmas wrappings saved and used again and again. At Mariana Mesa, large, unbroken Tularosa Black-on-white ollas have been found along with quantities of St. Johns Polychrome bowls, the hallmark of upland trade networks. Several fine jet and turquoise pendants turned up during excavation, along with shell from the Gulf of California.[76]

Not long after Site 616 fell silent, many other great mesa-top sites were abandoned throughout the Southwest. Few of these abandonments involved violence, but they must have been somber and reluctant. Many of the huge sites had been inhabited for only 20 to 40 years.[77] In most of them, life had been hard. The deceased were often interred in the outer walls as rebuilding or renovation took place. Their bones show abundant evidence of osteoporosis, and their teeth, hypoplasia, particularly in the densely settled districts at Mesa Verde and Bandelier. Most skeletons from the 1200s are marked by evidence of overwork and an inconsistent food supply.[78]

In spite of recurring hard times, the coalition of upland people after the 1230s had brought benefits. For the first time since the fall of Chaco, labor was available to plant enough different fields to produce community food surpluses in good years—and there were many good years in the first half of the thirteenth century. Between 1200 and 1250, precipitation increased in quantity and reliability. That combination apparently nurtured the first upland crops of larger-cobbed corn.[79] As corn harvests grew, trade networks also grew both more robust and farther flung. Traders at most of the big upland sites of the 1250s, as in Chacoan times, imported a dozen or more black-on-white trade wares from other districts, along with prized polychromes.[80]

But the rains were fickle and once again became erratic after 1250, just as regional population began to grow for the first time in more than a century. As the rains failed even more dramatically in the 1260s, a number of the fortified mesa-top settlements also failed. It was a case of too many people, too little corn, and not enough meat. The "mystery" of these abandonments is much discussed. While the particular reasons for abandonment at any one of these sites may forever elude us, the general pattern is clear.

As both the quantity and reliability of rainfall deteriorated in the 1260s, the drier west-facing mesas were hardest hit. In the Four Corners, the prevailing summer monsoon winds flow in from the Gulf of Mexico and are driven west, drenching the east faces of the high country while leaving the west faces much drier. One has only to look at the dry west face of Sandia Mountain, which rises another 5,000 feet above mile-high Albuquerque, and then drive to the lush, timbered east face of the same mountain on a dry July day to understand what must have happened in the 1260s and 1270s.

Most of the farmers who left the Chacoan world in desperation during the 1100s moved to upland localities where they could find land. True, a few actually returned to ancestral places even as others created new great houses in the shadow of Mesa Verde, but most simply took their chances on any available mountain meadow. The descendants of those who settled down to dry-farm the west-facing mesa country lost everything in the dry 1260s and 1270s. By mere chance, those who chose the east faces in the 1100s were lucky and won a reprieve from the droughts.

Ironically, Gallina highlanders on the west face of the Jemez Mountains had dug in and fought to the death during the 1100s in order to hold ancestral lands that were to become worthless only a century later. The winding canyons of the Gallina highlands and the west-facing Mesa Verde country emptied out as the 1260s bore on. The real mystery is not that some of those unable to farm left the Mesa Verde country north of the San Juan River, but that every last settler exited. The farmers there must have drawn together in cliff houses and large fortified mesa-top settlements during the mid-1200s for good reasons. Perhaps one of these was that Navajos or other hunters and gatherers were all too ready to take this prime hunting territory for themselves. Small clusters of Anasazi stragglers in the few well-watered side canyons may simply have been too vulnerable to stay after the majority retreated.

The ancestors of the Hopi, well to the west in Arizona, moved from mesa to mesa during this period, partially abandoning impressive sites such as the one called Chavez Pass.[81] They reestablished dry farming both on the mesas and in the valleys below, but their most permanent villages were built in the late 1200s atop three separate, fortresslike mesas—villages they live in to this day.[82] The Hopi may have been too far west to be in harm's way in the late 1200s, so they had time to adapt to the era of poor rainfall. Their region was also much less crowded than Mesa Verde.

Those on the east faces of the uplands fared best. The eastern districts included the Pajarito Plateau, populated partly by farmers displaced during the Gallina fighting and partly by others, possibly from Mesa Verde, who may have bypassed the upland conflicts altogether. Judging from details of pottery and kiva architecture on the Pajarito, survivors of other populations may also have been absorbed into the area around present-day Bandelier National Monument.[83] Yet life could not have been easy even for those who enjoyed this geographic reprieve. After about 1275, the erratic and declining rainfall turned into a series of deep, localized droughts.[84]

These severe droughts finally drove people from the mesa tops even in the east-facing localities. But instead of abandoning their land, they first moved down into the adjacent canyons, especially those with permanent streams. They innovated in their agriculture, reengineering entire gently sloping hillsides and mesa tops to create "grid gardens," cobble-mulched gardens, and cairn fields.[85]

Grid gardens, similar to the "waffle" gardens still in use at Zuni,[86] were small, cleverly designed microenvironments bordered by low walls of rough stone. The sun warmed these little walls, lengthening the growing season in the one- to two-meter-square plots. Plants were grown in small hillocks inside the grid and hand-watered as necessary.

In the cobble-mulched gardens, a covering of egg-sized gravel spread over the soil prevented the rapid evaporation of rainwater, kept it from running wastefully off the surface, and facilitated absorption. Dry, dusty soil just doesn't absorb water as well as the moist soil under a rock.

The rock cairns, often seen in aerial photographs as neat rows of tiny polka dots, were also ingenious. In the Southwest, humidity peaks in early morning, about 5:00 to 6:00 A.M. Even on a dry summer day a cubic yard of rock in a cairn stores enough of the daytime's sunny heat to precipitate several gallons of water from the moist predawn air. In the northern Rio Grande region, from La Bajada Mesa north to Chama and Taos, many square miles of mesa and hillside were cobble mulched or set with cairns beginning in the 1200s.[87]

In many of the lower mesa areas, these investments in infrastructure during the 1200s were expanded and refined by later Puebloan peoples. Such engineering projects, unlike Chacoan roads, produced food. Indeed, they were exceptionally clever and efficient, making the best use of every drop of available water, even precipitating it from moist air so that the size of a farm plot would not be limited by how many jars of water could be carried to it in the dry season.

Yet in spite of all these inventive responses to drought, by the 1270s the failing precipitation was seriously disrupting the vast upland trade network.[88] Tularosa Black-on-white bowls, Mesa Verde Black-on-white mugs, even St. Johns Polychromes were no longer widely available by the late 1270s. St. Johns bowls are occasionally found in later archaeological sites, but they were already heirlooms, often repaired. Surviving Anasazi pueblos, the majority of them in the northern Rio Grande, began to turn in on themselves and to make do with more restricted, local trading networks.

Tyuonyi, the great circular ruin at Bandelier National Monument, was probably founded in the 1290s.[89] In those days, it sat only a few feet from lovely Frijoles Creek, the permanent little stream that passed its southern outer wall. Most of Tyuonyi's pottery was local, but trade wares did come in from an area of several hundred square miles. This was a modest economic reach when compared with the upland trade network interconnecting 60,000 square miles just 20 years before. Both paled in comparison with the vast Chacoan economic machine, which had consistently pulled in exotic goods from at least half a million square miles during the A.D. 1000s.

By 1300 only the best-watered east-facing canyons were still permanently inhabited. The quantity and reliability of water flow in each canyon determined relative population density.[90] Wherever canyon-bottom streams began to dry up, farmers again moved out of the uplands, following the east-flowing rivulets and arroyos to permanent rivers. The Anasazi permanently abandoned the San Juan basin and all the uplands north of the San Juan River. All that remained of the Anasazi world was a thin, sweeping arc of surviving Pueblo settlements from Taos to Albuquerque and west to Zuni and the Hopi mesas.

The gods had forced yet another fundamental shift in settlement pattern upon the seventh generation to be born after the Chacoan exodus from the San Juan basin. Steeled by nearly two centuries of hardship since the fall of Chaco, the survivors accepted the judgment of the gods once more and did what was asked of them. They may not have realized it as they abandoned their lovely upland parks and trekked to new, largely uninhabited farmlands along the rivers, but they now possessed all the knowledge necessary to create an entirely new kind of society—a complex but efficient one.

Past and Present

The two centuries following the decline of Chacoan society were the most violent and tragic in the Southwest's entire human history up to that time. The whole structure of Chacoan society had been based on open, unfortified communities. Perhaps most households during the Chacoan heyday knew recurring hunger, but violence was comparatively rare until the late A.D. 1000s, when it became episodic at some outlying communities. Otherwise, Chacoan society was reasonably calm, orderly, and safe until the droughts of the 1090s, and perhaps even longer. Judging from the existence of way stations, people moved freely along the roads until then. Great kivas were not walled off from the populace, nor were great-house courtyards. That all changed shortly after 1100, when controlling walls were added at points where roads came into the great houses at Kin ya'a and Alto.[91] Courtyards were walled off, and defensively situated strongholds such as Bis sa'ani and El Faro were built at the same time.[92] These architectural changes announce incivility where order had once reigned.

Unable to sustain its population, and with its farmers already desperate, Chacoan society fractured into separate, competing groups. The remarkable increase in the number of kivas built during the early 1100s is a clear signal of this. Religious groups demand allegiance. When religions fracture, members must choose both dogma and leaders. The archaeologist Lynne Sebastian, who has written about power among the Chacoan elites, points out that large religious gatherings did not take place in Chaco Canyon after 1100.[93] Clearly, the elites' economic and religious power over an entire region had been destroyed, never to be reestablished. After 1100, ritual leaders could exercise power only over small, competing groups of followers.

These hungry remnants of the old order turned on one another and on nearby highlanders. Walls at Chacoan great houses were followed closely by palisades in the uplands. Decapitated bodies found in upland pit houses, warrior burials at Pueblo Bonito, and construction of elaborate fortifications in the uplands bordering the San Juan basin all point to fierce factional warfare.

As Chacoan society blossomed in the A.D. 900s and early 1000s, it probably incorporated several once-isolated tribal groups speaking different languages. To this day, Keres-, Tewa-, and Zuni-speaking Pueblo people all claim descent from Chacoan sites. All have oral histories that include fragments of events from Chacoan times. As Chacoan society came undone, those ancient linguistic, social, and religious differences would have been rich fodder for ethnic and tribal hatreds acted out in the uplands.

We have seen this same sort of fracturing elsewhere in modern times. Josip Broz Tito forged modern Yugoslavia from the ancient districts of Bosnia, Herzegovina, Montenegro, Croatia, Macedonia, Serbia, and Slovenia in the late 1930s.[94] World War II allowed Tito to create a "national" identity in response to both Nazi and Stalinist attempts to dominate the population. For a time, it worked. For two generations, people forgot, or simply discounted, religious and linguistic differences along with ancient enmities. This was easy while Yugoslavia grew in power, autonomy, and wealth. A generation of children born in the 1970s took little notice of their neighbors' differences—they were all Yugoslavs, and they carried the passport to prove it.

But their parents and grandparents remembered all too well. After Tito died, an unfettered Communist elite prospered more flamboyantly, even as living conditions among laborers and in traditional farming villages deteriorated. Yugoslavia, no longer expanding economically and unable to afford all the accoutrements and infrastructure of a modern nation-state, fragmented painfully along ancient religious and linguistic distinctions.

The costs of services, infrastructure, and organization needed to create and manage a large society are enormous. People bear them willingly only when they benefit. Just as an infant America drafted its Declaration of Independence in 1776 to protect itself from the costs of empire imposed by Britain's King George III, Yugoslavia in the mid-1990s threw off the costs of Tito's nation and returned to medieval society. Such destructuring almost always leads to violence as those who had benefited most seek to hold their advantage against those who have become desperate.

In 1996, the *Christian Science Monitor* published extensive accounts of massacres near Tuzla in Bosnia-Herzegovina. To quote but one ugly event, "Bosnian Serb soldiers systematically executed as many as 2,000 Muslim prisoners after taking the UN 'safe area' of Srebeniwĉa in July, according to credible eyewitness accounts."[95] The Bosnian Serb soldiers were Christian. Their hapless victims, once their neighbors, were Muslim. The graves have subsequently been located and confirmed. No one truly wins such wars of attrition, but it is terribly hard to convince the parties involved. As a consequence, Yugoslav students who came to the United States to study before their country splintered now have useless passports. In the blink of an eye Yugoslavia was gone, and those who had grown up with it as their national identity are having to decide who they really are and where they really belong.

Consider Northern Ireland and its appalling, neighbor-against-neighbor sectarian violence—Protestant versus Catholic. How on earth did the vigilante paramilitary groups on either side accurately recognize the "other" when they went shooting and bombing? Those people shared common appearance, language, customs, dress, and heritage. The vigilantes *could not* tell. So they attacked at places where they assumed "others" gathered—funerals, pubs, parties, and markets. This was a perfect formula for nurturing an unending cycle of injustice and rage.

The roots of this conflict go back to the A.D. 1200s, when Henry II of England tried to attach Ireland to his kingdom. He managed to control only the area around Dublin, known as "the Pale."[96] This gave rise to the phrase "beyond the pale"—moving from English-speaking (civilized) Ireland inside the Pale to Gaelic-speaking (primitive) Ireland beyond it. Over the next five centuries, England pushed harder and expanded its influence. Gaelic actually began to die out early in the 1900s. But when times are bad, memories are long. Gaelic is again on the rise—a chic political statement among young Irish Catholics, most of whom learn it at university.

Had Northern Ireland expanded economically as rapidly as other parts of northern Europe, we would not likely be reading about this sectarian violence, euphemistically called "the troubles." If you don't know that late-twentieth-century living standards still lag in Northern Ireland and to a lesser extent in the republic of Ireland, just rent the movie *The Commitments*.[97] The young Irish musicians in its rhythm-and-blues band, who are so fond of 1950s and 1960s America, make it painfully and coarsely clear that Ireland "is a … third world country." If Northern Ireland gets richer, the troubles will probably fade away. If it gets poor again, they will likely come back.

Prosperity, social integration, altruism, and generosity go hand-in-hand. Poverty, social conflict, judgmental cynicism, and savagery do, too.

And that brings us, well, to us. In the 1950s and 1960s, as the United States grew rapidly in power and wealth, social mobility and integration found greater favor. The civil rights movement blossomed with surprisingly little violence, considering the magnitude of the changes it wrought in the existing social order. America got more liberal, less judgmental, more accepting, and more generous.

But for the vast majority of Americans, the real purchasing power of median household income has been declining since the 1980s. To be precise, the median income of all American households declined from $33,452 in 1985 to $33,178 in January 1995, in constant 1995 dollars.[98] Poverty rates actually increased in the United States from 12.4 percent to 13.8 percent between 1980 and 1995.[99] Why should we worry about poverty and its effects on contemporary America? And what has Chaco Canyon got to do with conditions now?

We should worry because a male African American child born in the United States in 1990 was twice as likely to be dangerously underweight at birth than was a white baby boy born the same day. He was more than twice as likely to die in his first year, could expect to live nine years fewer, and was six times more likely to die of violence.[100] What might those differences eventually cost America? What is the possibility that our society, like Chaco's, will actually come undone someday?

These differences in infant mortality and longevity are not unlike those between a baby born at Pueblo Bonito and another born at Site 627 across Chaco Canyon in A.D. 1100. The Pueblo Bonito baby was three times more likely to live to adulthood than the farmhand's child a few hundred yards away.

What did those differences eventually cost the Anasazi? The fall of Chacoan society. The terrible exodus to the uplands. The atrocities and wars of attrition between 1150 and 1200. The need to create from scratch an entire new kind of upland community, economy, and trade network during the 1200s. Then the utter destruction of that new creation in the late 1200s, when nature refused to cooperate. Finally, nature again forced the survivors into their final exodus from the uplands to the rivers about 1300.

And just why was it their "final" exodus? Because from these tragedies the Anasazi had learned how to create different and enduring communities. That is the subject of the next chapter.

CHAPTER EIGHT

The Creation of Pueblo Society

EVEN AS SOME FARMERS LINGERED IN A FEW UPLAND VILLAGES LOCATED IN
favorable settings, such as Tyuonyi at Bandelier, others were displaced by the
droughts and moved on as the thirteenth century drew to a close. The decline
of upland society and the transformation to stable streamside villages was extraordinarily complex. This period, usually called Pueblo IV, spanned the years
from about A.D. 1290 to 1500.[1] The riverbank villages passed from prehistory into
history when they were described in the journals resulting from Coronado's
expedition of 1540–1542.[2] Because archaeological research has focused on excavation at a few very large pueblos of this period, there is still much research to
be done in order to complete our picture of the details. Nonetheless, the fundamental changes are clear.

Another Transformation

The thin arc of surviving Puebloan settlements shifted to the east and south
of the areas where most upland villages had been built in the 1200s. As in the
decline of Chacoan society, the first to depart the uplands escaped turmoil but
suffered isolation. These settlers started new farmsteads near points where side
creeks and arroyos joined the larger, permanent watercourses that emptied out
of the uplands. And again as in the 1100s, they built pit houses before constructing their pueblos.

This time the pit houses were dug in lower elevations, typically about 5,700
feet (1,805 meters) above sea level. They were both shallower and more rectangular than earlier ones, and these settlements were larger than those of the mid-

1100s. Averaging about nine pit houses apiece, they contained combinations of late upland pottery and new lowland styles decorated with lead glaze paint.[3]

Nearly 20 years ago, a team of archaeologists from the University of New Mexico partially excavated a number of pit-house sites typical of the Pueblo IV period in what is now Cochiti Reservoir.[4] One of these sites, LA 12522, now under Cochiti Lake, contained late upland Santa Fe Black-on-white and two varieties of early-fourteenth-century glaze-painted pottery, Cieneguilla Glaze Yellow and Espinoza Glaze Polychrome, a black-on-red ware. The settlement contained both shallow pit houses and surface rooms. Later Pueblo IV rooms were built atop several of the pit houses.[5]

Another nearby site in the Cochiti district, LA 6455, at 5,300 feet in elevation, contained 10 to 12 pit rooms arranged in an L-shaped alignment that partially enclosed a small central plaza. These pit rooms were 1.0 to 1.2 meters (just over a yard) deep. The site faced east and sat adjacent to a stream that flowed into the Rio Grande.[6] Surface storage rooms of poles and adobe were also constructed at this site. Probably built a few years later than LA 12522, it contained a wider variety of early glaze wares in addition to Galisteo Black-on-white and Biscuit A, two types of black-on-white pottery that superseded upland styles. Biscuit A, which became common after the upland trade network collapsed, was manufactured during the 1300s and 1400s in the area between Cochiti and Taos,[7] where the Tewa-speaking Pueblo Indians now live.

Collectively, these sites tell us an important story. By the time they were built in the early 1300s, St. Johns Polychrome was no longer being produced and imported from the Zuni area. It was being replaced in the Rio Grande district by new bowl designs in lead glaze paints—black, yellow, and red, or black, white, and red. The lead-bearing ores used to make the glaze paint were ground up into a slurry, painted on, and fired at a high temperature. They were mined from scattered local deposits along the Rio Grande. Some of the early glaze designs were stylized copies of the defunct St. Johns Polychrome patterns.[8]

The people who lived at these early Pueblo IV sites ate corn, beans, squash, turkeys (both wild and domesticated), rabbits, and other rodents such as pocket gophers and mice. A few years after the brief pit-house phase, most of these creekside settlements were renovated into above-ground pueblos.[9] This pattern is reminiscent of the practice of Anglo-American "sod-busters" who homesteaded the Oklahoma and New Mexico territories in the 1880s and 1890s. They built dugout houses and planted crops for a few years before erecting their typical Midwestern frame and clapboard houses.

To the south of the Cochiti district, life must have been more dangerous and the Puebloan population more vulnerable during the early 1300s. A number of fortified mesa and hilltop masonry room blocks stretched along the Rio Grande and the Rio San Jose (in the Acoma area) from Santo Domingo south to Socorro, New Mexico. On many of the mesas and isolated hillocks overlooking these rivers, people built compact, thick-walled citadels to overlook farmlands adjacent to the streams below. Most of these date from the 1320s to the 1350s. Some years ago, the late Mark Wimberly and his colleague Peter Eidenbach published important survey reports that identified many sites of this type along the middle Rio Grande and its tributaries. They all contained the distinctive early glaze wares that were under development in the river districts, and they provide strong evidence of yet another episode of conflict and social disintegration as upland society was replaced by a riverine one.[10]

One of these sites, known as Hidden Mountain (LA 415),[11] lies a few miles northwest of present-day Los Lunas on the lower Rio Puerco near its confluence with the Rio San Jose. It was built about three miles northwest of a huge later pueblo known as Pottery Mound (LA 416).[12] Hidden Mountain, first noted by Adolph Bandelier in the 1880s,[13] is not actually hidden at all. A substantial black basalt prominence visible for many miles, it rises nearly 500 feet (155 meters) above the surrounding valley floor. The mountain's slopes vary from merely steep and rugged to true cliffs. Its summit covers almost 35 acres, where 10 different house clusters enclose a total of 122 masonry and masonry-based jacal rooms. The hilly summit also contains 18 pit rooms, about 30 rock cairns, and several small reservoirs.[14] Hidden Mountain's scattered settlements ranged from as few as 3 rooms to as many as 38 at the rectangular complex called Casa de los Vientos ("windy house"), which also held the only kiva.[15] The varying architecture and site plans of the 10 separate clusters imply staggered building episodes and a series of different social groups living atop this summit in the early 1300s. A few of the rooms *might* have been built earlier, in the 1200s, but all of the pottery was either gray Rio Grande utility ware or "Glaze A" (Glaze I) pottery,[16] the hallmark of the early Pueblo IV, or riverine, period, which is dated to the 1300s.[17]

Another of these sites, San Pascualito, was built about two miles east of the Rio Grande in the Bosque del Apache on a prominent, isolated mesa fragment with steep, rocky sides and boulder-strewn sandstone cliffs. Its flat summit measures about 100 by 300 feet in area and offers spectacular views in every direction.[18] The fortified summit overlooks the ruins of the huge adobe pueblo called San Pascual Village (LA 757), which was built later. Some archaeologists think LA 757, the immense pueblo on the Rio Grande below, was founded just after the summit was fortified.[19]

San Pascualito, on the mesa top, includes two single-story, linear room blocks containing 37 rooms and a kiva. All were constructed right on the bedrock with walls made of brittle, reddish brown, irregular sandstone blocks. Several long defensive walls protected the talus slope, and on the northernmost cliff edge there is a large, heavily burned area that has discolored the sandstone—evidence of signal fires lighted long ago, perhaps to warn others living farther north of potential attack.[20]

Other, similar fortified sites are Indian Hill Pueblo (LA 287), overlooking the abandoned schoolhouse at San Acacia,[21] and a huge, later pueblo, LA 286, near the banks of the Rio Grande itself.[22] The single kivas, instead of pairs, at all of these fortified hilltop villages signal important religious changes. The early 1300s were the years when masked rain gods and the kachina cult, thought to have originated west of the Zuni area, began to penetrate the eastern pueblos and displace many older religious customs.[23]

Like the period just after Chacoan decline, the early to mid-1300s included a complex mix of pit houses and easily defended above-ground pueblos. A string of isolated and fortified sites, like an ancient Maginot line, overlooked the rivers on the southern frontiers of that fragile arc of settlements that had survived the upland period. At the same time, small pit-house communities were built in the creekside bottomlands of the safer and more heavily populated Puebloan core areas to the north of contemporary Albuquerque. After the mid-1300s, violence on the southern frontiers seems to have been largely sorted out, and settlements shifted downhill to the rivers' open floodplains. Evolving styles of glaze-painted pottery were manufactured, unfortified Pueblo villages near good farmland grew dramatically in size, and the compact hilltop forts were abandoned.

Take Me to the River . . .

By the end of the 1300s, a number of large pueblos had been founded in open settings near reliable rivers and creeks—the Rio Grande, Rio Jemez, Rio San Jose, Rio Puerco, and Rio Chama, the Zuni and Pescado rivers, Taos Creek, Galisteo Creek, and others. Lower arroyos emptying into these were also farmed. The densest concentration of these communities lay along the Rio Grande and its tributaries between Taos and San Marcial.[24] Other impressive clusters of large villages were founded along the Jemez River and along Galisteo Creek, southeast of Santa Fe.[25] Even though these towns were typically built at the hilly edges of each river's floodplain, few of them broke all connections with the nearby uplands. This fact is of dramatic importance.

By the end of the 1300s, a pueblo's land typically ran back from the rivers to adjacent foothills and then to the mountain crests. In the densely settled Rio Grande district between historic Isleta and Cochiti, there were once roughly 30 major villages, on both the east and west sides of the river. On average they sat two to three miles apart,[26] so each one's land was a long, narrow strip stretching away from the river into the adjacent uplands. Each of these territories included diverse topography and several distinct life zones—riparian, juniper, piñon-juniper parkland, and mixed piñon-ponderosa. Some pueblos adjacent to mountains such as the Jemez Caldera, Santa Fe Baldy, and Albuquerque's Sandias also had access to fir, aspen, and true alpine environments.[27]

As a practical matter, access to different ecological and altitudinal zones meant that a farmer could continue to plant some upland mesa-top fields in warmer years but could cultivate more fields in the lowlands during colder ones. It meant access to rabbits, prairie dogs, turkeys, fish, and mice within the main village's immediate precincts. It also meant access to deer and antelope along the grassy foothills and to elk, bear, and bighorn sheep in the high country.

Cottonwoods and willows grew along the rivers. In fact, the world's greatest natural stand of cottonwood *bosque* (forest) still grows along the Rio Grande from Santo Domingo to Los Lunas. Junipers and piñons grew on the low rolling hills above the river. Every few years, when temperature and moisture were benevolent, the piñon stands produced great harvests of nuts rich in protein and oils.

The Rio Grande district's volcanic mesas provided fine-grained black basalt for arrow points and sharp scrapers or gravers. Ancient gravel deposits, often exposed in arroyo cuts along the rivers, offered Puebloan toolmakers jasper, petrified wood, and chalcedony. The mesas provided volcanic tuff or sandstone for building, and the mountains around the Jemez Caldera provided some of the world's finest black obsidian — volcanic glass that formed when molten silica shot up from the numerous volcanoes of the Rio Grande rift. The obsidian was unsurpassed for stone tools and remarkable cutting blades. Eye surgeons in Russia still prefer to operate with obsidian when they can obtain it, because it is far sharper than any steel.

In short, each village attempted to maintain access to diverse ecological zones by holding and using the land. Alfonso Ortiz's introduction to San Juan Pueblo in the *Handbook of North American Indians* makes that very clear.[28] One method of holding the land was through tending shrines and offering prayers and feathered prayer sticks at both ancestral and holy places. The high mountain country was especially holy. At Tyuonyi in Bandelier this meant that Keresan speakers who had left "home" in the 1300s and gone downhill to farm at the river's edge in the Cochiti area came back regularly. Such pilgrimages were made to tend family shrines, replaster kivas, share in ritual feasts, and perform sacred dances with family members who had stayed behind.[29] Although most of the uplands throughout the Southwest had been vacated in the late 1200s, Pueblo peoples living at Taos and from San Juan Pueblo on the north to Cochiti Pueblo on the south had unusual access to the adjacent high mesa country, as did the people of Jemez. Most clung tenaciously to this access and used their old upland sites and cliff-face "cavate" rooms time and again over the next three centuries. Droughts and raids from nomadic tribes were the primary motivators of occasional retreats back into the forested mesa country.

The other important technique for extending a community's land holdings was to actively farm diverse and widely scattered fields. Some farm plots lay at the edges of the river bottoms; others were planted right on the floors of the arroyos that fed the rivers during the summer rainy season. Still other fields might sit on higher mesas several miles from the village. Sand dunes at the feet of those mesas were planted, too. By the late 1300s there were rapidly growing patches of grid gardens, cobble-mulch gardens, and cairn fields, productive engineering projects that helped maintain access to a village's surrounding landscape. Eventually, some farm plots lay so far from the central pueblo that the men and older boys seasonally moved out of the winter room blocks into outlying "field houses." These seasonal shelters, usually containing one to three small rooms, were often nestled against the great sandstone boulders that had fallen at the edges of canyon floors.[30]

Population at the main pueblos, even those with a thousand rooms or more, flowed outward each spring at planting time and back again for the winter's feasts, rituals, dances, and socializing. In winter the pueblo was full. In summer it was half empty, its farmers scattered across 20 or 30 square miles. In this sense, the riverine pueblos finally became a bit more like late medieval European communities—a central town with religious and civil functions surrounded by miles of farmsteads.

True, this new style of territorial holding did not necessarily guarantee everything people needed or desired, but it provided most of a village's essentials. There were particularly large and productive turquoise deposits in the Cerrillos Hills, known as Mount Chalchihuitl ("turquoise mountain") to the Aztecs, who actually had a place glyph for it.[31] The nearby Galisteo basin pueblos controlled most of this trade between the 1300s and 1500s, taking up where the Chacoan world had left off.[32]

Rich clay deposits in the area of modern Santo Domingo Pueblo provided another valuable trade good. So did a number of prized lead-bearing deposits for making glaze paint.[33] In all, a great deal of trading went on in the late 1300s and early 1400s. The new trade network interconnected nothing like the Chacoans' vast San Juan basin or even the later highlanders' widely scattered pockets of ponderosa-shaded mesas and mountain meadows. Rather, it created narrow corridors in which people and commerce flowed along the creeks and rivers much like the seasonal floods.

For this reason, the early Rio Grande glaze-painted trade wares are almost never found in large quantities more than a few miles from the rivers. Similarly, the Biscuit B series of black-on-white trade wares produced at ancient Tsama (now the Hispanic village of Chama) and nearby villages is seldom found more than several miles in either direction from the Chama River valley.[34] But the geographical reach of trade along these river systems should not be underestimated. Hopi pottery made it as far east as the Rio Puerco valley, and some Rio Grande glaze wares traveled as far as Kansas. Mogollon-style pottery from surviving remnants of that society in the Rio Abajo (lower Rio Grande) area between Socorro and Las Cruces found its way as far north as Santa Fe. Glaze wares traveled south down the Rio Grande,[35] a few even reaching Old Mexico near El Paso. Glaze wares also traveled down the Pecos River, and brown utility wares made in the middle Pecos valley traveled north.[36]

There was even some trade between the separate river districts. Polychromes such as the ones called Heshotauthla and Fourmile, made near Zuni, and others made in the Acoma-Laguna district were traded into the Rio Grande corridor, and glaze wares from the Rio Grande moved west to those settlements.[37] But the volume of east-west trade was quite low when compared with the movement of people and goods within those narrow riverside corridors.

Why did nearly all the Puebloan people tuck themselves into such confining corridors after 1300? The need for reliable water sources was one compelling factor, but there was also another. In the 1300s, the Puebloan descendants of the Chaco Anasazi were, by comparison with the 1000s, very few in number. Aggregation into larger communities discouraged raids by the nomadic peoples who had been moving into the Southwest since Mesa Verdean times.

Unlike the case with the Chacoan period, archaeologists have never tallied the total number of Pueblo IV sites in one place for purposes of comparison. Data were carefully compiled, however, for the heavily settled Cochiti Reservoir area in 1979.[38] Extrapolating from those data, the total of 1,293 Pueblo IV rooms created in more than 200 years in the Cochiti district represent approximately one-quarter of the residential space offered by the 2,972 Pueblo III rooms created in the same study area during 150 years. Not only were Pueblo IV rooms fewer in number, they were also much smaller. By whatever method we choose to estimate population on the basis of room numbers, it is clear that population had already dropped substantially by 1325–1350."[39]

Of course no one really knows the exact population of any of these prehistoric settlements because the square-footage-under-roof and room-count methods of "guesstimating" population have been proved inadequate.[40] But we do know that at least 4,500 Chacoan sites, and probably double that number, once existed in the San Juan basin.[41] Most of them were small farmsteads, and 100 to 200 were Chacoan great houses, or "towns." The number of persons living in any settlement fluctuated dramatically with that settlement's life cycle. Young families having babies generally translated into crowded conditions. Aging grandparents alone in the enlarged settlement translated into much more residential space per person and lower relative population.

Think of the population estimate "problem" as an extension of your own experience. How big was your grandparents' house, and how many people were living in it when you last visited? In contrast, how big was your first apartment when you took your first job or married? For many people, the first child arrives to great joy mixed with a profound sense of confinement. It was ever thus.

This is why the Cochiti study of residential space is an important yardstick. That yardstick clearly implies that between A.D. 1050 (Chaco) and 1350 (early Pueblo IV), population may have shrunk by as much as three-quarters.[42] Even if the data are skewed and this inference is off the mark, so that population had shrunk by, say, only one-half to two-thirds, it had been catastrophic. These possibilities are within the ranges of population loss once predicted for modern America if it suffered a nuclear war.[43]

Once again, surviving Puebloan farmers consolidated to maintain secure villages and access to a large labor pool. This time they rearranged their shrunken world into narrow riverine corridors during the 1300s. The enormous geographical and ecological diversity once enjoyed naturally by those in the Chacoan system and partially salvaged by the far-flung upland trade network was endangered by this consolidation into narrow corridors. In contrast to the hundreds of interconnected, widely spaced communities of the Chacoan era, which had once controlled a vast and diverse landscape, each of the Pueblo IV communities emphasized self-sufficiency and self-containment. Each achieved its individual needs for ecological diversity by holding dissimilar surrounding lands through farming, hunting, and ritual use.

That required the reduced population to aggregate in larger town cores from which they rhythmically spread out to the boundaries of each village's land every spring. They stayed on the land until the fall harvests had been brought back to the main village, where the pueblo's sheer numbers could protect the stored food from raids. It was *using* the land that held it for the community. Maximizing the ecological habitat of each major village had become crucial, because no far-flung political or economic system now existed to meet that need.

It was as if these survivors of the three hard centuries since the Red Mesa Valley had begun to empty were determined never again to want for firewood to warm them or for upland game to nourish pregnant women through the winter. During the upland period they had also learned that the warm lower basins were needed for growing large-cobbed corn during cold years. Clearly none intended ever again to live huddled in fear atop an isolated mesa like the Mesa Verdean inhabitants of CGP-56, mentioned in the last chapter.[44]

Having diverse land and diverse agricultural techniques also enabled them to grow far more varieties of corn, beans, squash, and gourds. These, along with cotton, tobacco, and turkeys, provided a richer, more secure overall harvest than could be gained by dry-farming merely one small dune field or a mesa top adjacent to the farmstead, as so many Chacoans had done. We "moderns" are also now beginning to realize, and our agricultural schools are teaching, that our vast monocropping systems are ecologically and economically more vulnerable to disaster than are complex, multicrop strategies. Pueblo IV farmers had begun to write their own "textbook" on this subject by the late 1300s. That knowledge was encoded into religious ceremonies, dances, chants, and harvest-time procedures that were reenacted annually for the benefit of the entire community.

Should you be tempted to doubt this, just attend a Pueblo feast dance open to the public. Look at the array of regalia in the different dances and the variety of terrains it represents: deer hooves or antlers (mountains), rattlesnake rattles (sand hills), gourds (farm plots), hand-loomed cotton sashes (farms), fox- or coyote-tail adornments (hill and mesa country), buffalo hides and heads (adjacent grasslands), pine or fir boughs (mountains), cottonwood drums (riverine woodlands) with deerhide drumheads (hills and mountains).[45] The list goes on and on. It takes regular access to *all* of the pueblo's distinct ecological zones to properly carry out its dances and rituals. How well did these emerging changes in Puebloan society succeed? Let us review the information available from several carefully excavated towns of the 1300s to 1400s.

Success, Failures, and the New Order:
A.D. 1300 to 1500

By Chacoan and upland standards, some of the Pueblo IV riverine sites were simply immense. But size isn't everything. More importantly, as the Pueblo IV period progressed, Puebloan villagers generally got better and better at sustaining themselves.

Arroyo Hondo ("deep wash") was a Pueblo IV town founded about A.D. 1310.[46] Its location, five miles south of Santa Fe on an upland piedmont west of the Sangre de Cristo Mountains, at 7,100 feet in elevation, was more a holdover from the upland period than a reflection of the emerging Pueblo IV riverine pattern. Still, a nearby canyonlike arroyo flowed seasonally, and a free-flowing perennial spring emerged in the canyon below the site.[47]

Beginning in about 1310, the core rooms at Arroyo Hondo, organized into seven room blocks and arranged around two plazas, were built of coursed adobe. In 1320, construction began to expand to the west and south as eight new room blocks and two additional plazas were added. By 1330, the site had become immense—24 room blocks, mostly two-storied, surrounded 10 plazas. At that zenith the town encompassed 1,000 rooms, and its population is estimated at 1,000 persons.[48]

Each of Arroyo Hondo's room blocks was 2 to 5 rooms wide and up to 15 rooms long. Each block was divided into apartments of four to five interconnected ground-floor rooms with associated storerooms and rooftop work areas above on the second story. Rooms averaged about 5 square meters of floor area (51 square feet).[49] These are very small by modern standards—about the size of either a large walk-in closet or the cheapest inside cabin with fold-down bunks found on a modern cruise ship. Most rooms were entered through the roof by ladder.

Rooftops and the adjacent plazas substantially amplified the confined indoor living spaces. Cooking, pottery-making, flint-knapping, corn-drying, basket-weaving, and a host of other daily activities took place in these spaces, in full public view. Most of the pots made at Arroyo Hondo were plain, everyday culinary wares. In addition, some black-on-white bowls were found. These were remarkably similar to ones manufactured at Rowe and Pecos pueblos some 25 miles to the northeast.[50] A few pieces of turquoise were unearthed during excavation, as were the bones of scarlet macaws. Moderate quantities of abalone and olivella shell, used to make heishe, pendants, and inlay work, came from both the Pacific coast of California and the bays of Sonora, just as they had for more than 500 years.[51] Apparently some of the trade networks disrupted during the end of the upland era were reemerging. These goods likely came to the Santa Fe district via the Colorado, Salt, or Santa Cruz drainage, thence to the Little Colorado River valley in Arizona, and finally to the Zuni River.

The diet at Arroyo Hondo included the standard corn, beans, and squash. The cobs were not particularly large, but arroyo farming there was apparently somewhat more reliable than dry-farming the mesa-top uplands in the ponderosa zone. The domesticated crops were supplemented by wild greens, seeds, roots, berries, and nuts. Other herbs were harvested as medicines. Pigweed (amaranth) seeds and those of other invasive "weeds," which had already been part of Anasazi agriculture for more than a thousand years, were also eaten. In addition, domesticated turkeys and nearly 50 species of wild game provided meat. As always, more meat came from jackrabbits and cottontails than from all else combined. Nonetheless, mule deer, pronghorn antelope, and elk were also hunted and consumed.[52]

Arroyo Hondo's prosperity was relatively short-lived. About 1335, precipitation decreased and population at the pueblo declined sharply. By 1345, the village was virtually abandoned. Then, in about 1370, it was resettled and reinvigorated until 1410, when another drought drove many away. The droughts persisted, and in 1420 a catastrophic fire burned much of the old pueblo not already vacated because of the protracted droughts. By 1425, this series of recurring droughts had effectively ended Arroyo Hondo's life as a viable community.[53] The compromise environment—neither truly upland nor truly riverine—no longer worked.

The burials excavated at Arroyo Hondo paint an important picture of this village's overall effectiveness at sustaining its population before it was abandoned. In all, 120 burials have been analyzed. One hundred eight of these individuals died and were buried in the early room blocks built between 1310 and 1330. Another 12 pertained to the smaller, second period of settlement after 1370.[54]

All but a few who apparently died in a kiva during the early Pueblo IV period had been formally buried, and about half of the formal burials were found in the plazas. The rest had been interred either in small subfloor crypts or in the midden areas.[55] Sixty-three percent had been buried with some kind of grave goods,[56] a far higher proportion than in the Chacoan farmsteads. Hide blankets and yucca mats were the most common grave accompaniments. Broken bowls and olla fragments were next, followed by modest gifts of heishe or stone beads. These people had a bit more to accompany them into the next world than had the Chacoan farmers of A.D. 1050. Unlike the Chacoan farmhands, about 10 percent of the deceased at Arroyo Hondo received food offerings at death.[57]

On the other hand, their children died at almost exactly the same 45-percent rate before age 5 as had the Chacoan farmhands' children 300 years earlier.[58] Owing to high infant mortality, life expectancy at birth in Arroyo Hondo was just 16 years. If a child born at the pueblo lived to age 15, it could expect to live another 19 years.[59]

Some 44 percent of all adults suffered from skeletal pathologies.[60] The adult males buried at the pueblo ranged in height from 157 to 172 centimeters. Their average height, in English measurement, was 5 feet 4 inches. Adult females ranged in height from 149 to 162 centimeters, with an average of 5 feet 1 inch.[61] In contrast, Chaco Canyon great-house males averaged 169 centimeters (5 feet 6 inches) tall, and females 162 centimeters (5 feet 3 inches). The nearby Chacoan farmers averaged 165 centimeters (5 feet 4 inches) tall, and their wives, 157 centimeters (5 feet 2 inches).[62] In this indirect measure of nutrition, Arroyo Hondo's inhabitants look more like the Chacoan farmhands than like the elites.

Still, there had been one clear demographic improvement. At Arroyo Hondo, "only" 58 percent of all those born died before reaching age 18.[63] Fully 80 percent of the farmers' children had died by that age in late Chacoan times. Yet a 22-percent improvement in survival to adulthood was not enough to carry the day for Arroyo Hondo. By 1425, its arroyo was not only deep but deserted. Human voices were not to be heard there again until after Spaniards settled Santa Fe in 1610.

The causes of Arroyo Hondo's demise were different from Chaco Canyon's. At Arroyo Hondo there were few of the status differences that were so prominent in Chacoan times. Only one adult male's burial at Arroyo Hondo implied unusual status. This man, who died in the 1330s, had been buried with 16 items: a well-made wooden bow, a stone ball, sheets of natural mica, a bone awl tip, an eagle claw, a raven skin and raven wings, and a number of projectile points.[64] This is reminiscent of several "warrior" burials at Chaco. The raven's wings are particularly interesting. Were they symbols of the Crow clan known at Pecos in historic times?[65] We may never know.

Whatever the story behind this one burial, the other burials suggest that Arroyo Hondo's demise was related to an unreliable local food supply. Arroyo Hondo represents one model of early Pueblo IV site location and adaptation that worked for a time but was not durable. A number of other sites built in this era employed the same geographical strategy—farming an arroyo while hanging onto a modified upland environment. Many similar sites were founded about 1300–1325, and like Arroyo Hondo, most were abandoned about 1425 during the deep droughts.

Another of these was Tijeras Pueblo, which was built next to a seep, or *cienega*, a few miles east of Albuquerque at an elevation of 6,300 feet.[66] Excavated by the University of New Mexico in the 1970s, its story is similar to Arroyo Hondo's, but it was a smaller settlement of only about 200 ground-floor rooms.[67] I find it especially interesting on several counts. It contained very early Rio Grande glaze wares and was one of the first pueblos in the northern Rio Grande to have a Mogollon-style kiva. Not surprisingly, research on its burial population indicates that its inhabitants may have been genetically mixed.[68] This implies amalgamation of surviving populations from both southern and central New Mexico in the 1300s.

In contrast to Arroyo Hondo, only an estimated 33 percent of Tijeras Pueblo's children had died by their eighteenth birthday. The average age of its adults at death was 32.4 years.[69] Apparently, smaller populations could be better supported by a combination of farming and foraging in these modified upland environments than the larger populations of sites like Arroyo Hondo, but daily life was not easy. Just consider the animals that were eaten at Tijeras Pueblo, and their percentages: cottontail rabbits (31.1 percent), pocket gophers (15.4 percent early, 23.2 percent late), prairie dogs (6.6 percent early, 7.1 percent late), turkeys (5.9 percent early, 7.7 percent late), mice (5.5 percent), and jackrabbits (5.9 percent).[70] Nearly 70 percent of the meat consumed at Tijeras Pueblo consisted of rodents! Bison, elk, and pronghorn were surprisingly rare, considering the village's location in the lower Manzano Mountains.

Nutritional status at Tijeras was grim by any modern standard, but only 12 percent of its adults suffered osteoporosis, and only about 15 percent of the infants buried there showed signs of pernicious anemia.[71] The gray bands in teeth, evidence of near starvation, were scarce compared with Chacoan times. Evidently famine was rarer, though lower-grade, day-to-day malnutrition was commonplace. Except at Pecos Pueblo and another nearby site, it was not until people moved to the rivers themselves and incorporated diverse adjacent lands that daily life and nutritional conditions improved dramatically.

Regrettably for archaeologists, few of the really large Pueblo IV riverine pueblos have been excavated using modern techniques, nor have many of them been properly reported. This is largely because the remaining riverside pueblos have either succumbed to modern sprawl—most people still live along rivers in the Southwest—or sit on land held by descendants of the original builders. Surviving Pueblo people have no intention of disturbing the resting places of their forebears.

So I use Pecos Pueblo as my last archaeological example of this period, partly because it survived into historic times. Pecos Pueblo isn't a perfect exemplar either—it lies on a small, prominent mesa at 6,950 feet in elevation, adjacent to the Arroyo del Pueblo some 18 air miles southeast of Santa Fe.[72] It is too high in elevation and too far from the Rio Grande to be a perfect model of the riverine period. But a well-watered arroyo flows by it, and it sits only about three-quarters of a mile from the Pecos River. It was in daily use from about 1300 until 1838, a span of five centuries. In the 1920s it was excavated by A. V. Kidder, who made it the location of the first Pecos Conference. This gathering of Southwestern archaeologists has taken place nearly every August since 1927.[73]

Pecos was founded in the early 1300s, just as the manufacture of local black-on-white pottery, a carryover from the upland period, was ending. The first room blocks atop its small mesa were isolated from one another, quite like those at Hidden Mountain and other fortified sites of the early 1300s located between 50 and 100 miles to the south along the Rio Grande. Like many villages of the early Pueblo IV period, these room blocks were of stone masonry and stood only one story tall. A surprising number of circular kivas were built on the mesa a short distance away from these early rooms.[74]

Like virtually all other villages of the early Pueblo IV period, Pecos suffered its share in the droughts of the 1330s and again during the protracted ones of 1410–1425. But Pecos was different from the other early Pueblo IV mesa-top strongholds, which did not survive. First, it was farther north, and second, it claimed and used the lion's share of its valley, which spread from the foothills of the Sangre de Cristos on the west (nearer to Santa Fe) to the Tecolote Mountains on the east, then south to Anton Chico.[75] As other, smaller Pueblo IV sites in its vicinity were either absorbed or abandoned, Pecos extended its hold on the surrounding territory. The Tecolotes separated Pecos from the nomadic Plains Indian tribes and were an important buffer against sudden raids. This territory may have been systematically expanded southward in historic times as other Indian populations declined in the lower valley after the Spaniards arrived. But the pueblo had held and used the entire upper Pecos Valley for half a millennium by the time its last survivors abandoned it and trekked to Jemez Pueblo in 1838.[76]

That access to the diverse environments bordering the valley and to the game hunted from the grasslands in the valley's wide southern end was what sustained the people of Pecos. In the early glaze-ware period (the 1300s), only 9.8 percent of Pecos's babies died in their first three years.[77] This is almost identical to survival rates for children born at Pueblo Bonito. After 300 years, the founders of Pecos had finally discovered another way to support their newborns at the standard set by the richest of Chaco's great-house elites. How? By holding and using this long, narrow, but ecologically diverse strip of land and the adjoining mountains.

The diet says it all. Pecos's diet included several varieties of corn (often stunted in the 1300s) and several varieties of beans, along with gourds, squashes, amaranth, squash and melon seeds, sunflower seeds, piñon nuts, yucca fruits and roots, various wild berries, and a wide variety of wild grass seeds. In contrast to middens at Arroyo Hondo, just 20 miles to the east, Pecos's middens contained large quantities of buffalo, antelope, deer, elk, and wild turkey bones. Like the people of Arroyo Hondo, Pecos residents regularly ate jackrabbits, cottontails, and other, smaller rodents.[78] Even in the difficult 1300s Pecos appears to have had as much meat as the Chacoan elites at the height of their power. The relatively high elevation at Pecos may have shortened the growing season in colder years, but corn could be harvested green if necessary and slowly roasted in earth ovens to preserve it, Zuni style.[79]

As Pecos struggled through the drought-stricken 1400s it shrank a bit, some people drifting away. This is unsurprising, for droughts in the early 1400s forced many people back into adjacent uplands where rain was more abundant. Huge new sites such as Otowi near Los Alamos were founded in the uplands at this time. Many others on the Parajito Plateau and in the Jemez Mountains, founded in the 1200s and then abandoned, were renovated and used again during these droughts.[80] Once more the uplands proved crucial in a time of crisis. This further reinforced each pueblo's desire to hold diverse lands.

The mid-1400s were unsettled years. At Pecos, some rooms were burned and large quantities of uneaten corn were destroyed at this time.[81] Had raiders temporarily breached the mesa? It is certainly possible, given that hungry nomadic Plains peoples lived nearby. But the crisis passed, and around 1440 or 1450, when "Glaze C" (or Glaze III) pottery was being produced, a huge, planned village was constructed at Pecos atop the older room blocks.[82] This building project consisted of four closely spaced room blocks laid out in a tight rectangle. Only four narrow, zig-zag passageways between each block gave entrance to the inner courtyard.[83] Kivas guarded three of the four entrances. The four room blocks contained roughly 600 ground-floor rooms, but portions of each block included terraced upper stories. Those upper rooms even sported shaded wooden galleries and small windows made of natural sheet mica. Kidder's excavations suggested a total of 1,020 masonry rooms.[84] Population estimates vary, as I have warned, but Kidder calculated 850 inhabitants.[85] Chroniclers accompanying Coronado's expedition estimated 500 "warriors" in 1540,[86] and Pérez de Luxan estimated 2,000 inhabitants in 1583,[87] just after a final, major house block had been constructed south of the aging main quadrangle built in the 1440s. By Spanish times, Pecos's entire mesa had been walled.

Nearby, its inhabitants farmed the arroyos, the mesa country, and sandy areas at the bases of low cliffs. Irrigation systems had been started in both the Arroyo del Pueblo at the base of the mesa and along the Pecos River nearly a mile away. Chaco Canyon's great-house elites had once started a small irrigation system designed to control runoff from the mesas,[88] but this system was different. In the 1400s at Pecos and elsewhere, a river or a fast tributary to it was actually diverted by a gravity ditch system to move water away from the river to adjacent low-lying fields.[89]

Irrigation was as crucial to these large, eastern, riverine pueblos as was holding land from mountain crest to river. Unlike the Chacoan roads, this investment in infrastructure produced food, as did miles of grid gardens, cairn fields, and cobble-mulched fields. In relatively dry years, some farming could be done in old oxbows, but when the summer rains came too abundantly, the Pecos River and the Rio Grande turned wild and destructive. In no time at all, raging waters could erase many acres of carefully planted bottomlands.

This is why the most successful of the large riverine pueblos sat on natural benches 10 to 20 feet above the rivers.[90] It is also why tributary streams and arroyos were often favored for farming—they were simply more manageable. The ditch systems created in the 1400s in the Chama, Española, White Rock, and middle Rio Grande districts opened up new riverside farmland and helped to control a previously unusable bounty.

Other pueblos along the Rio Grande and Chama rivers were even larger than Pecos. Kuaua, just north of Bernalillo on the west bank of the Rio Grande and now a state monument, was a coursed adobe town begun in the 1300s. It, too, went through several stages of development. At its height, when Coronado and his troops visited in the winter of 1540–1541, it contained more than 1,200 ground-floor rooms,[91] three large plazas, six elaborate underground kivas (one rectangular in Mogollon style),[92] and a number of smaller rectangular kivas built into the room blocks.[93] Its field houses and farms, both dry and irrigated, ran for several miles along the Rio Grande. The northern slopes of the Sandias rose up across the river as if placed there for Kuaua's benefit.

Another Pueblo IV town, Sapawe, on the west bank of El Rito Wash eight miles above its confluence with the Chama River, may be the largest adobe pueblo ever constructed. It contained an estimated 2,524 ground-floor rooms.

Second-story rooms may have increased this total to more than 4,000.[94] Five or six times larger than Pueblo Bonito, its room blocks once enclosed eight plazas. A modern football field would easily have fit into its largest plaza. Between 10 and 20 kivas were in use at Sapawe during the 1400s, though they were less complicated than the more "Chacoan" ones often found at other sites of the period.[95]

The late 1400s to early 1500s may have been a golden age for Puebloan peoples. Between 100 and 200 large pueblos, surrounded by their outlying field houses, constituted the Pueblo world. Living conditions were easier and more stable than they had been at any time in the previous 400 years. Population had increased markedly since the dark years after the droughts of the late 1200s and the horror of the 1100s.

The lonely western pueblos on the Hopi mesas continued to pursue dry farming in diverse environments,[96] and they maintained social patterns closer to the older Chacoan style. Zuni, a cluster of larger and less isolated settlements, practiced both creekside and dry farming.[97] But both of these groups also held unusually extensive surrounding lands, useful for hunting and gathering. All the remaining pueblos from the Acoma and Laguna area east to the Rio Grande and the Pecos River pursued complex combinations of dry farming and irrigation.[98] Each successful one also clung to adjacent uplands, both to farm and to hunt. The people of Jemez Pueblo used their uplands more intensively than did most of the others.[99] Taos Pueblo, too high and cool to permit farmers regularly to grow cotton or large crops of corn, also relied heavily on hunting and gathering.[100]

During the late Pueblo IV period, handicrafts—weaving of cotton, pottery production, jewelry manufacture—reached a zenith in quality and variety never to be surpassed. Adults made miniature pottery sets for children; tobacco pipes grew elaborate and diverse; even stone and bone tool manufacture had become intricate and more specialized.[101] Generally, the average age at death rose somewhat, and grave goods were a little more lavish, but there is surprisingly little evidence of the great differences in rank, nutrition, and stratification that characterized Chacoan times. By the early 1500s, life was still hard by our standards, but the population was growing. These Puebloans had learned to live as well as Chaco's elites without having created a true elite class among themselves. This, with the other dramatic transformations made between the time Chaco fell and the time the people came to the rivers, was fundamental to the very survival of Puebloan society.

Most books on Puebloan prehistory assume that the Spaniards arrived to find native communities that were nearly pristine reflections of a world little changed since ancient times. Some lament the changes wrought on the Pueblos by the Spaniards as if their arrival had robbed the world of a perfect living museum of societies who might still be acting out the daily rituals at Pueblo Bonito that had first brought the rains each summer about A.D. 1000. It is tempting to romanticize. Most humans, ourselves included, want to believe in an unending golden age—sometime or somewhere. For some romantics, all of Puebloan society represents such a golden age. Yet we need to give those Pueblo people who survived full credit for their actual accomplishments. Had they continued to behave exactly as their ancestors had in Chacoan times, they probably would not still be here today. The survivors of Chaco's fall held onto the best of the old ways, shaping them into new forms. In short, they innovated, adapted, and survived everything that was yet to come, and they survived as *functioning communities*. The Toltecs did not do that. Nor did the Phoenicians, the Assyrians, or the Incas. Archaeologists know a great deal about each of these ancient societies—but none has functioning communities today. The Pueblos have. How did they do it?

The Elements of Permanence

What had the riverine Puebloans learned from all that their forebears had suffered and experienced after Chaco's fall? The fundamental restructuring of their social, economic, and geographic concept of community fell into four categories: (1) a successful community is unified and egalitarian;[102] (2) a complex and diverse economy is more reliable than monocropping;[103] (3) investment in infrastructure must focus on producing necessities and conserving the environment;[104] and (4) efficiency is more valuable to survival than is power.[105] Each of these merits discussion.

COMMUNITY

For communities to become unified and egalitarian, the entire concept of community and its organization had to be reconstructed after the Chacoan decline. The Chacoan world had incorporated heterogeneous tribal and linguistic groups, then pitted farmers against elites as the regional system grew too large and too fragile. By the time Spaniards arrived in the Southwest, surviving pueblos were largely peaceful, and each shared a common language, customs, and religious practices particular to it. Except for a few marriages into a neighboring group, these societies were homogeneous and adamantly so. The pueblo and its customs and rules came first. One conformed. Nonconformists were often driven out.[106] The *koshare*, or clown, societies used jokes, ridicule, and buffoonery to focus peer pressure on those who did not accept the status quo.[107] Internal factionalism, though common, generally led to new communities hiving off and moving away, rather than to conflict turned inward.[108]

The religious elders—leaders of the two halves, or moieties, into which most pueblos were divided (winter people and summer people among the Tewa)[109]—were organizational overlays on the ancient clan system. So many of the clans had fragmented or even died out since the fall of Chaco that new layers or organizations grew up to fit everyone into a defined place in his or her group. The kiva elders, particularly the sun priests, the war (hunting) captain, the elders of the medicine societies, and the two moiety leaders, did form a small elite of sorts. But their status was based far more on knowledge and respect than on wealth. They were not a group apart from the others.[110] What had been created to replace separate Chacoan farming and great-house communities was a consolidated community in which all shared a common bounty in good times and common misery in bad.

A DIVERSE ECONOMY

Agriculture became far more varied and complex after 1300.[111] The most durable communities made a near fetish of planting more diverse crops in diverse locations and using diverse techniques, not merely planting more fields than would ever produce, as had the Chacoans. Experimentation with modest irrigation at Chaco,[112] and later experiments with cobble-mulching, grid gardens, and cairn fields in the terrible 1200s, formed the basis of far more complex agricultural practices in the 1300s and 1400s.[113] At a number of villages, different varieties of seed corn were carefully separated at harvest and kept in different storerooms,[114] so that valuable strains would not accidentally cross-pollinate by being planted too close together. This would have ruined the benefits of carefully selected characteristics—cold resistance, drought resistance, fast maturation, slow maturation, deep roots, large and mealy kernels, small and flinty ones, blue kernels, yellow, white, or mixed.[115] Dozens of such corn varieties had been developed and were being planted by the 1400s. The overall object was to plant different fields using different techniques and varieties.

This was another version of diversity equivalent to the market-basket of stocks held by modern mutual funds. The same general strategies were employed for beans, melons, and squashes. The Chacoans had created their risk pool by controlling vast, interconnected pockets of farming. The riverine Pueblos compacted that strategy into a greatly circumscribed space by increasing the number and kinds of cultigens and the microenvironments and techniques by which these were grown. It was then essential that social and economic mechanisms *internal* to each pueblo (as opposed to external in the Chacoan world) move a share of the harvest between those who had been fortunate in a given year and those who had not. In most of the surviving pueblos it is the act of actually farming an awarded plot for a year that gains someone the right both to continue using the land and to share in others' harvests.[116]

Puebloan concerns for those who till the soil but go hungry were so power-ful that Santa Ana Pueblo granted land, seed corn, and expertise in the 1700s to help hungry Spanish families farm successfully near the *angosturas* (narrows) of the Rio Grande. That Spanish hamlet is known today as Angostura, now part of contemporary Algodones.[117] It is testament to a value system more powerful than the enmity between conqueror and conquered.

The other economic activity to expand in Pueblo IV times was hunting and gathering. Just as agriculture was the organizational domain of the summer people's moiety captain among the Tewa, the winter people's leader organized hunting, gathering, and many winter-season rituals.[118] In most surviving Rio Grande pueblos, the war chief or war captain (once the hunt chief) organized the late fall hunts for deer, elk, pronghorn, and other large game. In early spring, villagers with access to extensive grasslands, such as the people of Pecos and Taos, hunted buffalo or traded pottery and jewelry to plainsmen for meat. To put it in cryptic modern terms, the summer people's activities among the Tewa brought in the fiber and carbohydrates. The winter people's activities brought in the fat and protein. The moieties needed one another to form a complete community and a complete diet. Unlike the case in Chacoan times, the interests of these social units converged rather than diverged. A more complex agricul-tural enterprise, combined with a reenergized hunting-and-gathering one, was key to the success of the late riverine Pueblos. Obviously, it worked well only when access to a diverse landscape was assured.

INFRASTRUCTURE

Though a lively ritual life continued in the riverine Pueblos, ritual was never again used to organize labor and create an infrastructure that supported one segment of society at the expense of another. Rituals, it was understood, could not be scheduled too closely together or enacted if their food requirements threatened to exceed the produce of one agricultural season.[119] In stark contrast to Chaco, this dictum kept the priests from imposing or gaining too much power.

Instead, labor was organized to create and extend the irrigation ditches (*ace-quias*, in Spanish) and to clean and repair them annually.[120] Cairn fields and cobble-mulched gardens on the hillsides undoubtedly were often group efforts, judging from the extent and regularity of the resulting projects as viewed in aerial photographs. Check dams and water catchments were also important community efforts.[121]

Each spring, as men cleaned the ditches, women organized to replaster the houses with adobe mud and renew roofs damaged by winter snowmelt. For new construction, builders poured adobe in courses or used post-and-adobe jacal. Adobe blocks did not appear until after the arrival of the Spaniards. In many communities, women built the walls of a structure while men cut ponderosa beams in the high country and finished the roofs.[122]

Many well-used trails can be found between pueblos in the Rio Grande, but no new roads were built after the fall of Chaco. Certainly the knowledge to do it remained with Chaco's descendants, but there was no real need. Each pueblo was as self-contained as possible, and ecological and economic diversity had been achieved locally at each. Some of the ancient road segments remained well known and were used ritually for pilgrimages to special places.

One of these was the Salt Road that went south to Zuni Salt Lake. Occasional Zuni pilgrimages along this Chacoan road to collect salt (the responsibility of the winter people in the Tewa pueblos to the east), continued into modern times.[123] Acoma people also travel to the salt lake using both prehistoric road segments and later ones that archaeologist Michael Marshall argues were built at the time Pueblo III transformed itself into Pueblo IV (about 1300). The kachinas, or ancient masked gods, of Zuni and Acoma return to those pueblos annually along these roads. They remain important ritual links to tribal origins and to sacred ancestral places. But the roads are not part of the daily economy. Indeed, Zunis make the pilgrimage down the ancient road only every four years.

EFFICIENCY VERSUS POWER

No powerful system like the Chacoan one was ever re-created by Chacoan descendants. Nevertheless, the Puebloan peoples knew how to engage in regional cooperation when they chose. They proved that amply in August 1680, when they mounted the Pueblo Revolt and drove every last Spaniard from New Mexico until 1692.[124] Had Spanish diseases (measles, smallpox, syphilis) not decimated Puebloan numbers, the Spanish might never have been able to return. This revolt involved planning among the war captains of the Keres, Tiwa, Tewa, and Tanoan pueblos from Taos south to Isleta. As a coordinated effort, it was utterly effective.[125]

But the Pueblo warriors were not hungry for power. They valued peace and stability more than vengeance. Some 400 Spaniards died in the first two days of the revolt, among them 21 or 22 priests.[126] But more than 2,000 Spaniards survived and, unattacked after the initial point had been made, marched south out of Santa Fe after forming a column at the plaza. As they moved south they gathered other Spaniards abandoning their *estancias* along the Rio Grande. After pausing near Isleta, they moved on to the El Paso area. Warriors from the various pueblos watched as the refugees went by, content that their desire to regain Indian lands and to practice their ancient Pueblo religion would be realized after 82 years of unhappy association with the outsiders.[127]

I believe that memories of war, conflict, and atrocities in the uplands after the fall of Chaco weighed heavily on the values of all those who survived to reform Puebloan society. Numerous early Spanish accounts refer to the Pueblos as peaceful and generous.[128] Pueblos themselves hold these values high, along with efficiency.[129] In fact, the drive for efficiency suffused nearly every aspect of economic life.

Most fall or spring rabbit hunts were communal.[130] The adolescents in particular were gathered for the hunts, running through the fields to chase rabbits. Such activities combined practicality and enjoyable social interaction, much as 4-H projects still meet those dual needs for Anglo and Hispanic farm children. Great quantities of meat and valuable rabbit furs were collected as the young hunters also rid the fields of rabbits that would eat freshly planted shoots. Young men engaged in competitive relay races.[131] They also got to show off for the young women and prove their mettle while bringing ponderosa beams in from the mountains for roof construction. Those beams were cut by stone axes more cleverly hafted than in earlier times. They were also made of harder, denser stone with more finely ground edges.[132] The roof beams were often finished to size by burning the ends to a desired length.[133] Quantities of corn were parched over fires from the burning beam ends, and the resultant ash was then mixed with clay to redo living room floors.

Women gathered side by side at progressively finer-grained metates, as in a production line, to grind corn from coarse to fine. The manos and metates of the 1400s had much larger grinding surfaces than those of earlier days.[134] Each sweep of the mano ground far more corn than before. The corn was generally much larger cobbed, and by the 1500s more ears were being produced per plant than had been the case at 1300.[135] It took the same labor to plant, weed, hoe, and water one cornstalk whether it produced two or three small ears or a half-dozen large ones. When one gets more product for the same investment of labor and materials, *efficiency* has increased.

The same held true for the ditch systems. Gravity carried thousands of gallons of irrigation water daily to young plants once nurtured by an endless succession of heavy water jars. Labor invested in the irrigation ditches was paid back year after year once they were established. Rock cairns atop La Bajada mesa near Cochiti went even one step better.[136] They "made" water from the cool morning air that would otherwise have been lost to the sun by 10:00 in the morning.[137] This made farming possible in areas where no nearby groundwater was to be found at all.

In the high, unirrigated fields, planting corn, beans, and squash together in little hillocks created a microenvironment in which the bean plants climbed the cornstalks and the ground-hugging squashes and gourds retarded weeds and shaded the bases of the plants from evaporation. Corncobs served as fuel. Turkeys were allowed to graze the stubble after harvest. Everything that could possibly enhance efficiency and stability was valued.

THE FINAL INVENTION: A DURABLE COMMUNITY

By 1500, large, peaceful communities along the rivers nurtured their populations as successfully as had Chaco's elites. But they had no separate elite class and were largely self-contained. Few were formally fortified, even though nomads, especially Navajos and Apaches, raided in bad years. Each thing done, each crop grown, each pot or bow made was made best at one's own pueblo.[138] Language, religion, and social rules were similar at a number of pueblos, but each town was the durable center of its own universe. Unlike Chacoan times, when "center place" was somewhere else for all but the canyon's great-house elites,[139] there were now as many center places as there were pueblos. One could walk daily to the central plaza and enjoy the surrounding cocoon of security and permanence at the best center place on the whole earth. One's role was defined by tiers of obligation—to kin, to ritual, to pueblo. All who conformed were guaranteed a place—a place to live, a place to marry, a place to raise children, a place to die.

When a village did move to "follow the rains," all things of importance, including the ancient kiva regalia, moved with it, and a new place became centered again. Pecos aside, villages often moved a few miles up to the mesa or to another bend in the river. But the old village often remained intact while vacant, just as "old Acoma" does today, and folks returned, recentered, and carried on again.[140] The *community,* its values, and its organizational structure were permanent— and portable when necessary. Until the Spaniards came, most Pueblos could live out their lives in peace so long as they believed in the community, worked hard and efficiently, sought no special wealth or glory for themselves, and worried after those who, despite hard work, found themselves less well off. Babies still died. Droughts still brought hunger now and again, and nomads raided from time to time. But no more lonely young men ever buried their dead, then walked away from a solitary farmstead to join a road crew among strangers.

No evidence of standing armies among the Pueblos has ever been found. And unlike the situation in Europe, no local magnates or kings rose up among them to demand tribute or a share of the harvests they had worked so hard to bring in. That all changed when the Spaniards arrived.

Photo 31.   The mesa-top Hopi pueblo of Shimopovi (also Shongopavi),
Second Mesa, Arizona, about 1896. Note the kiva (center) and the ladder
entryway-smokehole through its cribbed log roof, much like Anasazi ones.
The surrounding house blocks of adobe-plastered stone create a small plaza
area (foreground). Corn and other necessities dry on the rafters. Except for
the beams cut with steel axes and the plank doors (upper left and far right),
this scene could have been photographed any time after A.D. 1000.
(Courtesy NPS.)

Photo 32 (*opposite*).   Close-up of chimney and doorway at the Hopi pueblo
of Shipaulovi, Second Mesa, Arizona, about 1896. Note the chimneys built up
of bulging clay pots stacked one on another, then plastered. Again, dried corn
hangs from the house. A stone and adobe wall in the left background could
use a new coat of mud plaster. European implements are few—a bucket atop
one chimney, a broom, and a mattock (above head of animal at lower left).
(Courtesy NPS.)

Photo 33.   Oraibi, the Hopi's dominant village on Third Mesa, Arizona,
about 1896. Note the multistory, laddered room blocks, the plaza areas, and
the kiva (center). Although they are hard to see, some inhabitants have
gathered on a rooftop just above the "bush" (a bower of fresh-cut branches
for a traditional dance) to the left of the kiva. As at Shimopovi, the scene is
little changed from ancient times. (Courtesy NPS.)

Photo 34.   House and Hopi family near plaza at Walpi on high, narrow First Mesa, Arizona, about 1896. The boy at right wears his hair in the traditional style. His deerskin moccasins are locally made but his Levis are manufactured. (Courtesy NPS.)

Photo 35.   The traditional method of firing pottery at Zia Pueblo, about 40 miles northwest of Albuquerque, late 1890s. The fuel is a combination of wood, charcoal, and some cow chips—a post-Spanish addition. Note the old woman's traditional dress. The three pots cooling at right center are water canteens, not yet decorated. (Courtesy NPS.)

Photo 36. Traditional dancers at Acoma atop its high "enchanted mesa" about 70 miles west of Albuquerque, about 1898. Note the multistory house blocks, ladders to roofs, and contrasts in dress—traditional women's dance garb but manufactured clothing worn by male spectators along the rooftops. The cut branches are part of a shrine, similar to the brush bower near the kiva in the earlier scene at Oraibi. (Courtesy NPS.)

Photo 37 (*opposite, top*). Acoma plaza area and laddered, terraced house blocks. Note rooftop activities. The exposed dry-laid rock walls not only echo the Anasazi but remind us that adobe mud is not the universal building material in all surviving pueblos. In center foreground is a mud-plastered water cistern. The rock rubble (from cores of walls) and ponderosa beam behind the cistern will be salvaged for another building project. (Courtesy NPS.)

Photo 38 (*opposite, bottom*). An Acoma drummer in a flat, crowned hat cuts a majestic figure at a feast-day dance, about 1898. Note the combination of traditional and European garb on Acoma men in foreground and left—Levis, European hats, and store-bought shirts contrast with the Navajo blanket (bottom center) and buckskins (right of blanket). Here, too, the Acoma women (right of drummer) are more traditionally dressed. In right background, three women in Victorian dress (one with parasol) are tourists. (Courtesy NPS.)

Photo 39. Taos Pueblo about 1898. This view focuses on the adobe beehive
ovens used to bake bread—a Spanish influence after the introduction of
wheat. Most contemporary photographs of Taos show trees and vegetation.
Nearly all these Pueblo scenes in the 1890s are barren for the simple reason
that food was cooked and homes heated with firewood. Nowadays, most
Pueblo homes, including those in Taos, are supplied with propane and
electricity. (Courtesy NPS.)

Photo 40 (*opposite, top*).   Large storage jars (ollas) at Pojoaque Pueblo,
near Santa Fe. An archaeologist in George Pepper's party (kneeling at center)
is surrounded by women potters and men from the pueblo. Again, there is an
amalgam of the traditional (pottery) with outside influences (store-bought
clothing). (Courtesy NPS.)

Photo 41.   Kiva at San Felipe Pueblo, between Albuquerque and Santa Fe. In the crowded Rio Grande corridor, traditional elements (the kiva and the pole platform in front) blend with Spanish influences (the beehive bread oven and mold-formed adobe blocks at left of kiva). The kiva stair (right) appears to be somewhat modernized.
(Courtesy NPS.)

Photo 42.   A dance in a plaza at Isleta Pueblo, just south of Albuquerque, about 1898. Note the territorial-style door and window (left, center) and the mold-made adobe blocks (center). As at Acoma, some tourists in modern dress have come to see the dance. Eventually, curiosity seekers drove Pueblo people in the Rio Grande region to guard their religion more carefully. Nowadays, the most sacred dances are closed to outsiders. (Courtesy NPS.)

CHAPTER NINE

Enduring Communities

SEVERAL SPANISH EXPEDITIONS FROM MEXICO HAD ALREADY NIBBLED AT the edges of the Puebloan world before a party commanded by Francisco Vázquez de Coronado arrived at Zuni in July 1540 and "took" the pueblo.[1] Unfortunately for the Puebloans, Coronado's Spanish world was in a period of heady expansion and domination of others after centuries of humiliating religious and political repression under the Moors.[2]

Coronado reached Zuni just 48 years after Ferdinand and Isabella had founded the Spanish city of Santa Fe, near Granada, to celebrate the Moors' final expulsion from southern Spain in 1492. Four years after Santa Fe, Spaniards established the city of Santo Domingo on Hispaniola (now the Dominican Republic) in the Caribbean. From the waterfront at the foot of Santo Domingo's high, turreted walls, Hernán Cortés sailed down the narrow Ozama River in 1519 toward his destiny as conqueror of Mexico. Francisco Pizarro sailed down it 10 years later to become conqueror of the Incas and to found Lima, his victory city, in 1535. In that same year, Coronado arrived in Mexico City from Salamanca, Spain, where Cortés once studied law.

The fruits of these first conquests were stunning—gold, jades, emeralds, and thousands of Indian slaves to work Spanish plantations. But the sweetest fruits had already been picked, and latecomers like Coronado had to pursue possibilities farther afield. The fabled "golden cities of Cíbola" were his particular obsession,[3] and they certainly lay far afield. To his credit, he did find them, 1,600 miles to the north. But they proved to be only the Zuni district's adobe-walled Pueblo villages.[4] To Coronado's everlasting disillusionment, there were no riches—just corn, beans, and squash. He returned to Mexico no richer, but his exploits earned him a seat on the Council of Mexico City and a rich *encomienda*[5]—an award of many Indian serfs to work his land. Regrettably, he and his party left behind diseases to which the Puebloans had no immunity.[6]

Coronado's visit and the disease vectors took their toll and ended the Puebloans' brief golden age. Now and again, other Spanish parties passed through Rio Grande territory, but it was not until the summer of 1598 that Juan de Oñate and his party came to Pueblo country intent on staying.[7] Named "governor of New Mexico" by the viceroy in Mexico City, Oñate established himself at the Tewa pueblo of San Juan,[8] which is still located at the confluence of the Chama and the Rio Grande. The Spanish site is adjacent to modern-day Española and just a few miles down the Chama River from the great adobe pueblo of Sapawe.[9]

In disgust at the Rio Grande province's modest bounty, Oñate resigned as governor in 1607.[10] He, too, left disillusioned and no richer. Like Coronado, Oñate was tried under Spanish law for his mistreatment of New Mexico's Indians.[11] Unlike Coronado, he was convicted. But his parents in Zacatecas were rich silver barons, and he had married a granddaughter of Cortés's, the prestige match of his generation.[12] His conviction was eventually overturned.[13] Meanwhile, New Mexico remained a Spanish colony. Ironically, its second capital, established 30 miles south of San Juan in 1610, was also named Santa Fe—yet another victory city.[14] Still the capital of New Mexico, it has been continuously inhabited except for the 13 years during which it was vacated because of the Pueblo Revolt of 1680–1692.[15]

New Mexico's Spanish conquistadores arrived with what now would be described as "attitude." Centuries under the Muslim domination of the Moors had made Spanish culture both obsessively Catholic and hostile to other religions.[16] Many conquistadores were second or third sons of rich *hidalgos* (nobility) and would never inherit the family land and titles under the Spanish system of primogeniture.[17] Since no gold was to be got in the Rio Grande provinces, they settled for land, labor, and souls converted to Catholicism. The problem for the twenty-third generation of native farmers to be born in New Mexico after the fall of Chaco was that it was *Pueblo* land, labor, and souls that fueled the new Spanish colony.

When Coronado arrived in 1540, an estimated 150 sizable pueblos existed.[18] About 100 of these north of contemporary Socorro were populated primarily by direct descendants of the Anasazi. The others were formed of remnants from Mogollon society and are not part of the Chacoan story told here. Puebloan society included Hopi, Zuni, and the multivillage language groups Tiwa, Tewa, Towa, Tano, and Keres.[19] Population figures from the Spanish accounts range from Oñate's estimate of 16,000 to 60,000 persons in 134 villages at 1598 to Espejo's estimate of 130,000 to 248,000 Puebloans in 1582–1583. Oñate's estimate is generally considered too conservative, and Espejo's, exaggerated.[20]

It is important to remember, however, that the diseases first brought by Coronado's party had probably eroded peak population levels after 1540. Those same diseases struck again and again as exploring parties passed through the Rio Grande country in the late 1500s. The exact numbers will never be reconstructed definitively. But if one accepts Espejo's low estimate of 130,000 as plausible in 1582–1583, then one should also accept the possibility that Oñate's high figure of 60,000 in 1598, even if only a "guesstimate," could reflect a population roughly halved by disease by the time he took a census as governor. After all, Oñate's party was the fourth to arrive in the Rio Grande since 1540.[21] Three of those expeditions came between 1581 and 1598 and might have buffeted Pueblo people repeatedly with smallpox, whooping cough, measles, and syphilis.[22]

Tragically, the situation was only to worsen as disease, unreasonable demands on Indian labor, raiding nomads, and political unrest took their toll over the next two centuries. In the 1620s, Fray Alonso de Benavides estimated that 69,000 people survived in 64 pueblos. In 1638, just under 40,000 were believed to have survived a recent smallpox epidemic. In 1679, Spanish accounts mentioned only 46 pueblos with an estimated population of 17,000. And by 1706, the year Albuquerque was founded, only 18 pueblos, excluding the Hopi villages, survived, with a total population, by actual count, of 6,440.[23] Whether one accepts Espejo's "exaggerated" estimate of 130,000 Puebloans in 1582 or prefers Oñate's "conservative" one of 60,000 shortly after 1598, it makes little statistical difference for 1706. The loss of Puebloan society's pre-Spanish population base was something between 89 percent (on the basis of Oñate's estimate) and 95 percent (Espejo's estimate). In addition to the 18 New Mexico pueblos, four Hopi villages still existed far to the west in 1706.[24]

Amazingly, functioning *communities* survived, although cataclysmically reduced in number and size. How could these descendants of Chaco's fall have imagined that the thin arc of Pueblo survivors who had come to the rivers in the 1300s would seem numerous when compared with those who still endured at the beginning of the second century following Oñate's arrival?

Of the pueblos chartered by Spanish land grants in 1706, only one failed to survive. Pecos was abandoned in 1838, its last 20 members removing themselves to Jemez. To this day, one sees the surname Pecos among members of Jemez Pueblo, and Jemez reckons its modern Towa language to have been formed by a commingling of the older Jemez and Pecos dialects.[25] This survival rate is a remarkable show of endurance, especially considering that population specialists count any society of 500 or fewer members a candidate for extinction. Fully 14 of the 18 pueblos in 1706 were at or below that threshold.[26] These descendants of the Anasazi have not only survived, but in 1990 they numbered 55,330, according to the U.S. Bureau of the Census, and their numbers continue to grow.[27]

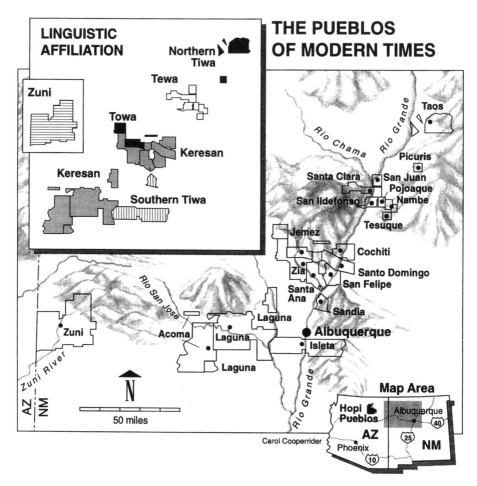

LINGUISTIC
AFFILIATION

Zuni

Northern
Tiwa

Tewa

Towa

Keresan

Keresan

Southern Tiwa

THE PUEBLOS
OF MODERN TIMES

Taos

Rio Chama

Rio Grande

Picuris

Santa Clara   San Juan
                Pojoaque
San Ildefonso   Nambe

Tesuque

Jemez

Cochiti

Zia

Santo Domingo
San Felipe

Santa
Ana

Sandia

Laguna

Albuquerque

Zuni

Acoma   Laguna

Isleta

Rio San Jose

Laguna

Zuni River

N

50 miles

AZ
NM

Rio Grande

Map Area

Hopi
Pueblos   Albuquerque

AZ

NM

Phoenix

Carol Cooperrider

Pueblo Arts of Survival

How did they do this? Again, enduring, functioning communities lay at the core of this feat of survival. The transformations made between the upland period (the 1200s) and late Pueblo IV (1500) were crucial. The Pueblos created a more productive infrastructure, greater economic diversity, and a more unified and egalitarian community. They disdained the pure growth model of the Chaco Anasazi era in favor of greater efficiency. Altogether they employed many strategies that enabled their communities to continue under conditions of catastrophic population loss.

Survivors of one pueblo could formally seek refuge with another, with the requirement that the refugees fully assimilate and accept the new pueblo and its customs as paramount.[28] In such cases—for example, the amalgam of Pecos with Jemez in 1838—kiva regalia and rituals came with the immigrants, and their "center place" was forever moved.[29] By the early historic period, different elements of Pueblo religion were known or owned through membership in religious societies and controlled by diverse social groups, even clan fragments. The monolithic control over ritual that seems to have held sway in Chacoan times never reemerged.

The risk of this system to a community threatened by rapidly declining population was the actual loss of a ritual or knowledge of an ancient shrine if "old So-and-So" died without passing on core religious information. This made knowledge of native religious elements simultaneously precious and precarious. Such knowledge was often an immediate ticket to entry into another pueblo. Rituals and chants had power—power necessary to tame the unpredictable climate of the Southwest. Those who possessed knowledge of revered ceremonies were desirable additions to a community. Since the knowledge of particular religious elements was dispersed among small groups and occasionally among individuals, it was necessary to draw them to, and keep them in, a complete community where all the necessary parts of a ritual could be performed as required.

The Pueblos' fight to hold onto their religion was not easy. The Spaniards detested Pueblo religion and attempted to stamp it out.[30] That only drove it underground and made it even more precious and more sacred. On Sundays in the 1600s and 1700s, most surviving Pueblo people went to mass and used Spanish names. At home in the pueblo, they stealthily practiced native religion and used Indian names.[31] It was inevitable that the Pueblos would attempt to hold onto their religion—they had suffused it not only with their social and spiritual values but with the knowledge of economic survival, which was encoded right into it. Without the proper prayers and ritual, there would be no rain, no sun, no corn, nor any of the other things the earth provided. There was no true world without the religious practices that meshed with it.[32] The natural world and religious practice were analogous to a jigsaw puzzle—the proper parts of each had to be carefully fitted together to form a complete picture. And that picture was of the very patterns of life itself.

Pueblo religious elements absolutely required knowledge of the native language.[33] Chants, prayers, and objects had power in the ancient languages, not in Spanish or in the English that was increasingly used on the street after the United States acquired the Southwest in 1848. Sustaining the community meant saving the language. Because the language was so intertwined with religion, it, too, became more precious and secretive over time in response to Spanish contact.

Pueblos and the United States

Even today, one of the Pueblos' greatest concerns is instilling the language in each new generation. It is not easy when parents live and work in cities such as Albuquerque, speaking English all week and watching television like the rest of us. The risks become even greater when the young people go away to work or to university. So deep are the instincts to protect the Pueblo languages and preserve them for the Pueblo community that they are not taught at any university.[34] No outsiders have knowledge of enough fragments to speak or to teach any of them properly, and ordinarily no Pueblo person will teach outsiders to speak his or her native language.[35] With the exception of the ancient Zuni tongue, which is unrelated to the other Pueblo languages and is spoken far away from the crowded Rio Grande corridor, the outside world has nothing more of these languages than fragments of a few poems, songs, and place names gathered by curious anthropologists a century ago.[36] Just think of it: we know the languages of the Pharaohs, the ancient Hebrews, and the Incas; we can even read ancient cuneiform tablets from the Middle East. But we don't know the languages spoken at home by thousands who walk among us each day in the Southwest.

The alloying of language and religious practice formed the key to knowing traditional economic, social, and healing practices. Add to these the enduring value system forged in the Pueblo IV period and one can argue that today's Pueblo communities have preserved a substantial core of traditional knowledge intact and protected from the outside world. Given four centuries of excruciating proximity to successive waves of outsiders—Spaniards, Mexicans, and Anglo-Americans, this is a security achievement worthy of the CIA or the KGB.[37]

What may be an even greater achievement is the Pueblos' ability to turn a strikingly conservative face inward, protecting their core languages, religion, and values, while turning another, more progressive face outward to deal with a changing surrounding world. As the anthropologist Edward Dozier of Santa Clara Pueblo explained, Pueblo society displays an unusual capacity to erect walls around its ceremonial life while being a generous host to outsiders.[38] I like to think that delightful capacity arises from ancient echoes of Chaco's open communities.

But adaptation to outsiders has not been limited to social superficialities. Alfonso Ortiz pointed out that Pueblo farmers were quick to adopt Spanish farm implements and metal tools that were more efficient than their own.[39] It is also unfair to credit the Spaniards with only strife and disease. In addition to metal, they brought wheat; with wheat came bread. They also introduced cattle, horses, mules, burros, pigs, goats, sheep, chickens, fruit trees (peaches and apples were prized), new varieties of melons, grapes, and barley. Construction techniques and architecture also changed somewhat under the Spaniards. Adobe blocks could be made in large wooden molds, production-line style. Because this was efficient, it was readily accepted. Corner fireplaces with chimneys also came into use, and as glass became more common, more and larger windows were added to houses. Nothing changed in the kivas, as you might suspect.

Yet access to new tools and crops did not compensate Puebloan people for the loss of much of their land to the Spaniards. These losses, which severely restricted access to the strips of diverse territory that had been a salvation in the 1400s, contributed to want during colonial times. When Spain at last gave land grants to most of the surviving Pueblos in the early 1700s, Zuni, Acoma, Laguna, Isleta, and Taos managed to be awarded the most extensive and diverse lands,[40] largely because they were in areas less heavily settled by Hispanics. Santa Clara, Jemez, and Santo Domingo made out comparatively well, but the other Rio Grande pueblos were squeezed by the many Spanish land claims between San Juan and Bernalillo.[41] Even more Pueblo land was effectively encroached upon as the Indian population dwindled in the seventeenth and eighteenth centuries. Then came the American reservation system, and most pueblos, except for Santo Domingo and Isleta, got squeezed again,[42] losing even more sustaining ecological diversity.

With modern Pueblo population again growing, the contemporary American judicial system regularly confronts court actions to reclaim Pueblo land. Currently, Sandia Pueblo is engaged in a dispute with some Albuquerque homeowners whose houses are perched on the face of the Sandia Mountains, where Sandians had traditional access.[43] In court, a pueblo's lawyers predictably emphasize religious rights to the area or the fact that the pueblo once "had a herd of bison on those lands." The landowners' lawyers just as predictably demand proof of title in "fee simple" or an original survey recorded on parchment a century ago. These claims are profoundly important to the Pueblos because they still need access to former lands for ritual items. They are simply trying to reestablish the diverse boundaries they once had. American courts fail to recognize that loss of the land means the community cannot be sustained forever. But the Pueblos have the modern United States to sustain them, right?

In the modern American era, virtually all the accoutrements of an industrial society have found their way into Pueblo homes. Trucks, autos, and televisions are probably the most widespread. Firearms long ago replaced the bow and arrow for ordinary hunting (they were more efficient),[44] just as Levis replaced traditional handmade or handsewn cotton pants once wage labor became widely available, just before and during World War II.[45] One could easily assume that Pueblo people run the risk of being entirely assimilated into contemporary American society. And nowadays, elders do worry about both the lure of nearby cities and the cultural pull of a university education on each new generation. But the deep tradition of dualities—first seen in paired Chacoan kivas, revered in the form of twin war gods,[46] and still seen in twin moiety organizations[47]—enables most Pueblo youths to adapt to our world, using one of "our" common names, our language, and our technology, and then return home on weekends or feast days using another name and another body of cultural knowledge.[48]

After all, American society requires little real commitment. Put in your 40 hours or take your classes, pay your taxes, and commit no major crimes. We ask little more. We do not really have communities in the Puebloan sense of the word. We don't even care what religion you practice or what language you speak so long as both are done on your own time and away from our few public institutions. And that explains why the Pueblos so badly want to regain their land, quietly hold onto language and religion, and teach their partly acculturated children to internalize the traditional value system of unified, self-contained, efficient, and relatively egalitarian *communities*.

America and an Enduring Community

It is not that Pueblo Indians hate modern America, especially since they find our modest cultural wants much easier to live with than colonial Spanish ones. Indeed, they don't hate us at all. It is just that our unchecked growth, lack of social cohesion, and flamboyant use of resources worries them as being unsustainable. They expect to outlast us. Recently, a local tribal elder appeared in an educational film about the Anasazi and commented that his people had to hold onto traditional Pueblo land, culture, and values because some day his descendants would look out across the Rio Grande Valley and modern Albuquerque would be gone.[49] He is in the mainstream of opinion among traditional Pueblo leaders. And with our wasteful ways, weak communities, and economically based class system, we may in fact not be a sure bet for long-term survival. Resist the temptation to scoff and consider that the Pueblos have been living in settled villages and have survived, with languages and identity intact, for 1,700 years. The United States has only two centuries under its belt. Even Rome, one of our cultural icons and a source of our literature, laws, architecture, and ideas, survived intact for only 1,000 years. In evolutionary terms, the score is 10 centuries for Rome, 17 for Puebloan society, and 2 for the United States. Advantage, Pueblos. Still unswayed?

Let me put it another way. When tourists go to see a late summer Pueblo feast day or corn dance, they often view the events as charming, delightful, or quaint. But the Pueblo people do not carry on these traditions either for our benefit or merely for their own amusement. They carry on because such practices sustain an enduring community. Maybe they don't all need to know how to plant and pollinate corn this year, so long as the rest of us and our huge economy surround them. But they know that when we are gone, they and their children will still need to know the basic things learned after their ancestors came to the rivers.

Having come 17 centuries, they intend to go the distance. If maintaining two worlds at once—a traditional one turned inward and a modern one turned outward—is what it takes, they will do it. They are utterly committed to survival and to their enduring communities.

In short, Pueblos are pragmatists because they know a society has to work at survival and invest in its communities. We are romantics for believing they are quaint or that our society will last forever. It won't, unless we take far better care of it than we do now. It is only two centuries old, and apart from the Civil War and the Great Depression, it is largely untested by any epic calamity. Why do Pueblo elders see us as so fragile? And are we?

Many of you may not agree with the Pueblo assessment that we are fragile. Your response might be to say, "Well, unless there is a nuclear war—which will destroy all of us including the Pueblos—we *will* be here." Fine, and Puebloan people understand that, too. Their viewpoint is based more on the fact that we are rapidly using up our water in the Southwest by wasting it on lawns and golf courses. They reckon that when the water is gone, our local high-technology jobs and industries will move elsewhere, and, uncommitted to any real community, so will most of the rest of us. Their view is not necessarily that the United States will vanish everywhere at once in a puff of smoke. Rather, it is that sooner or later the "America" now living in the American Southwest will use up its basic necessities, will shrink dramatically, and, uncommitted to permanence, will drift away to pick sweeter fruits elsewhere. Our own experts on population, industry, and environment are raising many of these same concerns.[50] So we need to ask, "Why aren't we more committed to our own communities?"

One reason is that the United States is currently experiencing a rapidly accelerating divergence in wealth, creating "haves" and "have nots." That trend began in 1968 and sped up after 1980, according to U.S. Census Bureau data.[51] So dramatic is the trend that widely read print news sources such as *USA Today* and *US News and World Report* have published special features on the phenomenon.[52] According to *US News and World Report,* the number of millionaire families in America *doubled* in the decade between 1983 and 1992, even though overall population increased only 9 percent.[53] Before you start applauding, consider a few more facts.

As the millennium neared, the rich in America were getting richer. In 1983, the richest 1 percent of households held 32 percent of the nation's wealth.[54] In 1989, that share had risen to 35 percent.[55] By 1992 it had grown to 42 percent.[56] One can safely guess that by the year 2000, which is almost upon us as I write this, the top 1 percent will have amassed nearly 50 percent of America's wealth. This shift in wealth is due partly to an increasing disparity in wage returns on labor. Why is this a worry?

The last time the wage spread between high-paying and low-paying jobs was so great, or inequality in wealth was accelerating so rapidly, came in the 1920s, right before the Great Depression.[57] To many of us that era seems remote, but ask a parent, a grandparent, or a retiree in the local coffee shop what the depression was like. It was a wrenching experience for a young nation still full of optimism, and of itself, after the Great War and America's rapid rise in political power among nations. Families lost farms, homes, and businesses. University graduates could find no work. Birth rates dropped and suicides rose.[58] Americans also became more rigid and judgmental. Social separation between classes and the races deepened and widened, after having narrowed in the "Roaring Twenties." The high-flying, socially and sexually permissive 1920s quickly turned into the somber, repressive, and bitter 1930s.[59]

Those bitter 1930s also nurtured outright hatreds. The Ku Klux Klan, founded in 1866 as a response to Reconstruction just after the Civil War, did not actually reach the height of its powers until the mid-1920s, when it boasted nearly five million members.[60] Because of the great wealth created in the late 1920s, the Klan had actually begun to lose its influence when the depression gave its hard core a new cause to pursue. Few people know that, apart from Florida, the die-hard Klan states weren't even in the South. They were Ohio, Indiana, and Oregon,[61] where competition for jobs inflamed feelings against immigrants and Catholics. A huge influx of immigrants had come to America between 1890 and 1924. They came believing in the power of the American economy. Disillusioned, some actually left the United States and returned to their home countries during the depression.[62] In fact, America had more emigrants than immigrants during the entire 1930s. Of course, blacks, Jews, and American Indians were also Klan targets. In short, the depression resulted in deep factionalism that tested the social fabric of the nation.[63]

The nation's social fabric was woven from the belief in a national community with shared values: democracy, capitalism, religious freedom, a middle class, and a public "American" identity. In the United States, the economic crisis of the 1930s cast serious doubts on both capitalism and the middle class—two cornerstones of our society. Had it not been for the controversial but inspired leadership of President Franklin Delano Roosevelt and the godsend of enormous, unexpected production demands placed on American industry in the late 1930s and early 1940s by the war in Europe (followed quickly by World War II), there is no telling what might have happened.

In the United States, the Great Depression lasted nearly 10 years—just a little longer than the Chacoan droughts of the A.D. 1090s. In both societies, "community" and the traditional formula for success, the "social contract," were disrupted. Both responded to the failure of their growth models by "pumping up the system." The Chacoans did it with rituals, roads, and great houses. America did it with CCC and WPA labor marshaled to create roads, monuments, parks, dams, and schools[64]—infrastructure that is still with us and is still used daily. In both societies, great social changes followed the crises. In the Chacoan world, farmers buried their loved ones and walked away, leaving the elites with no functioning system to manage. In the United States, the depression and World War II created equally dramatic population movements. Young men went to war, young women went to work, and the dust bowl "Okies" went to California. Thousands of once stable communities were disrupted by these massive population movements.[65]

Why does that all matter now? Isn't it good that America is again creating millionaires at record rates? It depends on *how* they are created. The fact is that since 1968, the growth in America's share of income has been limited *entirely* to the richest 5 percent of households. That growing share accruing to the rich actually represents a major transfer of wealth from the middle 60 percent of households. The poorest in America aren't getting poorer—the middle class is.[66] And that strikes at the heart of our social system. A far more intelligent mantra than "God bless the rich" would be "God bless the middle class."

Even more intelligent would be federal actions to protect and preserve America's middle class. Our huge middle class has been a moderating, stabilizing influence on the nation. Strong identification with a middle class is the closest thing America has to a national community with shared interests. In surveys and census rolls, even a high percentage of the working poor answer that they are "middle class." So do many of the near rich.[67] This only reinforces the notion that our shrinking middle class comes closest to an institution around which we could sustain a national community.

What is it like in countries without a large middle class? The answer can be seen in many countries of the developing world. In Mexico, where I once lived and studied, the small middle class that grew up in a few large cities is currently undergoing complete destruction. That will shortly leave Mexico with a small, extraordinarily rich elite class at daily odds with a huge proportion of its poor. These two groups have radically different values, politics, and interests.

Crime is rampant in contemporary Mexico.[68] Kidnapping the children of the rich and famous for stunning ransoms was a growth industry as recently as 1999, and "public" streets in Mexico City, the capital, have been gated off to protect entire blocks of the rich from their poor neighbors.[69] When the wealthy are forced to live behind walls and gates staffed by armed retainers, they are no longer living in a modern community—they are living in a feudal society supported by some accoutrements of modern technology. The interests of Mexico's rich and poor are easily as conflicted as were the interests of Chaco's farmhands and great-house elites at A.D. 1100. How big a calamity will it take to completely fracture Mexican society and turn the country into another Bosnia? Let us pray that we never find out.

And what has Mexico to do with us in the United States? First, it shares a huge border with us and has displaced millions of its poorer citizens into our society, both legally and illegally. Second, gated communities, symptomatic of social fragmentation, have also become common in America. Third, we are receiving Mexico's poor at the same time American low-technology industries are closing expensive factories here and are exporting jobs and factories in textiles, steel, autos, electronics, and machine tools to *maquiladoras* in Mexico. Those exported jobs once supported the lower middle class in many American communities that are now in despair. The abandoned American workers, ironically, must now compete with Mexican immigrants, legal and illegal, for poorer-paying American jobs in the service industries.[70] This fuels some of the same resentments against immigrants seen during the Great Depression, even as the ranks of America's rich become larger and even richer.

The view from the top and the view from the bottom in the contemporary American wage hierarchy are simply too different to dismiss with a glib "all's well" in annual state-of-the-union addresses. All is not well when the kind of work done matters so enormously. In 1973, the average American corporate CEO earned a salary 41 times larger than the average worker's. Twenty years later, in 1993, that had grown to a salary 225 times larger. No other industrial nation tolerates such vast differences.[71] Where you live also makes a huge difference in per capita income. In 1993, each Starr County Texan averaged an income of just $6,306, while New York County citizens averaged $52,277, more than eight times as much.[72] No wonder worldviews in McAllen, Texas, and New York City are so different. In truth, all is not well with the American community, and no one has said it better than *USA Today's* David Lynch: "The disparity [in wages] is shrinking society's shared outlook to the point that a common American experience becomes ever more remote, threatening not only a national sense of community, but, some experts feel, the underpinnings of stable democracy."[73] Amen! If a society will not invest in core institutions that draw people together into communities, eventually there will be no community and no society.

Even so, as a nation, we are still large, rich, envied, and the only remaining superpower. But while researching this book, it shocked me to discover just where we do rank in most other important measures of quality of life. Are we still "number one" in those?

Tragically, the answer is a resounding "no." In 1992, life expectancy at birth in the United States was 76 years. Fourteen countries did better (Australia, Austria, Canada, Cyprus, France, Iceland, Israel, Italy, Japan, Netherlands, Norway, Spain, Sweden, and Switzerland), and we tied with another eight for fifteenth place.[74] In 1994 we were in a seven-way tie for twenty-fourth place in infant mortality, at 0.8 percent. Iceland and Japan had but half the infant mortality we had.[75] Differences in infant mortality mattered at Chaco Canyon, and they matter now.

A recent study comparing 11 participating nations shows that general literacy is higher in Sweden and Canada than in the United States. More ominously, of those 11 nations (Belgium, Canada, Germany, Ireland, Netherlands, New Zealand, Poland, Sweden, Switzerland, United Kingdom, and the U.S.), only Poland and the U.S. had fewer than half of their adults scoring in the middle of four ranks.[76] In other words, there was much greater disparity between the poorly literate and the highly literate in the United States and Poland than in the other countries. Such disparities forge brittle class lines in a world where wages increasingly depend on knowledge.

And beyond income and literacy, other differences divide us in America and make it hard to establish real communities—local or national. Because of differences in infant mortality, the effects of violent crime, and access to medical care, an African American male born in the U.S. in 1990 could expect to live only 64.5 years, compared with 72.7 for his white counterpart.[77] In other words, a black man born in 1990 had the same life expectancy as a contemporary born in Ecuador, Peru, or the Philippines—not in America.[78] Even more sobering is the statistical reality that most black men born in 1990 will not live to collect Social Security awarded at age 67.

To be sure, overall life expectancy for the general population has increased dramatically in the United States, from about 54 years in 1920 to 75.4 years in 1990.[79] During most of that period, life expectancy among nonwhites grew a bit more rapidly than that among whites, who were better off, in terms of health, to begin with. But those gains have recently been eroded. Between 1970 and 1990, a black man's average life span grew from 60.0 to 64.5 years—a gain of 4.5 years. A white man's rose from 68.0 to 72.7, a gain of 4.7 years during the same period, showing an overall pattern similar to the recent divergence in wealth. Worse yet, federal government estimates of life expectancy to the year 2000 project no further gain in longevity for black men, but another 1.5 years of longevity (to age 74.2) for white men.[80] Gains once made are again slipping away, even as a foolish few continue to chant "God bless the rich."

The economic and demographic differences between blacks and whites in America are real. Emotions over these issues run deep, partly because the past still clutches at too many of us and partly because we spend too much time pointing fingers at one another rather than constructing solutions. So let us look to the future—our nation's children. It is much harder to assign blame to them. How are they doing? Again, it depends on who they are and where they were born.

Let us return to California and Mississippi, first mentioned in chapter 3. You may recall that folks in California were more prosperous and created more business ventures per capita but failed at them more frequently. The citizens of Mississippi were less prosperous and risked fewer new ventures but more successfully minimized their failures. Those "business" behaviors arose from daily worlds that were very different.

Consider children born in Marin County, California, just north of San Francisco, in 1993. Nearly 92 percent of those children's parents had graduated from high school. Fully 44 percent of those parents had also earned college degrees. Per capita income was $38,310 (in 1993 dollars), not as good as in New York but still nearly 55 percent above the national average. Infant mortality was 6.1 per thousand live births. Each child born in Marin County that year had a 99.4 percent chance of surviving to its first birthday, and only 1.1 percent of mothers were under age 20.[81]

Now consider the children born in Jefferson County, Mississippi's delta country, in 1993. Just 53 percent of their parents were high school graduates, and only 10.3 percent had earned a college degree. Per capita income was $9,686, better than Starr County, Texas, but more than 60 percent below the national average of $24,750.[82] Infant mortality was a shocking 24 per 1,000 live births. Each child born that year was four times likelier to die before its first birthday than a child born in Marin County, and 27.5 percent of the mothers of those children were under age 20.[83]

Babies born in these two counties live in very different worlds. Children born in Jefferson County, Mississippi, were half as likely as Marin County babies to have a high-school-educated parent and more than four times less likely to have a college-educated parent. They were four times less likely to survive to age one, and they lived in households earning approximately one-quarter as much income. A college-educated parent, on average, will earn 74 percent more money in a lifetime than will a high-school-educated one,[84] and teen-aged mothers are least able to provide for their children economically or socially.[85] The Mississippi child was also nearly three times more likely to be a victim of serious, violent crime.[86]

In short, there were greater disparities in life's possibilities between children born in Marin County, California, and Jefferson County, Mississippi, in 1993 than there were between the children of Chaco's great-house elites and those of Chacoan farmhands in A.D. 1100. True, both sets of modern children were nutritionally better off than any child born at Chaco Canyon, but the overall inequalities are stunning. The child born in Marin County lived in an economy much more like that of the richest northern European country, Switzerland, with a per capita wealth in 1993 of $36,410. The child born in Jefferson County lived in an economic world much more like that of Greece, Spain, or Ireland, with per capita wealth in 1993 ranging from $7,390 to $13,640.[87] The irony is that both sets of children carry the same American passport, obey the same national laws, and are supposed to believe equally in "one nation, under God, indivisible, with liberty and justice for all." The problem for America is how to sustain one national community, given such disparities.

Worse yet, the problem is not just the differences represented by those between California and Mississippi. As Thomas G. Mortenson, the editor of *Postsecondary Education Opportunity*, recently noted, among all Western nations "only poor children in Ireland and Israel are poorer than poor children in the United States."[88] The accompanying illustration makes that painfully clear, and the conclusion of Mortenson's article is genuinely distressing.

"Household income is highly unequally distributed in the United States and . . . has grown more unequal since about 1968. . . . Government . . . does less to alleviate poverty among poor children in the United States than [in] any other Western country. As a direct consequence, the resulting child poverty rate in the United States is 50 percent higher than the poverty rate in the next highest rate country."[89]

Mortenson goes on to point out that, as a nation, the United States is able to reduce child poverty but chooses not to do so, largely by maintaining an artificially low tax rate at the national scale.[90] The Chacoans undoubtedly used their roads, rituals, and great houses to redistribute pottery and seed corn. Had Chaco's elites shared more with the farmers from the outset, foregoing even a portion of the cost of maintaining their elite status and goods, Chacoan society might have survived. We Americans also redistribute some wealth. But the disparity between rich and poor in America is huge and growing in our own era. Hadn't we better be more proactive? And that brings us to infrastructure.

Child Poverty Rates in the United States
1959 to 1996

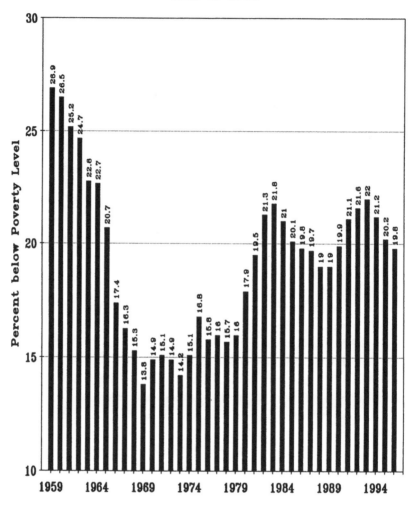

Child Poverty Before and After Government Intervention

Finland (1991) — 12 / 3

Sweden (1992) — 19 / 3

Denmark (1992) — 16 / 3

Switzerland (1982) — 5 / 3

Belgium (1992) — 16 / 4

Luxembourg (1985) — 12 / 4

Norway (1991) — 13 / 5

Austria (1987) — / 5

Netherlands (1991) — 14 / 6

France (1984) — 25 / 7

West Germany (1989) — 9 / 7

Italy (1991) — 12 / 10

United Kingdom (1986) — 30 / 10

Israel (1986) — 24 / 11

Ireland (1987) — 30 / 12

Canada (1991) — 23 / 14

Australia (1990) — 20 / 14

United States (1991) — 26 / 22

Before taxes and transfers

After taxes and transfers

0   5   10   15   20   25   30   35

Percent Below Poverty Level

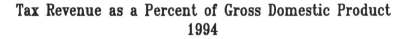

Tax Revenue as a Percent of Gross Domestic Product 1994

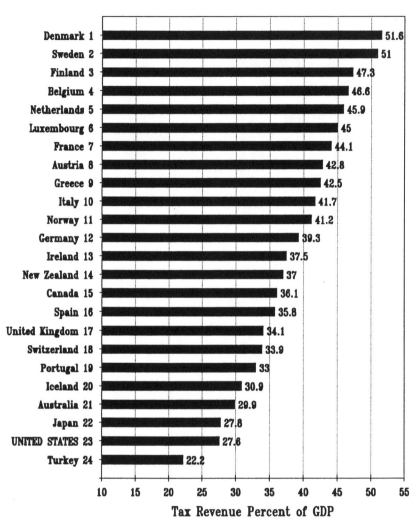

Country	Tax Revenue Percent of GDP
Denmark 1	51.6
Sweden 2	51
Finland 3	47.3
Belgium 4	46.6
Netherlands 5	45.9
Luxembourg 6	45
France 7	44.1
Austria 8	42.8
Greece 9	42.5
Italy 10	41.7
Norway 11	41.2
Germany 12	39.3
Ireland 13	37.5
New Zealand 14	37
Canada 15	36.1
Spain 16	35.8
United Kingdom 17	34.1
Switzerland 18	33.9
Portugal 19	33
Iceland 20	30.9
Australia 21	29.9
Japan 22	27.8
UNITED STATES 23	27.8
Turkey 24	22.2

Tax Revenue Percent of GDP

If a society will not invest in the core infrastructure and institutions that draw its people into communities, there will be no community and no nation. In another of Mortenson's diagrams, it is clear that the United States ranks twenty-third among 24 Western nations in taxes collected as a percentage of gross domestic product (GDP).[91] We beat only Turkey in funds made available to invest in the kinds of infrastructure and social programs necessary to sustain productivity and stability in our society. In 1994, the U.S. invested 27.6 percent of its GDP in tax revenues, whereas the average tax burden of those 24 industrial nations was about 40 percent of GDP. Can we really expect to be "number one" at such a steep discount on our tax base? Is this the reason we have no effective public transportation system, so that most of us are left to spend stunning amounts of money on private autos for nearly every trip? It may also be why we don't have universal access to health services. In 1995, 41 million American citizens had no health insurance, and therefore no guaranteed access to health care.[92] Another 10 to 20 million temporarily gain and lose access due to changing job status each year.[93] The number of Americans without assured access to health services in any given year is nearly equal to the population of the United Kingdom.

We all know that sustaining infrastructure takes resources. Currently, the United States is suffering from deteriorating roads, schools, bridges, dams, waterworks, and sewage disposal systems. Some cities, such as New York, are carrying on with infrastructure created nearly a century ago. Others carry on with aging schools, roads, bridges, and dams built with cheap labor during the Great Depression.

Since we tax ourselves at such a low rate compared with other industrial nations,[94] do we really intend to build infrastructure only episodically, when millions are out of work? There are huge, real costs to sustaining the fabric of an industrial nation-state—the costs of schools, health services, and transportation are among them. Are we willing to bear them? Mexico currently isn't, and judging from recent massacres of Indian farmers in the state of Chiapas,[95] such unwillingness can well lead down a path filled with hatred, horror, and sorrow—rather like the 1150s, when Chacoan society came undone.

We Americans are different, are we not? After all, ancient Chaco and present-day Mexico have in common a far more agrarian society than that of the contemporary U.S. Yes, there was another kind of infrastructure that played a crucial role in the Chacoan decline—farmland. And it was clear that the Chacoans used up forests, overhunted game, and pushed some farmland too hard in its core area during the 1000s. In this sense, the United States has been blessed. Throughout most of our short history we have had sufficient reserves of farm and forest land to overcome regional droughts and the effects of erosion and misadventure due to thoughtless urban development and foolish farming practices. Even now we are able to feed a population at least four times larger than our current 260 million citizens.[96] But it may not always be that way.

In 1997, the U.S. had an estimated 945 million acres of land in production.[97] As immense as that number is, it is sobering that we annually convert 1 million acres to serve less useful urban sprawl. Converting prime farmland to parking lots, shopping malls, and housing developments is short-sighted in the extreme. At current rates of destruction and current population levels, our farmland will vanish altogether in about 900 years. But nothing stays the same.

A recent study shows that 79 percent of the nation's fruits, 69 percent of its vegetables, and 52 percent of its dairy goods are currently harvested on very high quality farmland in immediate danger of being swallowed up by urban sprawl.[98] That means as American population increases, the future will increasingly depend on less productive land. Given our current behavior, 500 years is a more likely outer limit at which we will be able to feed ourselves, *if* our population does not grow rapidly. But we will grow, at least moderately. So when will we have a food crisis? When some combination of perverse climate, loss of prime farmland, diminishing fossil fuels, and increasing population "surprises" us. That could be 100, 300, or even 500 years from now. It is a matter of when—not if—given current behavior.

Since 1968, when Paul Ehrlich's *The Population Bomb* predicted disaster as world population passed 3.5 billion, the planet's population has actually grown to 6 billion. There was no world crisis because unexpected new plant varieties, fossil-fueled farm equipment, and new technologies boosted yields of staples such as wheat and corn by 80 percent during that period.[99] That has forestalled worldwide disaster and made America's export of food even more important. Ironically, American farmers have not benefited proportionally from this demand. In order to compete internationally, they have had to increase production and lower prices. Because of this, American farmers earn less now than in 1980, when they received 37 cents of every consumer dollar spent on food. In 1998, they received only 23 cents of every dollar spent on food.[100]

Does this erosion in farm income spell trouble? Yes. In 1978, when farm income was greater, there were 2.3 million farms in the United States. By 1998, after income declined, 300,000 of those farmers had given up.[101] Discouraged farmers, often unable to convince their children to carry on, are currently selling prime farmland near cities and abandoning farming each year. Every acre they abandon now means that half the world away, some child will be a little hungrier and staples a little costlier. Every acre they abandon now may also mean that some American child will starve 100 years from now.

We know how the disappearance of farmland will end, given surging population. We just don't know when it will end for us, so we put off worrying about it for another day, or another generation. Can we afford to take the same risks the Chacoans took, until all our farmers have walked away as theirs once did?

A More Durable Community

As America matures, it must work at the arts of survival if it is to be the model of prosperity, democracy, and stability a century from now that it is today. The model of historic Pueblo society — efficient, egalitarian, homogeneous, and self-sufficient — is not one we can or should mimic in detail. The United States is far too large, heterogeneous, polyglot, and growth-oriented to justify such mimicry. We probably cannot achieve their level of efficiency or egalitarianism and would not want to if we could. But the means of Pueblo success at survival points the way toward some essential improvements.

First, we can no longer accept the troubling fact that the U.S. is actually "number one" among industrial nations only in the sheer size of its economy and in the disparity of wealth between its citizens. America has been so obsessed with its short-term power that it has forgotten the long-term value of efficiency. We must become more efficient and less wasteful. Americans use more than twice as much energy per person as citizens of the other rich, industrial nations of Europe.[102] Their standards of health, education, public transportation, infant mortality, longevity, and literacy are generally higher than ours. We do not use twice as much because we are twice as rich — we aren't. We just plain waste it. That means we are horribly inefficient by comparison. If we can save a portion of those wasted resources by increasing our efficiency, we *will* be able to invest more in the core institutions that draw our citizens into real communities.

Perfect egalitarianism in the Pueblo fashion is not achievable in a population of 260 million, either. Besides, we have a national aversion to anything that smacks of socialist or communist schemes. The real risk is not that we will become socialists — we won't — but that the extremes of wealth will continue to accelerate in America until we have accidentally created a Third World society. Think about the children from Marin County, California, and Jefferson County, Mississippi. Should they not at least share the major benefits of living in the same country? Would we not have more of a national community if both had access to the same standards of education, nutrition, and health care? Would it destroy the fabric of a capitalist democracy if the Californians were only twice as rich, instead of four times as rich, as the Mississippians? I don't think so.

And we must rethink our national tax policies. Is it sensible that a disproportionate share of our nation's taxes are paid by the shrinking American middle class? For that matter, why are American corporations taxed less than their counterparts in other industrial nations? Should we be emulating a relatively undeveloped country such as Turkey in our overall tax effort? Or does it make more sense to tax corporations and the growing numbers of ultra-rich just a little more in order to guarantee all our citizens a reasonable level of health care, good schools, and good public transport?

Suppose we increased the national tax burden by about 3 percent, from 27.6 percent of GDP in 1993 to just 31 percent, still far below the 40-percent average for other Western nations. In 1993, that would have generated about 200 billion dollars annually to invest in those core institutions that enhance communities. If 200 billion dollars were carefully invested each year only in health, education, and public transport, we would soon have a richer, healthier, better-educated, and more efficient country. Corporations might scream, but can we really justify tax breaks for businesses that manufacture nonessential "widgets" or that export American jobs overseas? I believe not. If we had any sense at all, we would tax corporations for every job they exported. We also need to conserve farmland, so we need to give tax breaks to family farms and local food processors. We simply are not better off when rich land becomes parking lots. We actually lose valuable export business for every acre lost. Right now that food export demand merely gets met elsewhere, often at cheaper prices.

Economists and business mavens argue that a completely open, capitalist market is perfectly efficient. Obviously, efficiency's meaning depends on its definition. Most Americans think it simply means "cheaper." This definition implies that a factory, or a farmer, must create more product for a fixed quantity of labor or materials than another in order to sell at a lower price. It doesn't focus on sustainability. If that factory or farmer sells a product below cost, or one based on nonrenewable resources, eventually it won't just be "cheaper." The farmer or factory will be out of business. Extinct. Short-term definitions of efficiency don't provide for the future.

The themes of this book are transformation and survival. The marketplace's question "Can you buy it cheaper today than yesterday?" needs to be transformed into "If it is essential to survival, can you get it today, tomorrow, and forever?" The Chacoans did not fail because they ran short of turquoise and macaws, which they prized. They failed because they ran out of essentials, so that their growth could not be sustained. At the end, they did not have enough water, corn, meat, or fuel. If modern societies fail, ours included, it will not be because they taxed widgets another 3 percent to create infrastructure or because they could import fewer Mercedes sedans. It will be either because, besotted by the idea of growth, they ran out of irreplaceable resources—fossil fuel, water, farmland—or because they so flamboyantly increased the disparity in wealth that the moderating middle class vanished and cities burned in an orgy of rage and desperation. Both scenarios are preventable.

Can we again have a national community with shared values? Yes—if we can learn to share more than just a lecture about values. America works surprisingly well, considering the chances we have taken with our resources and our social order. That luck cannot last forever. The old idea of a strong *public* American identity based on common language, tolerance, flag, and fair play still has merit. Most immigrants to this nation still want a real chance at that identity. They want a share, not a lecture. So do the descendants of America's former slaves.

We *can* waste less. We *can* re-create safe and satisfying communities that Puebloan society would understand. They would be communities where all who worked hard and believed in the community were guaranteed a place—a place to live, a place to marry, a place to raise children, and a place to die, secure in the knowledge that their children's children would enjoy the same. But to have such a community requires us to work at it, to invest in it, and to think strategically rather than just about the near term. We must now build our own version of a durable community and invest far more heavily in survival than we have so far been willing to do. That means we must support a robust middle class and again build infrastructure designed to last a century rather than a decade. It will not be easy. But it must be done.

We can start by accepting the lesson left to all of us by the Anasazi of Chaco Canyon and their adaptable descendants—that survival means establishing a durable community. A durable community is one that balances growth with efficiency and refuses to be seduced by greed and power. Even the business world, currently astray on its own path to short-term profits, knows this. On Wall Street, veterans of the business cycle know that "bulls get rich, bears get rich, pigs get slaughtered." As the Chacoans, too, discovered nearly a millennium ago, greed is not a badge of honor. It is the signature of a dying society.

Epilogue

The Spirit of Community

DANIEL, THIS IS YOUR ANCESTORS' STORY, TOLD AS I PERCEIVE IT THROUGH the filter of my own culture. It is a remarkable journey that your people have taken in the 17 centuries since they became farmers and invented the first stable communities to exist in the Southwest. They grew impressively in numbers and in knowledge before creating their second version of a community—the interconnected, open communities of the Chaco Anasazi spread across the vast San Juan basin. It worked for a time, but the elites seem to have been seduced by their own power, and the needs of common farmers could not be met. Your ancestors paid dearly for this mistake, but they did not repeat it.

Instead, they formed a new and fragile society in the uplands following a period of hunger and conflict. The cliff houses they created were majestic solutions to the need for more efficiency, but nature was impatient with them. Their third version of farming and foraging communities also failed, not through their own fault but through bad luck.

Finally, they came to the rivers and created the fourth version of their communities. They increased the diversity of the lands they held and improved the technology of farming. They wove the essence of religion and of egalitarianism into virtually all of their undertakings. These values, along with changes in land-holding and farming technology and the creation of food-producing infrastructure, finally gave them enduring communities. A brief but important "golden age" ensued.

Then came the Spaniards, bearing both good and bad. Anglo-American society followed some two centuries later, bringing a different mix of outside influences. In response, your elders created their fifth kind of community — one with a face turned inward and another turned outward.

And that brings us to now — and to you.

You asked how to make a perfect Folsom point and worried that some lack of spirituality in you blocked the solution. I don't think the Folsom point is that important — your people have gone far beyond that need, and the kind of spirituality you seek is not the kind an ordinary American teacher can impart to you. I am helpless in this matter. My own society is still in its first great age. Yours is now in its fifth. We have yet to discover how one creates a community requiring real commitment. We are rich in "things" but poor in the skills of survival and in the spirit of "community."

I wrote this book to tell you that it is your own elders who can help you in this matter of spirituality. Listen to them. They know things about survival that you need to learn. They know things about sustaining the spirit of true communities. *That* is your heritage. Take advantage of it. America may yet learn how to create enduring communities with its own version of your elders' values. Then again, maybe it won't. In that case, you had better learn from them how to sustain your ancestral community so that you, too, can pass that knowledge on to your children. What we know and what we have created in Anglo-American society may not matter in another few centuries. Time will tell.

Notes

Chapter 1

1. Cordell 1997: 306.
2. Frazier 1986: 171–173.
3. Frazier 1986: 205.
4. Young and Morgan 1987.
5. Frazier 1986: 25–35.
6. Frazier 1986: 25.
7. Frazier 1986: 27.
8. Frazier 1986: 23.
9. Beck 1962: 131.
10. Beck 1962: 134.
11. Frazier 1986: 33, 35.

Chapter 2

1. Powledge and Rose 1996: 58–68.
2. Cordell 1997: 68–71.
3. Haynes 1993: 219; Meltzer 1995: 21–45.
4. Cordell 1997: 76; Gore 1997: 92–99.
5. Powledge and Rose 1996: 58–68.
6. Adovasio 1993: 205–213; Adovasio, Donahue, and Stuckenrath 1990: 348–354; Dillehay et al. 1992: 145–204; Powledge and Rose 1996: 61.

7. Gore 1997: 92–99.
8. S. Plog 1997: 44–45 (see illustrations).
9. S. Plog 1997: 43–44.
10. Cordell 1997: 85–86; Frison 1993: 240.
11. *Information Please Almanac* 1993: 779.
12. *Information Please Almanac* 1993: 237.
13. Lee 1968: 37.
14. Stuart 1986a.
15. Houghton 1959; Vivian 1990: 21–22.
16. Martin and Klein 1984.
17. Cordell 1997: 115.
18. Houghton 1959; Vivian 1990: 21–22.
19. Cordell 1997: 108; Stuart and Gauthier 1981: 29–33.
20. Cordell 1997: 101–102; S. Plog 1997: 46–47.
21. Cordell 1997: 84–85; Stuart and Gauthier 1981: 29–30.
22. Irwin-Williams 1973; Irwin-Williams 1979: 36, 39.
23. Odum 1955: 53–55.
24. Cordell 1997: 108; Irwin-Williams 1979: 36–37; Vivian 1990: 83.
25. Bryan and Toulouse 1943: 271–272.
26. Bryan and Toulouse 1943: 275.
27. Stuart 1980: 269–284.

28. *Information Please Almanac* 1993: 237.
29. *Information Please Almanac* 1993: 178.
30. Irwin-Williams 1973; Vivian 1990: 84.
31. Irwin-Williams 1979: 56; Irwin-Williams and Pippen 1969.
32. Irwin-Williams 1968: 48–54.
33. Keynes 1965.

Chapter 3

1. Hevly 1964.
2. Dick 1965; Wills 1988.
3. Dick 1965: 10.
4. Haury 1962: 106–131.
5. Cordell 1997: 129.
6. Cordell 1997: 129.
7. Irwin-Williams 1973: 13.
8. Stuart 1980: 269–284.
9. Cordell 1997: 141–142.
10. Cordell 1997: 119.
11. Ford 1981: 14; Kaplan 1965: 153–155.
12. Cordell 1997: 131.
13. Kaplan 1965; S. Plog 1997: 65, 68.
14. S. Plog 1997: 65, 68.
15. Lee and DeVore 1968: 36.
16. Cordell 1997: 132.
17. Cordell 1997: 386; Gumerman 1988.
18. Steward 1938: 20.
19. S. Plog 1997: 70.
20. Stuart 1986a.
21. See the discussion in Cordell (1997: 128) summarizing the theoretical work of Binford, Boserup, and others.
22. Stuart 1986a.
23. Lister and Lister 1968: 8.
24. Dittert et al. 1961; Eddy 1966.
25. Skinner et al. 1980: 47–59.
26. Bice and Sundt 1968; Reinhart 1967: 459.
27. Eddy 1961.
28. Bice and Sundt 1968.
29. Eddy 1966: 132–134.
30. Stuart and Gauthier 1981: 179.
31. Roberts 1929: 40, 91.
32. Cordell 1997: 49.
33. Cordell 1997: 244; Wills and Windes 1989: 355.
34. Cordell 1997: 381–382; Eddy 1966: 478–484; Vivian 1990: 117–118.
35. Larson 1995: 185–213.
36. El Najjar et al. 1976: 480–481.
37. Cordell 1997: 133.
38. Stuart and Gauthier 1981: 66.
39. The data base is now much larger, but no new overall analysis has been done.
40. Intel Corporation 1998.
41. Microsoft Corporation 1998.
42. U.S. Department of Commerce 1997: 547.
43. U.S. Department of Commerce 1997: 547.
44. U.S. Department of Commerce 1997: 547.
45. U.S. Department of Commerce 1997: 28.
46. U.S. Department of Commerce 1997: 457–458.
47. *Information Please Almanac* 1993: 833.
48. *Information Please Almanac* 1993: 833.
49. *Information Please Almanac* 1993: 833 (see "Household Size in 1990").

Chapter 4

1. Stuart and Gauthier 1981: 66.
2. Stuart and Gauthier 1981: 66.
3. Eldredge and Gould 1972: 82–115.
4. Brew 1946.
5. Eddy 1966.
6. R. Lightfoot 1992: 215; Wilshusen and Blinman 1992: 252–253, 264.
7. Stuart and Gauthier 1981: 39, 82.

8. Cordell 1997: 283.

9. Eddy 1966: 266; Vivian 1990: 138.

10. Cordell 1997: 280.

11. Cordell 1997: 282–283.

12. R. Lightfoot 1992: 227; Wilshusen and Blinman 1992: 261–263.

13. Duke 1985: 286.

14. Ellis 1988: 14–26.

15. Vivian 1990: 157.

16. Vivian 1990: 158.

17. Wiseman 1979: 42.

18. Eddy 1966: 485.

19. Cordell 1997: 280.

20. Cordell 1997: 385–387.

21. Cordell 1997: 133.

22. Gumerman and Dean 1989: 99–148.

23. Vivian 1990: 181.

24. McKenna and Truell 1986: 71.

25. McKenna 1984: 352.

26. McKenna 1984: 353–357.

27. McKenna 1984: 97–99.

28. Vivian 1990: 201–202.

29. McKenna 1984: 261–285, 323.

30. Vivian 1990: 275.

31. Vivian 1990: 194–205 (see figs. 7.18, 7.19).

32. Vivian 1990: 204.

33. Cordell 1997: 36–38.

34. Ruppe 1953: 313–314.

35. Akins 1982, 1984, 1985; Vivian 1990: 214–215.

36. Vivian 1990: 163.

37. *USA Today,* December 11, 1998.

38. Charles A. Schwab and Company 1998.

Chapter 5

1. Vivian 1990: 472, 478.

2. Cordell 1997: 305–306.

3. Cordell 1997: 306.

4. Previté-Orton 1966.

5. Vivian 1990: 115.

6. Frazier 1986: 174; Vivian 1990: 206.

7. Vivian 1990: 177–178.

8. Vivian 1990: 178–179.

9. Vivian 1990: 181.

10. Stuart 1997: 41; Stuart and Gauthier 1981: 42.

11. Marshall et al. 1979: 141.

12. Marshall et al. 1979: 155.

13. Vivian 1990: 178.

14. Marshall et al. 1979: 155.

15. Marshall et al. 1979: 157.

16. Marshall et al. 1979: 155–156.

17. Peckham 1958: 161–163; Marshall et al. 1979: 155.

18. Peckham 1958: 161–163; Marshall et al. 1979: 155.

19. Marshall et al. 1979: 157.

20. Cordell 1997: 37–38 (see fig. 2.2).

21. Marshall et al. 1979: 155, 157.

22. Ortiz 1969: 105, 114–115.

23. Marshall et al. 1979: 143.

24. Marshall et al. 1979: 133.

25. Marshall et al. 1979: 131.

26. Marshall et al. 1979: 131–132.

27. Marshall et al. 1979: 134.

28. Marshall et al. 1979: 134.

29. Marshall et al. 1979: 133.

30. Vivian 1990: 266.

31. Marshall et al. 1979: 133.

32. Marshall et al. 1979: 134 (see "Ceramic Notes").

33. Pepper 1920.

34. Marshall et al. 1979: 134.

35. Marshall et al. 1979: 131–140.

36. Vivian 1990: 266.

37. Frazier 1986: 27–37.

38. Marshall et al. 1979: 201.

39. Marshall et al. 1979: 206.

40. Marshall et al. 1979: 73.

41. Vivian 1990: 243.

42. Marshall et al. 1979: 202.

43. Marshall et al. 1979: 203.

44. Marshall et al. 1979: 16; Vivian 1990: 287.

45. Fransted 1979: 40–41; Kluckhohn 1967: 159; Reichard 1944: 153.

46. Marshall et al. 1979: 206.

47. Marshall et al. 1979: 205.

48. Marshall et al. 1979: 206.

49. Bannister et al. 1970: 25; Marshall et al. 1979: 204.

50. Marshall et al. 1979: 75.

51. Marshall et al. 1979: 73.

52. Marshall et al. 1979: 73.

53. Marshall et al. 1979: 67.

54. Marshall et al. 1979: 75.

55. Vivian 1990: 31.

56. Frazier 1986: 31.

57. McNitt 1957: 113.

58. Vivian 1990: 157.

59. Frazier 1986: 182, 151.

60. Cordell 1997: 308.

61. Cordell 1997: 306–309.

62. Cordell 1997: 308.

63. Sofaer 1997: 100.

64. Frazier 1986: 179; Lekson 1986.

65. Stein, Suiter, and Ford 1997: 133–134.

66. Lekson 1986.

67. Powers et al. 1983; Vivian 1990: 185.

68. Marshall et al. 1979: 201; Powers et al. 1983.

69. Marshall et al. 1979: 241; Powers et al. 1983; Vivian 1990: 185.

70. Marshall et al. 1979: 308; Powers et al. 1983; Vivian 1990: 185.

71. Breternitz et al. 1982: 1247; Vivian 1990: 346–347.

72. Frazier 1986: 33.

73. Vivian 1990: 275.

74. Vivian 1990: 275–276; Windes 1984: 192–209.

75. Lekson 1986; Vivian 1990: 276.

76. Lekson 1986; Vivian 1990: 278.

77. Vivian 1990: 280, 282.

78. Lekson 1986: 70.

79. Judd 1954: 151; Vivian 1990: 280, 285.

80. Vivian 1990: 291–292.

81. Frazier 1986: 33.

82. Sofaer 1997: 100.

83. Sofaer 1997: 88–120.

84. Marshall 1997: 62–66.

85. Marshall 1997: 70.

86. White 1960: 89.

87. Stevenson 1884: 67–68.

88. Frazier 1986: 125–126.

89. Frazier 1986: 115; Schreiber 1997: 84; Vivian 1990: 323.

90. Marshall 1997: 70.

91. Marshall 1997: 68.

92. Schreiber 1997: 84.

93. Nials 1983: 6.1–6.51.

94. Vivian 1990: 321.

95. Marshall et al. 1979: 243–244.

96. Marshall et al. 1979: 243; Vivian 1990: 194.

97. Marshall et al. 1979: 244.

98. Cordell 1997: 324; Frazier 1986: 135.

99. Frazier 1986: 133; Stuart and Gauthier 1981: 82.

100. Vivian 1990: 23–24.

101. Irwin-Williams 1980; Vivian 1990: 414.

102. Vivian 1990: 379.

103. Vivian 1990: 316.

104. Frazier 1986: 133–134.

105. Lekson 1997.

106. Marshall 1997: 70.

107. Frazier 1986: 135; Vivian 1990: 237.

108. Vivian 1990: 237.

109. Stuart and Gauthier 1981: 82; Vivian 1990: 388.

110. Vivian 1990: 350.

111. Vivian 1990: 237, 335, 347.

112. Frazier 1986: 177, 179.

Chapter 6

1. Lekson 1984: 271; Vivian 199: 443.

2. Lekson 1984: 70, 271; Marshall et al. 1979: 337–338; Vivian 1990: 445.

3. Cordell 1997: 310–311.

4. Cordell 1997: 281.

5. Cordell 1997: 308 (see fig. 10.3).

6. Cordell 1997: 306–307 (see fig. 10.2).

7. McKenna and Truell 1986: 274; Vivian 1990: 178–181.

8. McKenna and Truell 1986: 132–135 (see table 2.1).

9. McKenna and Truell 1986: 82, 274–276.

10. McKenna and Truell 1986: 77–78.

11. McKenna and Truell 1986: 82.

12. McKenna and Truell 1986: 82.

13. McKenna and Truell 1986: 79 (see fig. 1.19), 82.

14. McKenna and Truell 1986: 80 (see fig. 1.20), 82–83.

15. McKenna and Truell 1986: 266.

16. McKenna and Truell 1986: 88.

17. McKenna and Truell 1986: 88.

18. Cordell 1997: 49; McKenna and Truell 1986: 225–227; Vivian 1990: 306.

19. Archives of the Chaco Center 1974.

20. McKenna 1984: 2, 97–101.

21. McKenna 1984: 16–17 (see table 2.1), 349 (see table 7.1); McKenna and Truell 1986: 71–72.

22. McKenna 1984: 107.

23. McKenna 1984: 307.

24. McKenna 1984: 103, 117.

25. McKenna 1984: 321.

26. McKenna 1984: 352.

27. McKenna 1984: 66; Vivian 1990: 201–202.

28. McKenna 1984: 352.

29. McKenna 1984: 355–357, 358.

30. McKenna 1984: 352.

31. McKenna 1984: 352, 353.

32. McKenna 1984: 358.

33. McKenna 1984: 355.

34. McKenna 1984: 355.

35. McKenna 1984: 353–357.

36. Akins 1986: 62.

37. Akins 1986: 61.

38. Akins 1986: 61.

39. Tainter and Gillio 1980: 85, referring to a dissertation by W. Dexter Wade. Archaeologists use "life tables" created by paleodemographers from ancient burial populations. These are not as accurate as the contemporary life tables prepared by insurance companies and demographers who have modern statistical data at their disposal. Estimates from the archaeological tables are just that—estimates.

40. Tainter and Gillio 1980: 86, referring to Wade dissertation.

41. U.S. Department of Commerce 1997: 90.

42. Tainter and Gillio 1980: 85, referring to Wade dissertation.

43. Akins 1986: 62.

44. Akins 1986: 62.

45. Akins 1986: 61.

46. Akins 1986: 61.

47. Cordell 1997: 324.

48. Akins 1986: 135.

49. Akins 1986: 136.

50. Judd 1954: 61–64; Vivian 1990: 314–315.

51. Cordell 1997: 318–319.

52. Palkovich 1984: 107.

53. Judd 1954: 254.

54. Judd 1954: 325.

55. Akins and Schelberg 1984: 93.

56. Pepper 1920: 194–195.

57. Pepper 1920: 164, 169 (see fig. 71).

58. Pepper 1920: 120–126.

59. Stuart 1996: viii.

60. Judge 1989: 239–240.

61. Cordell 1997: 324–326.

62. Vivian 1990: 224 (see fig. 8.1).

63. Cordell 1997: 36–37.

64. Vivian 1990: 215.

65. Vivian 1990: 215–216.

66. Eggan 1979: 229.

67. Akins 1986: for examples see 161

(table B-1: burials 32708A and 327111), 163.

68. Marshall et al. 1979: 117–195.

69. Vivian 1990: 328–329.

70. Vivian 1990: 225.

71. Michael P. Marshall, personal communication, 1983.

72. Vivian 1990: 478–486 (see "A.D. 1020–1120: The Growth of the Chacoan System," specifically p. 479).

73. Vivian 1990: 364–365, 375.

74. Steinbeck 1939.

75. Vivian 1990: 238–239 (see fig. 8.6).

76. Bannister et al. 1970: 25; Marshall et al. 1979: 201.

77. Marshall et al. 1979: 303; Robinson 1974: 60.

78. Powers et al. 1983: 252.

79. Powers et al. 1983: 164–167.

80. Powers et al. 1983: 161–164.

81. Marshall et al. 1979: 195; Vivian 1990: 348–349 (see fig. 9.6).

82. This statement is summarized from data contained in Marshall et al. 1979.

83. Vivian 1990: 351.

84. Vivian 1990: 347–348.

85. Frazier 1986: 123–124.

86. Judd 1954: 28–29.

87. Vivian 1990: 334.

88. Vivian 1990: 350.

89. U.S. Department of Agriculture 1998.

90. U.S. Department of Agriculture 1998.

91. Stuart 1989: 52.

92. Mitchell 1936.

93. Stuart 1989.

94. Feldman 1996.

Chapter 7

1. That some elites stayed on in the great-houses after 1130 is remarked in Vivian 1990: 347.

2. Breternitz et al. 1982: 1247.

3. Hayes 1964.

4. Stuart 1989: 39.

5. Stuart and Farwell 1983.

6. Farwell 1981: 43–47.

7. Klodt 1985: 252.

8. Wendorf and Reed 1955: 141–142.

9. Stuart and Farwell 1983: 119–138 (see table 7).

10. Farwell and Oakes n.d.: see "Excavation at LA 12697"; Stuart and Farwell 1983: 143.

11. Stuart and Farwell 1983.

12. Hayes 1964; Stuart and Gauthier 1981: 42, 49, 51 (see table 3.2).

13. Hayes 1964.

14. Seaman 1976.

15. Stuart and Farwell 1983: 148–151 (many original excavation reports are cited throughout).

16. Dick 1976; Stuart and Farwell 1983: 152.

17. Dick 1976.

18. Dick 1976.

19. Green 1956.

20. Stuart and Farwell 1983: 152.

21. Blumenschein 1956: 53–56.

22. Schroeder and Wendorf 1954.

23. Stuart and Farwell 1983: 139.

24. Stuart and Farwell 1983: 119–138 (see table 7).

25. Stuart and Farwell 1983: 139.

26. Author's conclusion based on a reading of Vivian 1990.

27. Although the elevation of each of these is well-known, current textbooks fail to note the elevational differences between the scion communities and the pithouses and early Pueblo III pueblos on the mesas above. Thus the differing ecological settings of the two groups of sites have gone largely unnoticed.

28. Eddy 1977; Hallasi 1979; Vivian 1990: 76.
29. Vivian 1990: 369, 370, 371.
30. Vivian 1990: 384.
31. Akins 1984: 225–240; Akins 1985: 305–445; Vivian 1990: 379.
32. Powers et al. 1983: 161–164; Vivian 1990: 370.
33. Powers et al. 1983: 252.
34. Powers et al. 1983: 167–170, 387; Reed et al. 1979: 251–252.
35. Reed et al. 1979: 310–311.
36. Vivian 1990: 379.
37. Stuart and Farwell 1983: 153–154; Stuart and Gauthier 1981: 172–173 (see table 4.9).
38. Stuart 1989: 64.
39. Stuart and Farwell 1983: 119–138 (see table 7).
40. Stuart 1989: 57; Stuart and Gauthier 1981: 57–59 (see tables 3.6 and 3.8).
41. Hewitt 1938; Stuart 1989: 60; Stuart and Gauthier 1981: 51–52.
42. Stuart and Farwell 1983 (see "Subsistence," 148–152).
43. Hewett 1938; Stuart 1989: 58.
44. Shepard 1965: 385–387.
45. Stuart 1989: 57.
46. Mathien 1997: 127–129.
47. Stuart 1989: 61.
48. Stuart 1985: 90; Stuart 1989: 61.
49. Worman 1967.
50. Wendorf and Reed 1955: 143–154.
51. Wiseman 1980.
52. Marshall et al. 1979 (see ceramic inventory sections for each site visited).
53. Stubbs and Stallings 1953.
54. Stuart and Farwell 1983: 153.
55. Vivian 1990: 386.
56. Cordell 1997: 368; Vivian 1990: 386–388.
57. Cordell 1997: 368; Windes 1984: 75–87.
58. Vivian 1990: 383–389.
59. Reher 1977: 79.
60. Reher 1977: 79.
61. Kelley and Frances 1995.
62. Christy G. Turner, personal communication, 1998.
63. Donoho n.d.: 5–6; Marshall and Hogan 1991; Towner 1996.
64. Wendorf and Reed 1955.
65. Stuart and Gauthier 1981: 58–59.
66. Stuart 1985: 86; Stuart 1989: 68–69.
67. Stuart 1985: 86–92.
68. Stuart and Gauthier 1981: 50 (see fig. 3.5).
69. Stuart 1985: 86.
70. McGimsey 1980: 1, 43.
71. Stuart 1985: 80–82.
72. Stuart 1985: 82.
73. McGimsey 1980: 49–54.
74. McGimsey 1980: 105.
75. Stuart 1985: 80–82.
76. McGimsey 1980: 60–105; Stuart 1985: 82.
77. Cordell 1997: 367–368, 378–379.
78. Cordell 1997: 210; Dittert 1959; Lambert 1954; Stuart and Gauthier 1981: 152–153; Tainter and Gillio 1980.
79. Vivian 1990: 376–377, 387, 486–487.
80. McGimsey 1980: 42, 60–105.
81. Cordell 1997: 422; F. Plog 1979: 123.
82. Brew 1979: 514–515.
83. Stuart 1989.
84. Vivian 1990: 387.
85. D. Lightfoot 1990; Stuart 1989: 69, 71.
86. Ladd 1979: 497.
87. Cordell 1997: 294–296 (see illustration); D. Lightfoot 1990.
88. Stuart 1989: 74.
89. Hewitt 1953; Stuart 1985.
90. Stuart 1989: 73–74.
91. Morgan 1994: 46, 47, 51; Frazier 1986: 116, 117.
92. Vivian 1990: 347–349.
93. Sebastian 1992: 135.

94. *Encyclopaedia Britannica* 1977 (vol. 18): 472.
95. Rohde 1995.
96. Darby 1995.
97. Randall-Cutler and Myles (producers) 1991.
98. U.S. Department of Commerce 1997 (see table 468).
99. United States Fact Sheet, USDA Economic Research Service March 1998.
100. U.S. Department of Commerce 1997 (see tables 89, 126, 119, 136).

Chapter 8

1. Stuart and Gauthier 1981: 44.
2. Simmons 1979: 178.
3. Stuart and Farwell 1983: 157.
4. Biella and Chapman 1977–1979.
5. Chapman and Biella 1977.
6. Lange 1968a.
7. Rory P. Gauthier, personal communication, 1981.
8. Shepard 1965: 178–180; Stuart 1989: 84, 85.
9. Stuart and Farwell 1983.
10. Eidenbach 1982; Wimberly and Eidenbach 1980.
11. Marshall et al. 1981: 116.
12. Marshall et al. 1981: 101.
13. Lange and Riley 1970.
14. Marshall et al. 1981: 116. See also Marshall and Walt 1984 for more on Hidden Mountain and nearby sites.
15. Marshall et al. 1981: 118.
16. Marshall et al. 1981: 130–131 (see table 12).
17. Stuart and Gauthier 1986: 89–91.
18. Marshall et al. 1981: 101–105.
19. Marshall et al. 1981: 102.
20. Marshall et al. 1981: 104.
21. Marshall et al. 1981: 111.
22. Laboratory of Anthropology site files, n.d.
23. Adams 1991; Cordell 1997: 425.
24. Stuart and Gauthier 1986.
25. Lang 1977; Stuart and Gauthier 1981: 99–103.
26. Schroeder 1979: 242–248.
27. Eggan 1979: 225 (see map).
28. Ortiz 1979: 279.
29. Stuart 1989: 71, 77, 89.
30. Cordell 1997: 263; Pruecel 1990: 55–56.
31. Weigand et al. 1977: 22; Williams 1986: 117.
32. Schroeder 1979: 247; Stuart 1989: 109.
33. Shepard 1965: 178–180.
34. Stuart and Gauthier 1981 chronicles several hundred sites.
35. Marshall and Walt 1984: 95–115 (see especially pp. 104–105).
36. Jelinek 1967.
37. Dittert 1949.
38. Hunter-Anderson 1979: 181.
39. Stuart and Gauthier 1981: 53.
40. Eighmy 1981: 225–233.
41. Stuart and Gauthier 1981: 65–68.
42. Eighmy 1981: 225–233.
43. Daughtery et al. 1986.
44. Reher 1977.
45. See articles on the Pueblo Indians in *Handbook of North American Indians* 1979 (vol. 9): 225–467.
46. Schwartz 1980: xii.
47. Schwartz 1980: x.
48. Creamer 1993; Schwartz 1980: xii.
49. Schwartz 1980: xii.
50. Schwartz 1980: xvii.
51. Schwartz 1980: xvi.
52. Schwartz 1980: xii.
53. Schwartz 1980: xvi.
54. Palkovich 1980: 1–2.
55. Palkovich 1980: 1–2.

56. Palkovich 1980: 1–2.
57. Palkovich 1980: 16–17.
58. Palkovich 1980: 23.
59. Palkovich 1980: 30–31.
60. Palkovich 1980: 25.
61. Palkovich 1980: 24.
62. Akins 1986: 136.
63. Palkovich 1980: 30–31.
64. Palkovich 1980: 16–17.
65. Schroeder 1979: 435.
66. Personal communication with Tijeras Ranger station.
67. Cordell 1980: 9.
68. Cordell 1980: 11.
69. Ferguson 1980: 130.
70. Young 1980: 99–101.
71. Ferguson 1980: 132.
72. Schroeder 1979: 430.
73. Woodbury 1993.
74. Schroeder 1979: 430–432; Kidder 1958: 14–15.
75. Schroeder 1979: 430 (see fig. 1).
76. Schroeder 1979: 432.
77. Akins 1986: 61.
78. Kidder 1932: 6, 302.
79. Kidder 1932: 5.
80. Stuart 1989: 88–89.
81. Morgan 1994: 226.
82. Morgan 1994: 226.
83. Morgan 1994: 228.
84. Kidder 1958: 121.
85. Kidder 1958: 122.
86. Hammond and Rey 1940.
87. Hammond and Rey 1929.
88. Vivian 1990: 309.
89. Arnon and Hill 1979: 303.
90. Author's summary of many specific site reports.
91. Stuart and Gauthier 1981: 105.
92. Hewitt 1938: 21–28.
93. Morgan 1994: 205.
94. Morgan 1994: 216.
95. Morgan 1994: 216.
96. Dozier 1970: 24; Whiteley 1982: 99.
97. Woodbury 1979: 468–469.
98. Ellis 1979: 441.
99. Sando 1979: 419.
100. Bodine 1979: 259.
101. Kidder 1932 (see plates).
102. Bunzell 1938: 352.
103. Ortiz 1969: 111.
104. Dozier 1970: 39.
105. Ortiz 1969: 39, 118.
106. Dozier 1970: 117.
107. Ortiz 1994: 32.
108. Dozier 1966: 172–185.
109. Ortiz 1969: 9–10.
110. Ortiz 1969: 79–98.
111. Whiteley 1982: 99.
112. Vivian 1990: 309.
113. Ladd 1979: 497; Stuart 1989: 69, 71, 75.
114. Cordell 1984: 186; Alfonso Ortiz, personal communication, early 1990s.
115. Cordell 1997: 133.
116. Ortiz 1969: 100–101; Whiteley 1982: 99.
117. Pearce 1965: 8, 6.
118. Ortiz 1969: 112–113.
119. Ortiz 1969: 39.
120. Ortiz 1969: 112, 115.
121. Dozier 1970: 65.
122. Ortiz 1994: 49.
123. Marshall 1997: 65.
124. Silverberg 1970: 131, 165.
125. Sando 1979: 194–197.
126. Sando 1979: 196.
127. Sando 1979: 196–197.
128. Bunzell 1938: 352.
129. Ortiz 1994: 14–15.
130. Brandt 1979: 343; Kennard 1979: 557; Ortiz 1969: 112; Strong 1979: 402.
131. Lange 1968b: 338–339; Ortiz 1969: 108–111.
132. Kidder 1932; Stuart 1989: 83.

133. Alfonso Ortiz, personal communication, 1991.
134. Cordell 1997: 224–225; Silverberg 1970: 26; Stuart 1989: 83–84.
135. Cordell 1997: 131–133.
136. Stuart 1989: 75.
137. D. Lightfoot 1990; Stuart 1989: 71.
138. Dozier 1970: 209.
139. Frazier 1986: 19; Marshall 1997: 69.
140. Garcia-Mason 1979: 450.

Chapter 9

1. Simmons 1979: 178.
2. Beck 1962: 39.
3. Bolton 1949: 38.
4. Bolton 1949: 118.
5. Bolton 1949: 403–404.
6. Ramenofsky 1987.
7. Simmons 1979: 179.
8. Simmons 1979: 179.
9. Schroeder 1979: 239 (see map).
10. Simmons 1979: 181.
11. Beck 1962: 60; Simmons 1979: 178, 181.
12. Beck 1962: 52.
13. *Encyclopaedia Britannica* 1977 (vol. 7): 534.
14. Beck 1962: 62.
15. Ortiz 1994: 54–55.
16. Beck 1962: 39.
17. Beck 1962: 40; Bolton 1949: 55.
18. Schroeder 1979: 238.
19. Schroeder 1979: 239.
20. Schroeder 1979: 254.
21. Ortiz 1994: 21–35.
22. Ramenofsky 1987; Simmons 1979: 184–185.
23. Schroeder 1979: 254 (compilation of all population data).
24. Brew 1979: 521–522; Schroeder 1979: 254.
25. Schroeder 1979: 430.
26. Simmons 1979: 185.
27. U.S. Bureau of the Census 1995.
28. Schroeder 1979: 434–435.
29. Sando 1992: 30; Stuart 1989.
30. Ortiz 1994: 46–47.
31. Ortiz 1994: 49–50.
32. Ortiz 1994: 50.
33. Dozier 1970: 26–27.
34. Garland Bills, personal communication, 1998.
35. Lange and Riley 1970: 88, 92, 100.
36. Dozier 1970: 181–182.
37. Cordell and Stuart 1986: 90–91.
38. Eggan 1970: ix.
39. Ortiz 1994: 96.
40. Sayles and Williams 1986 (see table 105 and map 106).
41. Eggan 1979: 225 (see maps).
42. Simmons 1979: 183 (see fig. 2).
43. Paskind 1998.
44. Dozier 1970: 160; Lange 1979: 202.
45. The changes in clothing are obvious from dated photographs reproduced in *Handbook of North American Indians* 1979 (vol. 9).
46. Arnon and Hill 1979: 298–300.
47. Ortiz 1969: 4.
48. A number of my Pueblo Indian students over the years have given me their "Indian" names to use when I visit them at the pueblo. This is simply because many of their elders, the most permanent residents of the pueblo, often do not know these young people by their outside names. Alfonso Ortiz and I used to discuss this duality in names as well.
49. Friedberg, Wells, and Fuchs, producers, 1997.
50. Ehrlich 1968.
51. Mortenson 1998: 11.
52. *USA Today*, September 20, 1996; *U.S. News and World Report*, Janu-

ary 22, 1996: 47–54; *U.S. News and World Report,* May 26 1997.

53. Glassman 1997.
54. Mortenson 1998: 11.
55. Glassman 1997.
56. Boroughs et al. 1996.
57. Boroughs et al. 1996.
58. Garrett 1988: 228–229.
59. Garrett 1988: 226–227.
60. Bernardo 1981: 352.
61. Chalmers 1965.
62. Garrett 1988: 54–55.
63. Watkins 1993.
64. Garrett 1988: 229.
65. Garrett 1988: 229.
66. Mortenson 1998: 14.
67. Newman 1988.
68. U.S. Department of State 1998.
69. Dillon 1998; Robinson 1996.
70. Holstein 1997.
71. Boroughs et al. 1996.
72. Wright 1996: 249.
73. Lynch 1996.
74. Wright 1996: 370–371.
75. Wright 1996: 372.
76. Organization for Economic Cooperation and Development 1994, 1996.
77. U.S. Department of Commerce 1997: 88 (see table 117).
78. Wright 1996: 370–371.
79. Wright 1996: 221.
80. U.S. Department of Commerce 1997: 88 (see table 117).
81. U.S. Bureau of the Census 1996.
82. U.S. Department of Commerce 1997: 452.
83. U.S. Bureau of the Census 1996.
86. U.S. Department of Justice 1997.
84. U.S. Department of Labor and Council of Economic Advisors 1995.
85. *National Geographic,* October 1998.
87. Wright 1996: 365–372.
88. Mortenson 1998: 14.
89. Mortenson 1998: 15.
90. Mortenson 1998: 12.
91. Mortenson 1998: 16.
92. U.S. Department of Commerce 1997: 109.
93. U.S. Department of Commerce 1997: 397–421(see tables 619, 638, 652, 653, 658).
94. Mortenson 1998: 16.
95. U.S. Department of State 1998.
96. This is my estimate based on individual commodities exported, compared with industry data on food production. On the United States' ability to feed a larger population, see U.S. Department of Commerce 1997: 989.
97. American Farmland Trust 1997.
98. American Farmland Trust 1997.
99. *National Geographic,* October 1998.
100. U.S. Department of Agriculture 1998.
101. U.S. Department of Agriculture 1998.
102. Wright 1996: 272, 374–375.

Glossary

Anasazi. Archaeologist's name for prehistoric farmers who lived in the American Southwest from about A.D. 300 to 1500. They are ancestors of the historic and contemporary Pueblo peoples.

Apache. Nomadic hunters and gatherers of the Athapascan language group who migrated into the Southwest sometime after A.D. 1200. See also *Navajo.*

Archaic. The name archaeologists have given to hunting and gathering peoples who lived in North America from roughly 5000 B.C. to A.D. 1. The term *Desert Archaic* refers specifically to hunters and gatherers of the desert Southwest. They are considered the ancestors of later Anasazi and Mogollon farmers.

Basketmaker. Archaeologist's name for the eastern Anasazi between A.D. 1 and about 700. During much of this period, basketry was especially important and elaborate, since pottery was either absent or in the process of development.

Chaco Anasazi. Anasazi who formed a complex regional society centered on Chaco Canyon, New Mexico, from the early A.D. 800s to the 1100s.

Four Corners. Geographic place where the modern states of Utah, Colorado, New Mexico, and Arizona join. It was the geographic homeland of the eastern Anasazi, who eventually gave rise to Chacoan society after A.D. 800.

Great house. A multistoried, sandstone masonry building of the A.D. 800s to 1100s, built by the Chaco Anasazi. It usually contained habitation rooms, storerooms, and paired ceremonial chambers, or *kivas.* The most famous is Pueblo Bonito at Chaco Canyon.

Hopi. Descendants of the Anasazi, many of whom still maintain a relatively traditional lifestyle in northern Arizona.

Kitchen midden. The refuse pile of an ancient village or farmstead. It was usually located to the east of an Anasazi settlement.

Kiva. A ceremonial-religious chamber used by the Anasazi and their Puebloan descendants. Anasazi kivas were usually circular in plan, and later Puebloan ones, either circular or squarish. Most kivas were semisubterranean, but others were enclosed circles within above-ground rooms.

Mano and metate. A handpiece pestle and mortar, typically made of sandstone and used for grinding corn or other seeds into flour. These implements were in daily use from about the A.D. 1 into the 1960s and are still used on special occasions in traditional Pueblo Indian households.

Mogollon. Archaeologist's name for the prehistoric farmers of southern New Mexico and southeastern Arizona, who were culturally distinct from the Anasazi. Their society flourished from about A.D. 200 to 1400. Some survivors from Mogollon villages may have made their way north after the 1300s and become amalgamated into Anasazi and later Puebloan society.

Navajo. Nomadic hunters and gatherers of the Athapascan language group who migrated into the Southwest sometime after A.D. 1200 and now form the largest tribal nation in North America. They are closely related to Apache people, who also still live in the same general area.

Pit house. An efficient, semisubterranean dwelling dug into the earth and roofed with timbers, bark, and clay-rich soil. Pit houses were typically used between A.D. 200 and 800, then again in the 1100s to 1300s.

Pueblo. Refers to the Anasazi after they began to build above-ground farmsteads and multistoried villages about A.D. 700-800, and to their town-dwelling descendants, who were first encountered by Spaniards in 1540 and still live in New Mexico and Arizona.

Suggested Readings

There are hundreds of good books about the Chaco Anasazi and their Pueblo Indian descendants. My own favorites follow.

The People of Chaco, by Kendrick Frazier (W. W. Norton, 1986). Written by an accomplished science writer, this enjoyable and well-referenced book tells how archaeologists pieced together evidence for the "Chaco phenomenon" in the 1970s and 1980s. It summarizes Chacoan research to 1986. If you read only one other book about Chaco, make it this one.

Chaco Canyon: Archaeology and Archaeologists, by Robert H. Lister and Florence G. Lister (University of New Mexico Press, 1981). Written by the first director of the National Park Service's Chaco Center and his talented collaborator and wife, this book tells you just about everything that happened in research at Chaco Canyon from 1896 to the early 1970s. It is both readable and a classic.

Anasazi Architecture and American Design, edited by Baker Morrow and V. B. Price (University of New Mexico Press, 1997). This collection of essays is the product of an interdisciplinary symposium at Mesa Verde National Park that included archaeologists, historians, architects, and urban planners. As a consequence, the articles step beyond the traditional textbook boundaries of each of those disciplines. If your taste runs to the bold, provocative, thoughtful, and insightful, this volume will deliver.

The Chacoan Prehistory of the San Juan Basin, by R. Gwinn Vivian (Academic Press, 1990). This magisterial technical reference is the definitive work on pure Chacoan archaeology. It summarizes the remarkable life's work of its much loved and admired author, a distinguished professor at the University of Arizona.

Archaeology of the Southwest, second edition, by Linda S. Cordell (Academic Press, 1997). This is the best advanced-level reference-textbook overview ever written about Southwestern archaeology, which includes much more than the Chaco area. Although not light reading, it is readable, it explains both fact and theory, and it has a killer bibliography. It is the current "bible" among advanced undergraduate and graduate archaeology majors on two continents.

The Tewa World (University of Chicago Press, 1969) and *The Pueblo* (Chelsea House, 1994), by Alfonso Ortiz. Why get it second-hand, when you can read about the Rio Grande Pueblo descendants of the Chacoans from an eminent Native American anthropologist who was born at San Juan Pueblo?

The Southwest, published as volume 9 of the *Handbook of North American Indians,* edited by Alfonso Ortiz (Smithsonian Institution, 1979). This is another classic source that is absolutely indispensable. The writing is straightforward, and the photographs and bibliography are fabulous.

References Cited

Adams, Charles E.

1991   *The Origin and Development of the Pueblo Katsina Cult.* University of Arizona Press, Tucson.

Adovasio, James M.

1993   "The Ones That Will Not Go Away: A Biased View of Pre-Clovis Populations in the New World." In *Kostenki to Clovis: Upper Paleolithic-Paleo-Indian Adaptations,* edited by Olga Soffer and N. D. Praslov, pp. 199–218. Plenum Press, New York.

Adovasio, James M., J. Donahue, and R. Stuckenrath

1990   "The Meadowcroft Rock Shelter, 1977: An Overview." *American Antiquity* 43: 632–651.

Akins, Nancy J.

1982   "Perspectives on Faunal Resource Utilization, Chaco Canyon, New Mexico." *Newsletter of the New Mexico Archaeological Council* 4 (5–6): 23–28. Albuquerque.

1984   "Temporal Variations in Faunal Assemblages from Chaco Canyon." In *Recent Research on Chaco Prehistory,* edited by W. James Judge and John D. Schelberg, pp. 225–240. Reports of the Chaco Center, no. 8. Division of Cultural Research, National Park Service, Albuquerque.

1985   "Prehistoric Faunal Utilization in Chaco Canyon: Basketmaker III through Pueblo III." In *Environment and Subsistence of Chaco Canyon,* edited by Frances Joan Mathien, pp. 305–445. Publications in Archeology 18-E. Chaco Canyon Studies. National Park Service, Washington, D.C.

1986   *A Biocultural Approach to Human Burials from Chaco Canyon, New Mexico.* Reports of the Chaco Center, no. 9. Division of Cultural Research, National Park Service, Santa Fe.

Akins, Nancy J., and John D. Schelberg

1984   "Evidence for Organizational Complexity as Seen from the Mortuary Practices at Chaco Canyon." In *Recent Research on Chaco Prehistory,* edited by W. James Judge and John D. Schelberg, pp. 89–102. Reports of the Chaco Center, no. 8. Division of Cultural Research, National Park Service, Albuquerque.

American Farmland Trust
1997 "Why Save Farmland?" http://www.farmland.org.

Archives of the Chaco Center
1974 Field season reports. Various preparers. On file at the National Park Service Chaco Center, Zimmerman Library, University of New Mexico, Albuquerque.

Arnon, Nancy S., and W. W. Hill
1979 "Santa Clara Pueblo." In *Handbook of North American Indians, vol. 9: Southwest,* edited by Alfonso Ortiz, pp. 296–307. Smithsonian Institution, Washington, D.C.

Bannister, Bryant, William Robinson, and Richard Warren
1970 *Tree-Ring Dates from New Mexico A, G-H, Shiprock-Zuni-Mount Taylor Area.* Laboratory of Tree-Ring Research, University of Arizona, Tucson.

Beck, Warren A.
1962 *New Mexico: A History of Four Centuries.* University of Oklahoma Press, Norman.

Bernardo, Stephanie
1981 *The Ethnic Almanac.* Doubleday, Garden City, New Jersey.

Bice, Richard A., and William M. Sundt
1968 *An Early Basketmaker Campsite: Report on Site AS-1, a Field Project of the Albuquerque Archaeological Society.* Albuquerque Archaeological Society, Albuquerque.

Biella, Jan V., and Richard C. Chapman, editors
1977– *Archeological Investigations in Cochiti Reservoir, New Mexico.* 4 vols. Office of
1979 Contract Archeology, University of New Mexico, Albuquerque.

Blumenschein, Helen
1956 "Excavations in the Taos Area, 1953–1955." *El Palacio* 63: 53–56.

Bodine, John J.
1979 "Taos Pueblo." In *Handbook of North American Indians, vol. 9: Southwest,* edited by Alfonso Ortiz, pp. 255–267. Smithsonian Institution, Washington, D.C.

Bolton, Herbert Eugene
1949 *Coronado: Knight of Pueblos and Plains.* Whittlesey House, New York.

Boroughs, Don. L., Monika Guttman, Maria Mallory, Scott McMurray, and David Fischer
1996 "Winter of Discontent." *U.S. News and World Report,* January 22, 1996, pp. 47–54. From U.S. News Online, http://www.usnews.com.

Brandt, Elizabeth A.
1979 "Sandia Pueblo." In *Handbook of North American Indians, vol. 9: Southwest,* edited by Alfonso Ortiz, pp. 343–350. Smithsonian Institution, Washington, D.C.

Breternitz, Cory D., David E. Doyel, and Michael P. Marshall (editors)
1982 *Bis sa'ni: A Late Bonito Phase Community on Escavada Wash, Northwest New Mexico.* Papers in Anthropology, no. 14. Navajo Nation, Window Rock, Arizona

Brew, John O.
1946 *Archaeology of Alkali Ridge, Southeastern Utah.* Papers of the Peabody Museum

of American Archaeology and Ethnology, no. 21. Harvard University, Cambridge, Mass.

1979 "Hopi Prehistory and History to 1850." In *Handbook of North American Indians, vol. 9: Southwest,* edited by Alfonso Ortiz, pp. 514–532. Smithsonian Institution, Washington, D.C.

Bryan, Kirk, and J. H. Toulouse, Jr.

1943 "The San Jose Non-Ceramic Culture and Its Relation to Puebloan Culture in New Mexico." *American Antiquity* 8: 269–290.

Bunzell, Ruth L.

1938 "The Economic Organization of Primitive Peoples." In *General Anthropology,* edited by Franz Boas, pp. 327–488. D. C. Heath, Boston.

Chalmers, David M.

1965 *Hooded Americanism: The First Century of the Ku Klux Klan, 1865–1965.* Doubleday, Garden City, New Jersey.

Chapman, Richard C., and Jan V. Biella (editors)

1977 *Archeological Investigations in Cochiti Reservoir, New Mexico, vol. 2: Excavations and Analysis, 1975 Season.* Office of Contract Archeology, Department of Anthropology, University of New Mexico, Albuquerque.

Charles A. Schwab and Company, Inc.

1998 "Average Percentage Returned This Century, New York Stock Exchange." December 11, 1998. Research on Request. Schwab Website: http://www.stockup.com.

Cordell, Linda S.

1980 "The Setting." In *Tijeras Canyon: Analyses of the Past,* edited by Linda S. Cordell. Maxwell Museum of Anthropology and University of New Mexico Press, Albuquerque.

1984 *Prehistory of the Southwest.* 1st edition. Academic Press, Orlando, Florida.

1997 *Archaeology of the Southwest.* 2d edition. Academic Press, San Diego.

Cordell, Linda S., and David E. Stuart

1986 "Archaeology and Anthropology." In *From Sundaggers to Space Exploration,* edited by David Shi and Janda Panitz, pp. 65–96. Special issue of *New Mexico Journal of Science* (vol. 26, no. 1). New Mexico Academy of Science, Las Cruces, New Mexico.

Creamer, Winifred

1993 *The Architecture of Arroyo Hondo Pueblo, New Mexico.* With contributions by Catherine M. Cameron and John D. Beal. School of American Research Press, Santa Fe, New Mexico.

Darby, John H.

1995 "Conflict in Northern Ireland: A Background Essay." In *Facets of the Conflict in Northern Ireland,* edited by Seamus Dunn. Macmillan Press Ltd. As found on CAIN Web Service, http://cain.ulst.ac.uk.

Daugherty, William, Barbara Levi, and Frank Von Hippel

1986 "Casualties Due to the Blast, Heat, and Radioactive Fallout from Various Hypothetical Nuclear Attacks on the United States." In *The Medical Implications of Nuclear War,* edited by Fredric Solomon and Robert Q. Marston, pp. 207–337. Institute of Medicine, National Academy of Sciences. National Academy Press, Washington, D.C.

Dick, Herbert W.

1965 *Bat Cave.* School of American Research Monograph 27. University of New Mexico Press, Albuquerque.

1976 *Archeological Excavations in the Llaves Area, Santa Fe National Forest, New Mexico, 1972–1974, part 1: Architecture.* Archaeological Report 13. USDA Forest Service, Southwest Region, Albuquerque.

Dillehay, T. D., G. A. Calderon, G. Politis, and M. C. Peltrao

1992 "Earliest Hunters and Gatherers of South America." *Journal of World Prehistory* 6: 145–204.

Dillon, Sam

1998 "With Brutality and Bribes, Mexican Suspect Thrived." *New York Times,* May 31, 1998. From archives on the *Times*'s Website: http://www.nytimes.com.

Dittert, Alfred E.

1949 "The Prehistoric Population and Architecture of the Cebolleta Mesa Region, Central Western New Mexico." Master's thesis, Department of Anthropology, University of New Mexico, Albuquerque.

1959 "Cultural Change in the Cebolleta Mesa Region, New Mexico." Ph.D. diss., Department of Anthropology, University of Arizona, Tucson.

Dittert, Alfred E., J. J. Hester, and F. W. Eddy

1961 *An Archaeological Survey of the Navajo Reservoir District, Northwestern New Mexico.* Monographs of the School of American Research and the Museum of New Mexico, no. 23. Santa Fe.

Donoho, Kathy

n.d. "Navajo Origins: Archaeological Indicators of the Diné." Senior thesis, Department of Anthropology, University of New Mexico, Albuquerque. Manuscript in the possession of David Stuart.

Dozier, Edward P.

1966 "Factionalism at Santa Clara Pueblo." *Ethnology* 5 (2): 172–185.

1970 *The Pueblo Indians of North America.* Waveland Press, Prospect Heights, Illinois.

Duke, P. G.

1985 *Fort Lewis College Archaeological Investigations in Ridges Basin, Southwestern Colorado, 1965–1982.* Center of Southwest Studies, Fort Lewis College, Durango, Colorado.

Eddy, Frank W.

1961 *Excavations at Los Pinos Phase Sites in the Navajo Reservoir District.* Papers in Anthropology, no. 4. Museum of New Mexico, Santa Fe.

1966 *Prehistory in the Navajo Reservoir District, Northwestern New Mexico.* Papers in Anthropology, no. 15, part 2. Museum of New Mexico Press, Santa Fe.

1977 *Archaeological Investigations at Chimney Rock Mesa, 1970–72.* Memoirs of the Colorado Archaeological Society, no. 1. Denver.

Eggan, Fred

1970   "Forward." In *The Pueblo Indians of North America,* by Edward P. Dozier. Waveland Press, Prospect Heights, Illinois.

1979   "Pueblos: An Introduction." In *Handbook of North American Indians, vol. 9: Southwest,* edited by Alfonso Ortiz, pp. 224–235. Smithsonian Institution, Washington, D.C.

Ehrlich, Paul R.

1968   *The Population Bomb.* Ballantine Books, New York.

Eidenbach, Peter L. (editor)

1982   *Inventory Survey of the Lower Hidden Mountain Flood Pool, Lower Rio Puerco Drainage, Central New Mexico.* Submitted by Human Systems Research, Inc., to the U.S. Army Corps of Engineers, Albuquerque.

Eighmy, Jeffrey L.

1981   "The Archaeological Significance of Counting Houses: Ethnoarchaeological Evidence." In *Modern Material Culture: The Archaeology of Us,* edited by Richard A. Gould and Michael B. Schiffer. Academy Press, New York.

Eldredge, N., and S. J. Gould

1972   "Punctuated Equilibria: An Alternative to Phyletic Gradualism." In *Models in Paleobiology,* edited by T. J. M. Schopf, pp. 82–115. Freeman, Cooper and Co., San Francisco.

Ellis, Florence Hawley

1979   "Laguna Pueblo." In *Handbook of North American Indians, vol. 9: Southwest,* edited by Alfonso Ortiz, pp. 438–449. Smithsonian Institution, Washington, D.C.

1988   *From Drought to Drought: An Archeological Record of Life Patterns as Developed by the Gallina Indians of North Central New Mexico (A.D. 1050–1300).* Volume 1: *Canjilon Mountain Hunting and Gathering Sites.* Sunstone Press, Santa Fe.

El Najjar, M. Y., Dennis J. Ryan, Christy G. Turner II, and Betsy Lozoff

1976   "The Etiology of Porotic Hypertosis among the Prehistoric and Historic Anasazi Indians of the Southwestern United States." *American Journal of Physical Anthropology* 44: 477–488.

Encyclopaedia Britannica

1977   Volumes 7 and 18. Encyclopaedia Britannica, Inc., London.

Farwell, Robin E.

1981   "Pithouses: Prehistoric Energy Conservation." *El Palacio* 87 (3): 43–47.

Farwell, Robin E., and Yvonne Oakes

n.d.   "Pueblo III Occupations in the Sacramento Mountains of New Mexico." *Laboratory of Anthropology Note.* Museum of New Mexico, Santa Fe.

Feldman, David Lewis

1996   *The Energy Crisis: Unresolved Issues and Enduring Legacies.* Johns Hopkins University Press, Baltimore.

Ferguson, Cheryl

1980   "Analysis of Skeletal Remains." In *Tijeras Canyon: Analyses of the Past,* edited by Linda S. Cordell, pp. 123–140. Maxwell Museum of Anthropology and University of New Mexico Press, Albuquerque.

Ford, Richard I.
1981   "Gardening and Farming before A.D. 1000: Patterns of Prehistoric Cultivation North of Mexico." *Journal of Ethnology* 1 (1): 6–27.

Fransted, Dennis
1979   "An Introduction to the Navajo and History of Anasazi Sites in the San Juan Basin Area." Unpublished manuscript on file at the Chaco Center, National Park Service and University of New Mexico, Albuquerque.

Frazier, Kendrick
1986   *People of Chaco: A Canyon and Its Culture.* W. W. Norton, New York.

Friedberg, Lionel, Richard Wells, and Thomas Fuchs (producers)
1997   "The Pueblo Cliff Dwellers." Film in *The Secrets of the Pueblo* series. FilmRoos, Inc., New York City.

Frison, George
1993   "North American High Plains Paleo-Indian Hunting Strategies and Weaponry Assemblages." In *Kostenki to Clovis: Upper Paleolithic-Paleo-Indian Adaptations,* edited by Olga Soffer and N. D. Praslov, pp. 237–249. Plenum Press, New York.

Garcia-Mason, Velma
1979   "Acoma Pueblo." In *Handbook of North American Indians, vol. 9: Southwest,* edited by Alfonso Ortiz, pp. 450–466. Smithsonian Institution, Washington, D.C.

Garrett, Wilbur E. (editor)
1988   *Historical Atlas of the United States.* Centennial edition. National Geographic Society, Washington, D.C.

Glassman, James K.
1997   "The Rich Really Aren't Different." *U.S. News and World Report,* April 14, 1997. From U.S. News Online, http://www.usnews.com.

Gore, Rick
1997   "The Most Ancient Americans." *National Geographic,* October 1997, pp. 92–99. National Geographic Society, Washington, D.C.

Green, R. C.
1956   "A Pithouse of the Gallina Phase." *American Antiquity* 22: 188–193.

Gumerman, George J. (editor)
1988   *The Anasazi in a Changing Environment.* Cambridge University Press, Cambridge, U.K.

Gumerman, George J., and Jeffrey S. Dean
1989   "Prehistoric Cooperation and Competition in the Western Anasazi Area." In *Dynamics of Southwest Prehistory,* edited by Linda Cordell and G. J. Gumerman, pp. 99–148. Smithsonian Institution Press, Washington, D.C.

Hallasi, Judith A.
1979   "Archeological Excavation at the Escalante Site, Dolores, Colorado, 1975 and 1976." In *The Archeological Stabilization of the Dominguez and Escalante Ruins,* pp. 197–404. Cultural Resources Series, Colorado State Office, Bureau of Land Management, Denver.

Hammond, George P., and Agapito Rey (editors)
1929   *Expedition into New Mexico made by Antonio de Espejo, 1582–1583, as Revealed*

in the Journal of Diego Pérez de Luxán, a Member of the Party. Quivira Society, Los Angeles.

1940   *Narratives of the Coronado Expedition, 1540–1542.* University of New Mexico Press, Albuquerque.

Haury, Emil W.

1962   "The Greater American Southwest." In *Courses toward Urban Life: Some Archaeological Considerations of Cultural Alternates,* edited by Robert J. Braidwood and Gordon R. Willey, pp. 106–131. Viking Fund Publications in Anthropology, New York.

Hayes, Alden C.

1964   *The Archaeological Survey of Wetherill Mesa.* Archaeological Research Series 7-A. National Park Service, Washington, D.C.

Haynes, C. Vance

1993   "Clovis-Folsom Geochronology and Climatic Change." In *Kostenki to Clovis: Upper Paleolithic-Paleo-Indian Adaptations,* edited by Olga Soffer and N. D. Praslov, pp. 219–236. Plenum Press, New York.

Hevly, Richard H.

1964   "Pollen Analysis of Quarternary Archaeological and Lacustrine Sediments from the Colorado Plateau." Ph.D diss., University of Arizona, Tucson.

Hewitt, Edgar L.

1938   "Frescoes of Kuaua." *El Palacio* 45: 21–28.

1953   *Pajarito Plateau and Its Ancient People.* 2d edition., revised. University of New Mexico Press, Albuquerque, and School of American Research, Santa Fe.

Holstein, William J.

1997   "The New Economy." In "As High Tech Firms Boom, Old Theories Totter." *U.S. News and World Report,* May 27, 1997. From U.S. News Online: http://www.usnews.com.

Houghton, Frank E.

1959   "Climate of New Mexico." U.S. Department of Commerce, National Oceanic and Atmospheric Administration, Environmental Data Service, Silver Spring, Maryland.

Hunter-Anderson, R. L.

1979   "LA 13326, LA 13329, LA13331, LA13332, and LA 13333." In *Archeological Investigations in Cochiti Reservoir, New Mexico, vol. 3: 1976–1977 Field Seasons,* edited by J. V. Biella, pp. 208–216. Office of Contract Archeology, University of New Mexico, Albuquerque.

Information Please Almanac: Atlas and Yearbook

1993   44th edition. Houghton Mifflin, Boston.

Intel Corporation

1998   "Intel 1997 Annual Report: Financial Summary." Intel Corporation Website, http://www.intel.com.

Irwin-Williams, Cynthia

1968   "Archaic Culture History in the Southwestern United States." *Contributions in Anthropology* 1 (4): 48–54. Eastern New Mexico University, Portales, New Mexico.

1973   *The Oshara Tradition: Origins of Anasazi Culture.* Contributions in Anthropology 5 (1). Eastern New Mexico University, Portales, New Mexico.

1979   "Post-Pleistocene Archaeology, 7000–2000 B.C." In *Handbook of North American Indians, vol. 9: Southwest,* edited by Alfonso Ortiz, pp. 31–42. Smithsonian Institution, Washington, D.C.

1980   "Investigations at Salmon Ruin: Methodology and Overview." In *Investigations at the Salmon Site: The Structure of Chacoan Society in the Northern Southwest,* edited by Cynthia Irwin-Williams and Phillip H. Shelley, pp. 135–211. Eastern New Mexico University, Portales, New Mexico.

Irwin-Williams, Cynthia, and L. C. Pippen

1969   *Excavations at the Armijo Shelter.* Contributions in Anthropology 1 (5). Eastern New Mexico University, Portales, New Mexico.

Jelinek, Arthur J.

1967   *A Prehistoric Sequence in the Middle Pecos Valley, New Mexico.* Anthropological Papers, no. 31. Museum of Anthropology, University of Michigan, Ann Arbor.

Judd, Neil M.

1954   *The Material Culture of Pueblo Bonito.* Smithsonian Miscellaneous Collections 124. Washington, D.C.

Judge, W. James

1989   "Chaco Canyon-San Juan Basin." In *Dynamics of Southwest Prehistory,* edited by Linda S. Cordell and George J. Gumerman, pp. 209–262. Smithsonian Institution Press, Washington, D.C.

Kaplan, Lawrence

1965   "Beans of the Wetherill Mesa." In *Contributions of the Wetherill Mesa Archaeological Project,* edited by D. Osborne, pp. 153–155. Society of American Archaeology Memoirs, no. 19. Salt Lake City, Utah.

Kelley, Klara, and Harris Frances

1995   "The Turquoise Trail." Paper prepared for the Durango Conference in Southwest Archaeology. Fort Lewis College, Durango, Colorado.

Kennard, Edward A.

1979   "Hopi Economy and Subsistence." In *Handbook of North American Indians, vol. 9: Southwest,* edited by Alfonso Ortiz, pp. 554–563. Smithsonian Institution, Washington, D.C.

Keynes, John Maynard

1965   *The General Theory of Employment, Interest, and Money.* Harcourt, Brace and World, New York.

Kidder, Alfred V.

1932   *The Artifacts of Pecos.* Yale University Press, New Haven, Connecticut.

1958   *Pecos, New Mexico: Archaeological Notes.* Papers of the Robert S. Peabody Foundation for Archaeology, vol. 5. Phillips Academy, Andover, Massachusetts.

Klodt, Gerald G.

1985   *Earth Sheltered Housing.* Restin Publishing Co., Restin, Virginia.

Kluckhohn, Clyde

1967   *Navajo Witchcraft.* Beacon Press, Boston.

Ladd, Edmund J.
1979 "Zuni Economy." In *Handbook of North American Indians, vol. 9: Southwest*, edited by Alfonso Ortiz, pp. 492–498. Smithsonian Institution, Washington, D.C.

Lambert, Marjorie
1954 *Paa-Ko: Archaeological Chronicle of an Indian Village in North Central New Mexico, Parts I-V.* School of American Research Monograph 19. Santa Fe.

Lang, Richard W.
1977 *Archaeological Survey of the Upper San Cristobal Arroyo Drainage, Galisteo Basin, Santa Fe County, New Mexico.* School of American Research Contract Archaeology Program, Santa Fe.

Lange, Charles H.
1968a *The Cochiti Dam Archaeological Salvage Project, Part 1.* Museum of New Mexico Research Records, no. 6. Museum of New Mexico Press, Santa Fe.
1968b *Cochiti.* Southern Illinois University Press, Carbondale.

Lange, Charles H., and C. L. Riley (editors)
1970 *The Southwestern Journals of Adolf E. Bandelier, 1883–1884.* University of New Mexico Press, Albuquerque.

Larson, Clark Spencer
1995 "Biological Changes in the Human Populations with Agriculture." *Annual Review of Anthropology* 24: 185–213.

Lee, Richard B.
1968 "What Hunters Do for a Living." In *Man the Hunter*, edited by Richard B. Lee and I. DeVore, pp. 30–48. Aldine, Chicago.

Lekson, Stephen H.
1986 *Great Pueblo Architecture of Chaco Canyon, New Mexico.* University of New Mexico Press, Albuquerque.
1997 "Rewriting Southwestern Prehistory." *Archaeology* 50 (1): 52–55.

Lightfoot, Dale R.
1990 "The Prehistoric Pebble-Mulched Fields of the Galisteo Anasazi: Agricultural Innovation and Adaptations to Environment." University of Michigan Dissertation Services, Ann Arbor.

Lightfoot, Ricky R.
1992 *Architecture and Tree-Ring Dating at the Duckfoot Site in Southwestern Colorado. The Kiva* 57: 213–236.

Lister, Florence C., and Robert H. Lister
1968 *Earl Morris and Southwestern Archaeology.* University of New Mexico Press, Albuquerque.
1981 *Chaco Canyon: Archaeology and Archaeologists.* University of New Mexico Press, Albuquerque.

Lynch, David J.
1996 "Rich, Poor World: Widening Income Gap Divides America ... Dying Dreams, Dead-End Streets." *USA Today,* September 20, 1996. Final edition. From USA Today Premium Archives, http://www.usatoday.com.

Marshall, Michael P.

1997 "The Chacoan Roads: A Cosmological Interpretation." In *Anazasi Architecture and American Design,* edited by Baker H. Morrow and V. B. Price, pp. 62–74. University of New Mexico Press, Albuquerque.

Marshall, Michael P., and Patrick Hogan

1991 *Rethinking Navajo Pueblitos.* Cultural Resources Series no. 8. Bureau of Land Management, Albuquerque and Farmington, New Mexico.

Marshall, Michael P., John R. Stein, Richard W. Loose, and

Judith E. Novotny (editors)

1979 *Anasazi Communities of the San Juan Basin.* Public Service Company of New Mexico, Albuquerque, and New Mexico Historic Preservation Bureau, Santa Fe.

Marshall, Michael P., Bill Kight, Charlotte Ann Hollis, John Stein,

and Carol Cooperrider.

1981 "Fortified Pueblo Architecture in the Rio Abajo District in New Mexico." *The Artifact* 19 (3–4): 101–132. El Paso Archaeological Society, El Paso, Texas.

Marshall, Michael P., and Henry J. Walt

1984 *Rio Abajo: Prehistory and History of a Rio Grande Province.* New Mexico Historic Preservation Program, Santa Fe.

Martin, Paul S., and Richard G. Klein (eds.)

1984 *Quarternary Extinctions: A Prehistoric Revolution.* University of Arizona Press, Tucson.

Mathien, Frances Joan (editor)

1997 *Ceramics, Lithics, and Ornaments of Chaco Canyon, vol. 1: Ceramics.* Publications in Archeology 18-G, Chaco Canyon Studies. National Park Service, Santa Fe.

McGimsey, Charles R. III

1980 *Mariana Mesa: Seven Prehistoric Settlements in West-Central New Mexico.* Papers of the Peabody Museum of Archaeology and Ethnology, no. 72. Harvard University, Cambridge, Massachusetts.

McKenna, Peter J.

1984 *The Architecture and Material Culture of 29SJ1360.* Reports of the Chaco Center, no. 7. Division of Cultural Research, National Park Service, Albuquerque.

McKenna, Peter J., and Marcia L. Truell (editors)

1986 *Small Site Architecture of Chaco Canyon, New Mexico.* Publications in Archeology 18-D, Chaco Canyon Studies. National Park Service, Santa Fe.

McNitt, Frank

1957 *Richard Wetherill: Anasazi.* University of New Mexico Press, Albuquerque.

Meltzer, David J.

1995 "Clocking the First Americans." *Annual Review of Anthropology* 24: 21–45.

Microsoft Corporation

1998 "Microsoft Fast Facts." Website http://microsoft.com.

Mitchell, Margaret

1936 *Gone with the Wind.* Macmillan, New York.

Morgan, William N.

1994 *Ancient Architecture of the Southwest.* University of Texas Press, Austin.

Mortenson, Thomas G.
1998   "Growing Income, Inequality, Public Selfishness, and Consequences for America's Children (and our Future)." *Postsecondary Education Opportunity,* August 1998, pp. 11–16, Thomas G. Mortenson, Oskaloosa, Iowa.

Newman, Katherine S.
1988   *Falling from Grace: The Experience of Downward Mobility in the American Middle Class.* Free Press, New York.

Nials, Fred L.
1983   "Physical Characteristics of Chacoan Roads." In *Chaco Roads Projects, Phase 1: A Reappraisal of Prehistoric Roads in the San Juan Basin,* edited by Chris Kincaid, pp. 6.1–6.51. Bureau of Land Management, Albuquerque.

Odum, Eugene P.
1955   *Fundamentals of Ecology.* W. B. Saunders and Company, Philadelphia.

Organization for Economic Cooperation and Development
1994   "International Adult Literacy Survey." Unpublished tabulations. Website http://nces.ed.gov.
1996   "International Adult Literacy Survey." Unpublished tabulations. Website http://nces.ed.gov.

Ortiz, Alfonso
1969   *The Tewa World: Space, Time, Being, and Becoming in a Pueblo Society.* University of Chicago Press, Chicago.
1979   "San Juan Pueblo." In *Handbook of North American Indians, vol. 9: Southwest,* edited by Alfonso Ortiz, pp. 278–295. Smithsonian Institution, Washington, D.C.
1994   *The Pueblo.* Chelsea House, New York.

Palkovich, Ann M.
1980   *The Arroyo Hondo Skeletal and Mortuary Remains.* School of American Research Press, Santa Fe.
1984   "Disease and Mortality Patterns in the Burial Rooms of Pueblo Bonito: Preliminary Considerations." In *Recent Research on Chaco Prehistory,* edited by W. James Judge and John D. Schelberg, pp. 103–113. Reports of the Chaco Center, no. 8. Division of Cultural Research, National Park Service, Albuquerque.

Paskind, Martin
1998   "Sandia Pueblo and the Sandia Mountains." *Albuquerque Journal,* September 21, 1998.

Pearce, T. M. (editor)
1965   *New Mexico Place Names: A Geographical Dictionary.* University of New Mexico Press, Albuquerque.

Peckham, Stuart L.
1958   Salvage Archaeology in New Mexico, 1957–1958: A Partial Report. *El Palacio* 65 (5): 161–163.

Pepper, George H.
1920   *Pueblo Bonito.* Anthropological Papers of the American Museum of Natural History, no. 27. New York. Reprint 1996, University of New Mexico Press, Albuquerque.

Plog, Fred
1979 "Prehistory: Western Anasazi." In *Handbook of North American Indians, vol. 9: Southwest,* edited by Alfonso Ortiz, pp. 108–130. Smithsonian Institution, Washington, D.C.

Plog, Stephen
1997 *Ancient Peoples of the American Southwest.* Thames and Hudson, London.

Powers, Robert P., William G. Gillespie, and Stephen H. Lekson
1983 *The Outlier Survey: A Regional View of Settlement in the San Juan Basin.* Reports of the Chaco Center, no. 3. Division of Cultural Research, National Park Service, Albuquerque.

Powledge, Tabitha M., and Mark Rose
1996 "The Great DNA Hunt, Part 2: Colonizing the Americas." *Archaeology,* Nov.-Dec. 1996, pp. 58–68.

Preucel, Robert W., Jr.
1990 *Seasonal Circulation and Dual Residence in the Pueblo Southwest: A Prehistoric Example from the Pajarito Plateau, New Mexico.* Garland Publishing, New York.

Previté-Orton, C. W.
1966 *The Shorter Cambridge Medieval History, vol. 1: The Late Roman Empire to the Twelfth Century.* Cambridge University Press, Cambridge, U.K.

Ramenofsky, Ann F.
1987 *Vectors of Death: The Archaeology of European Contact.* University of New Mexico Press, Albuquerque.

Randall-Cutler, Roger, and Lynda Myles, producers
1992 *The Commitments.* Film. Twentieth Century Fox (Fox Video), Hollywood, California.

Reed, Alan S., Judith Ann Hallasi, Adrian S. White, and David A. Breternitz
1979 The Archaeology and Stabilization of the Dominguez and Escalante Ruins. Bureau of Land Management, Colorado State Office, Denver.

Reher, Charles A. (editor)
1977 *Settlement and Subsistence along the Lower Chaco River: The CGP Survey.* University of New Mexico Press, Albuquerque.

Reichard, Gladys A.
1944 *The Story of the Navajo Hail Chant.* Columbia University Press, New York.

Reinhart, Theodore R.
1967 "The Rio Rancho Phase: A Preliminary Report on Early Basketmaker Culture in the Rio Grande Valley, New Mexico." *American Antiquity* 32 (4): 458–470.

Roberts, Frank H. H., Jr.
1929 *Shabik'eschee Village: A Late Basketmaker Site in the Chaco Canyon, New Mexico.* Bureau of American Ethnology Bulletin 92. Smithsonian Institution, Washington, D.C.

Robinson, Linda
1996 "Rebellion, Mexican Style." *U.S. News and World Report,* September 23, 1996. From U.S. News Online, http://www.usnews.com.

Robinson, William J.

1974 *Tree-Ring Dates from New Mexico B: Chaco-Gobernador Area.* Laboratory of Tree-Ring Research, University of Arizona, Tucson.

Rohde, David

1995 "Bosnian Muslims Were Killed by the Truckload." *Christian Science Monitor,* October 2, 1995. From the Pulitzer Prize Board Website, http://www.pulitzer.org.

Ruppe, R. J.

1953 "The Acoma Culture Province: An Archaeological Concept." Ph.D. diss., Department of Anthropology, Harvard University, Cambridge, Massachusetts.

Sando, Joe S.

1979 "The Pueblo Revolt in the Southwest." In *Handbook of North American Indians, vol. 9: Southwest,* edited by Alfonso Ortiz, pp. 194–197. Smithsonian Institution, Washington, D.C.

1992 *Pueblo Nations: Eight Centuries of Pueblo Indian History.* Clear Light Publishers, Santa Fe.

Sayles, Stephen, and Jerry L. Williams

1986 "Land Grants." In *New Mexico in Maps,* 2d edition, edited by Jerry L. Williams, pp. 105–107. University of New Mexico Press, Albuquerque.

Schreiber, Stephen D.

1997 "Engineering Feats of the Anasazi: Buildings, Roads, and Dams." In *Anasazi Architecture and American Design,* edited by Baker H. Morrow and V. B. Price, pp. 77–87. University of New Mexico Press, Albuquerque.

Schroeder, Albert H.

1979 "Pueblos Abandoned in Historic Times." In *Handbook of North American Indians, vol. 9: Southwest,* edited by Alfonso Ortiz, pp. 236–254. Smithsonian Institution, Washington, D.C.

Schroeder, Albert H., and Fred Wendorf

1954 "Excavations near Aragon, New Mexico." *Highway Salvage Archaeology* 1: 53–105. New Mexico State Highway Department and Museum of New Mexico, Santa Fe.

Schwartz, Douglas W.

1980 "Foreword: The Arroyo Hondo Project." In *The Arroyo Hondo Skeletal and Mortuary Remains,* by Ann M. Palkovich, pp. ix-xix. School of American Research Press, Santa Fe.

Seaman, Timothy J.

1976 *Archaeological Investigations on the San Juan-to-Ojo 345x Transmission Line for the Public Service Company of New Mexico: Excavation of LA 11843, an Early Stockaded Settlement of the Gallina Phase.* Laboratory of Anthropology Notes, no. 111g. Museum of New Mexico, Santa Fe.

Sebastian, Lynne

1992 *The Chaco Anasazi: Sociopolitical Evolution in the Prehistoric Southwest.* Cambridge University Press, Cambridge, U.K.

Shepard, Anna O.

1965 *Ceramics for the Archaeologist.* Carnegie Institute of Washington Publication 609. Washington, D.C.

Silverberg, Robert
1970   *The Pueblo Revolt.* Weybright and Talley, New York.

Simmons, Marc
1979   "History of Pueblo-Spanish Relations to 1821." In *Handbook of North American Indians, vol. 9: Southwest,* edited by Alfonso Ortiz, pp. 178–193. Smithsonian Institution, Washington, D.C.

Skinner, S. Alan, Chester Shaw, Carol Carter, Maynard Cliff, and Carol Heathington
1980   *Archaeological Investigations at Nambé Falls.* Archaeological Research Program, Research Report 121. Department of Anthropology, Southern Methodist University, Dallas.

Sofaer, Anna
1997   "The Primary Architecture of the Chacoan Culture: A Cosmological Expression." In *Anasazi Architecture and American Design,* edited by Baker H. Morrow and V. B. Price, pp. 88–132, University of New Mexico Press, Albuquerque.

Stein, John R., Judith E. Suiter, and Dabney Ford
1997   "High Noon in Old Bonito: Sun, Shadow, and the Geometry of the Chaco Complex." In *Anasazi Architecture and American Design,* edited by Baker H. Morrow and V. B. Price, pp. 133–148. University of New Mexico Press, Albuquerque.

Steinbeck, John
1939   *The Grapes of Wrath.* Viking Press, New York.

Stevenson, Mathilda Coxe
1884   *The Sia.* Eleventh Annual Report of the Bureau of American Ethnology. Smithsonian Institution, Washington, D.C.

Steward, Julian H.
1938   *Basin Plateau Socio-Political Groups.* Bureau of American Ethnology, Bulletin 20. Washington, D.C.

Strong, Pauline Turner
1979   "Santa Ana Pueblo." In *Handbook of North American Indians, vol. 9: Southwest,* edited by Alfonso Ortiz, pp. 398–406. Smithsonian Institution, Washington, D.C.

Stuart, David E.
1980   "Kinship and Social Organization in Tierra del Fuego: Evolutionary Consequences." In *The Versatility of Kinship,* edited by Linda S. Cordell and S. J. Beckerman, pp. 269–284. Academic Press, New York.

1985   *Glimpses of the Ancient Southwest.* Ancient City Press, Santa Fe.

1986a "The Rise of Agriculture: An Essay on Science, the Rule of Unintended Consequences, and Hunter-Gatherer Behavior." In *Award-Winning Essays,* pp. 11–16. New Mexico Humanities Council, Third Annual Humanities Award Program. Albuquerque.

1986b "Prehistory: The Upland Period." In *New Mexico in Maps,* 2d edition, edited by Jerry L. Williams, pp. 86–88. University of New Mexico Press, Albuquerque.

1989   *The Magic of Bandelier.* Ancient City Press, Santa Fe.

1996   "Preface." In *Pueblo Bonito,* by George H. Pepper, pp. v–ix. Reissued by University of New Mexico Press, Albuquerque.

1997 "Power and Efficiency in Eastern Anasazi Architecture: A Case of Multiple Evolutionary Trajectories." In *Anasazi Architecture and American Design,* edited by Baker H. Morrow and V. B. Price, pp. 36–52. University of New Mexico Press, Albuquerque.

Stuart, David E., and Robin E. Farwell

1983 "Out of Phase: Late Pithouse Occupations in the Highlands of New Mexico." In *High-Altitude Adaptations in the Southwest,* edited by Joseph C. Winter, pp. 115–158. USDA Forest Service, Southwest Region, Albuquerque.

Stuart, David E., and Rory P. Gauthier

1981 *Prehistoric New Mexico: Background for Survey.* New Mexico Historic Preservation Bureau, Santa Fe. Reprint 1988, University of New Mexico Press, Albuquerque.

1986 "The Riverine Period." In *New Mexico in Maps,* 2d edition, edited by Jerry L. Williams, pp. 89–91. University of New Mexico Press, Albuquerque.

Stubbs, Stanley A., and W. S. Stallings, Jr.

1953 *The Excavation of Pindi Pueblo.* Monographs of the Laboratory of Anthropology and School of American Research, no. 18. Santa Fe.

Tainter, Joseph A., and D. A. Gillio

1980 *Cultural Resources Overview: Mount Taylor Area, New Mexico.* USDA Forest Service and Bureau of Land Management, Albuquerque. U.S. Superintendent of Documents, Washington, D.C.

Towner, Ronald H., editor

1996 *The Archaeology of Navajo Origins.* University of Utah Press.

U.S. Bureau of the Census

1995 "Top 25 American Indian Tribes for the United States, 1990 and 1980." Racial Statistics Branch, Population Division, 1990, CP-3–7. As found on Website http://www.census.gov/population/socdemo/race/Indian.

1996 "USA Counties." Website http://www.census.gov.

U.S. Department of Agriculture

1998 *A Time to Act.* National Commission on Small Farms, Miscellaneous Publication 1545 (MP-1545). Washington, D.C.

U.S. Department of Commerce

1997 *Statistical Abstracts of the United States,* 117th edition. Economics and Statistics Administration, Bureau of the Census, Washington, D.C.

U.S. Department of Justice

1997 *Crime Victimization in the United States, 1994.* A National Crime Victimization Survey Report, May 1997, NCJ-1622126. Washington, D.C. As found on Website http://www.usdoj.gov.

U.S. Department of Labor and Council of Economic Advisors

1995 "Educating America: An Investment for Our Future." White paper, Washington, D.C. As found on Website http://www.whitehouse.gov.

U.S. Department of State

1998 "Mexico Advisory (April 29, 1998), Washington." As found on U.S. News Online, http://www.usnews.com.

Vivian, R. Gwinn
1990   *The Chacoan Prehistory of the San Juan Basin.* Academic Press, San Diego.

Watkins, T. H.
1993   *The Great Depression: America in the 1930s.* Little, Brown, Boston.

Weigand, Phil C., Garman Harbottle, and Edward V. Sayre
1977   "Turquoise Sources and Source Analysis: Mesoamerica and the Southwestern USA." In *Exchange Systems in Prehistory,* pp. 15–34. Academic Press, New York.

Wendorf, Fred, and Eric K. Reed
1955   "An Alternative Reconstruction of Northern Rio Grande Prehistory." *El Palacio* 62 (5–6): 141–142.

White, Leslie A.
1960   "The World of the Keresan Pueblo Indians." In *Culture in History: Essays in Honor of Paul Radin,* edited by Stanley Diamond, pp. 55–64. Columbia University Press, New York.

Whiteley, Peter Michael
1982   "Third Mesa Hopi Social-Structural Dynamics and Sociocultural Change: The View from Bacavi." Ph.D. diss., Department of Anthropology, University of New Mexico, Albuquerque.

Williams, Jerry L.
1986   "Mining and Stagecoaching, 1846–1912." In *New Mexico in Maps,* 2d edition, edited by Jerry L. Williams, pp. 117–119. University of New Mexico Press, Albuquerque.

Wills, Wirt H.
1988   *Early Prehistoric Agriculture in the American Southwest.* School of American Research Press, Santa Fe.

Wills, Wirt H., and Thomas C. Windes
1989   "Evidence for Population Aggregation and Dispersal during the Basketmaker III Period in Chaco Canyon, New Mexico." *American Antiquity* 54: 347–369.

Wilshusen, R. H., and E. Blinman
1992   "Pueblo I Village Formation: A Reevaluation of Sites Recorded by Earl Morris on the Ute Mountain Tribal Lands." *The Kiva* 57: 251–269.

Wimberly, Mark, and Peter Eidenbach
1980   *Reconnaissance Study of the Archaeological and Related Resources of the Lower Puerco and Salado Drainages, Central New Mexico.* Human Systems Research, Inc., Tularosa, New Mexico.

Windes, Thomas C.
1984   "Pueblo Alto." In *Great Pueblo Architecture of Chaco Canyon, New Mexico,* by Stephen H. Lekson, pp. 192–209. Publications in Archaeology 18-B, Chaco Canyon Studies. National Park Service, Washington, D.C.

Wiseman, Regge N.
1979   *The Naschitti-North Project: The Excavation of Two Small Pueblo II Sites near Sheep Springs, San Juan County, New Mexico.* Laboratory of Anthropology, Museum of New Mexico, Santa Fe.

1980   *The Carnue Project: Excavation of a Late Coalition Period Pueblo in Tijeras Canyon, New Mexico.* Laboratory of Anthropology Notes, no. 166. Museum of New Mexico, Santa Fe.

Woodbury, Richard B.

1979   "Zuni Prehistory and History to 1850." In *Handbook of North American Indians, vol. 9: Southwest,* edited by Alfonso Ortiz, pp. 467–473. Smithsonian Institution, Washington, D.C.

1993   *Sixty Years of Southwestern Archaeology.* University of New Mexico Press, Albuquerque.

Worman, F. C. V.

1967   *Archaeological Salvage Excavations on the Mesita del Buey, Los Alamos County, New Mexico.* Los Alamos National Laboratories.

Wright, John W. (editor)

1996   *The Universal Almanac.* Andrews and McMeel, Kansas City.

Young, Gwen

1980   "Analysis of Faunal Remains." In *Tijeras Canyon: Analyses of the Past,* edited by Linda S. Cordell. Maxwell Museum of Anthropology and University of New Mexico Press, Albuquerque.

Young, Robert W., and William Morgan, Sr.

1987   *The Navajo Language: A Grammar and Colloquial Dictionary.* Revised edition. University of New Mexico Press, Albuquerque.

Index

Photographs are indicated by ph; graphs by gr; diagrams by diag; lithographs by litho.

Acoma Pueblo: dancers at, 174(ph); drummer at, 175(ph); plaza area at, 175(ph)
acorns, 21
agriculture, 35–50; expansion of, 58, 62–63; experimentation in, 57; and foraging, 46; increasing importance of, 41; and multicrop strategies, 155; reasons for adopting, 38; rise of complex practices of, in 1300s and 1400s, 164; rise of small settlements due to, 40; riskiness of experimentation in, 51; small-scale, 38–39; and status, 39; techniques of, 37, 154; transition from hunting and gathering to planting and harvesting, 35–39. See also farming
Albino village, 40
Alkali Ridge, 52
Altithermal, 16; camp sizes during, 19; population increase during, 20
Alto great house, controlling walls built at, 142
Anasazi: and Four Corners, 9; unknown date of ancestral arrival in Four Corners, 13

ancient ones, 9
anemia, 113, 114, 115, 158
Angostura, 165
Archaic people, Paleo-Indians more efficient than, 22
Archaic tool kit, 17
arrowheads, 40
Arroyo del Pueblo, 161
Arroyo Hondo, 155–58; burials at, 156; causes of demise of, 157–58; diet at, 156
arthritis, 113, 114
asphyxiation deaths, 112
atlatl, 14, 19; bow and arrow replaces, 42
axes, 45, 167
Aztec great house, 104(ph), 120, 135

bancos, 59
Bandelier National Monument, 131
basalt, 151
basins, 133–37; brief period of Anasazi reuse of, 136
Basketmakers, 25, 39–48; and cultural developments, 47; diet of, 42; geographical and ecological setting of, 56; growth of settlements of, 46–47; importance of time to, 48; and osteoporosis, 44; and overwork, 46
Bat Cave, 35
Bayo Canyon Ruin, 136
beads, turquoise, 115

beans, 37–38, 40, 41, 42, 57, 84, 86
Benavides, Alonso de, 181
Beringia, 13
Biscuit A pottery, 148
Biscuit B pottery, 152
Bis sa'ani, 85, 101(ph): citadel at, 121;
    South House at, 101(ph)
blankets, thermal, 43
bow and arrow, 42
bowls, decorated pottery, 54
brokerage role (of Chaco Canyon), 58
burials, 41, 45, 47, 110, 113, 157; at great
    houses compared to farmsteads, 115;
    and proximity to habitations, 44
business cycles, 87
business failures, 48

cairn fields, 141
"California" model of economic
    development, 48–49, 191
Canyon del Muerto, 25(ph)
carbon-based paint, 130–31
Casa de los Vientos, 149
Casamero Draw, 70, 72
Casamero great house, 70, 120; dating of,
    72; pottery found at, 72
Casa Rinconada, 29(ph)
Catholicism, conversions to, 180
center places, 168
Chacoan society: area dominated by, 7;
    Cliff palace sites, 131–132; and effi-
    ciency, 132; compared to contempora-
    neous Europe, 66; compared to United
    States, 122; dispersal of, 127; downfall
    of, 121–24; fracturing of, 142; and
    growth in stages, 75; and number of
    sites in San Juan basin, 153; pinnacle
    of, 67; ritual and religion as organizing
    principle in, 119; socioeconomic hier-
    archy of, 108; tradition of land owner-
    ship missing from, 67; transformation
    of, 8; varied fates of families in, 8
Chaco Canyon, 7, 27, 28(ph), 29(ph), 58,
    66, 75–79, 76(map): construction in,
    84; expansion projects at great houses
    in, 107, 119; and lack of large religious
    gatherings, 143; mortality at, 113; as
    nerve center of Anasazi culture, 108;
    ten great houses on floor of, 78

Chaco Canyon National Historic Park, 59
Chaco country, 71(map)
Chaco emigrants, 127
Chaco phenomenon, 65–106
Chaco River, 26(ph), 27(ph), 28(ph): as
    seasonal wash, 77
Chacra Mesa, 77
chapalote, 35, 36, 41
Chavez Pass, 140
Chetro Ketl great house, 28(ph), 79,
    94(ph, diag): abandonment of, 121
Chiapas, Mexico, 197
child mortality, 118; at great houses
    compared to farmsteads, 115; during
    Chacoan period compared to modern
    United States, 145, 193
child poverty before and after
    government intervention, 195(gr)
child poverty rates in the United States
    1959 to 1996, 194(gr)
Chile, 13
Chuska Mountains, 52
Chuska Valley, 60, 77
Cibola, golden cities of, 179
cienega, 158
Cienguilla Glaze Yellow pottery, 148
citadels, 149
clay deposits, 152
cliff palaces, 131–32; dating of, 136; period
    of inhabitation of, 131
climate, 55; change in, 16–18; and fauna, 14
Clovis camps, 13
Coalition period sites, 137–42
cobble-mulched gardens, 141
Cody hunters, 14
Commitments, The, 144
communities: building more durable,
    199; as center places, 168; and
    conformity, 163; connecting of
    farming, 108; consolidated, 164;
    cooperative efforts in, 165; disruption
    of, 189; earliest, 35; five versions of,
    203–204; four categories of
    restructuring of, 163; functioning, 163,
    181; gated, 190; geographically
    expansive, 67; interconnected, 66, 67,
    203; lack of commitment to, 187; and
    language, 184; national, 200–201; open,
    70, 203; organization of, 43–44;

permanence of values of, 168; pit-house, 127; preservation of, 186; tradition as a sustainer of, 187
community house, 43
community organization, 53
construction, 78, 85; D-shaped, 79
cooking, effect of pottery upon, 42
cooking techniques, 40
Coolidge great house, 70
coprolites, 37
Cordell, Linda S., XII, 57
corn, 35–38, 40, 41, 57, 84, 86, 110; development of varieties of, 164; dry-farming of, 109; effect of, upon late Archaic foragers, 36; effect of sandstone grit in ground meal of, 45; experimentation with, 58; fresh-roasted, 42; grinding of, 42, 44, 45; increased efficiency in raising, 167; and increase in cob size, 42; lack of seed, 119; metabolization of, 37; rituals associated with, 117; stored, 36; surplus of, exchanged for meat and bowls, 58; upland restrictions on, 126; varieties of, 46
corncobs, as fuel, 42, 167
Coronado, Francisco Vazquez de, 179
Cortés, Hernán, 179
cosmology, 80
Crownpoint, 73
culture wars, 123

dance, 178(ph)
dart points, 13–14, 40; diversification of, 21
decapitation, 127
dental caries, 113, 114
Dick, Herbert W., 35, 127
diet, 37, 42–43, 84, 114, 129, 156, 158
diseases, 180, 181
dislocations from ancestral farms, 118
displacement, 120
diverse enviroments, use of, 160
dogs, 112; raising, 111
Dozier, Edward, 185
droughts, 83, 119–20, 121, 140, 156; and corn varieties, 37; and retreats to forested mesa country, 151
dunes, 109

east-facing mesas, and precipitation, 140
ecological diversity, loss of, 185
economy, diversity in, 164–65
ecotones, 46
efficiency, 132, 141, 183; forgotten value of, 198; versus power, 166
egalitarianism, 199
Ehrlich, Paul, 198
Eidenbach, Peter, 149
elders, 164, 203
El Faro pinnacle, 81, 102(ph)
encomienda, 179–80
energy, wasting of, 62
En Medio period, 36
Escalante Ruin great house, 120, 128–30; diet of residents of, 129–30; lack of roads leading to, 129
Espejo, 180–81
Espinoza Glaze Polychrome pottery, 148
ethnic violence, 143
exotic goods, 116

family size, declining, 49–50
famine, 110
farmers: and abandonment of Chaco Canyon, 123–24; in United States, 122
farm income, erosion in, 198
farming, 77; and access to diverse ecological zones, 151; expansion of, 61–62, 68; and limitations found in uplands, 125; and rain, 161; and sharing of harvests, 164. See also agriculture
farming centers, 60
farmland, 197–98
farmsteads, 30(ph), 31(ph), 32(ph), 33(ph), 66, 68; abandonment of, 120; contrasted with associated great houses, 108; daily life in, 70; proximity to watercourses, 147; ratio of residential to storage space at, 107; sizes and construction of, 109; unfortified, 118
Farwell, Robin, 128
fear, 135
field houses, 152
fire-cracked rock, 18
food-processing technologies, 21

foraging: and agriculture, 46; decline of, 39
fortified sites, abandonment of, 150
Fort Wingate great house, 69
Four Corners: bow and arrow introduced to, 40; and climate change, 16; as homeland of Anasazi, 9; introduction of pottery to, 42; and Jay lance points, 17; map of, 10; population in, 20; temperature extremes in, 15
Fourmile polychrome pottery, 153

Galisteo Black-on-white pottery, 148
Gallina district, lack of Red Mesa Black-on-white pottery at, 128
Gallina highlands, and drought, 140
Gallina pit-house sites, dismembered bodies found at, 127
game, 84, 110
Gila Cliff Dwellings, 131
golden age, 203
Gould, Stephen Jay, 52
Grand Gulch, Utah, 77
grave goods, 44, 157, 162
Great Depression, 188, 189
great-house architecture, 66
great houses, 7, 8, 11, 68, 114–16; abandonment of, 85–86; Chaco Canyon origin of, 107; compact, 129; curving, 79; evidence of wealth at, 115–16; expansion of, 119; export of, 119; growth of food storage in, 108; portion of space devoted to living in, 107; role in maintaining trade with farming communities, 107; and scion communities, 125; shoddy construction of, 134. *See also named great houses*
Great North Road, 81
greed, 201
Greenlee great house, 98 (ph, diag)
grid gardens, 141
grinding rooms, 60
groundwater, 79
growth, 49, 51–52, 78; and economy, 22–23; seduction by, 87; unchecked, 186
Guaje Canyon Ruin, 137
Guisewa Ruin, 43

Handbook of North American Indians, 151
health services, universal access to, 197
heishe, 111, 156, 157
herraduras, 82
Heshotauthla polychrome pottery, 153
hidalgos, 180
Hidden Mountain settlement, 149
hogans, 70; dating of Navajo, 136
Hogback great house, 78, 82, 119
Hopi family, and house, 172(ph)
Hopi Indians, 140, 180
Hopi pottery, 153
Hopi village, 171(ph)
Horse Camp Canyon, 138
horses, 81
horticulture, transition to, 35–36
house forms, evolution of, 52
house mounds A and B at Fort Wingate great house, 69; dating of, 70
housing starts, 87
hunting, 165; and change in technology, 40; communal, 167; gathering supplants, 19
hybrids, 58
Hyde, Talbot, 77
hypoplasia, 59, 139

Ice Age, 14
Ida Jean great house, 120, 128–29
Indian Hill Pueblo, 150
Indians: mistreatment of, 180; seen as threat, 9
infanticide, 20
infant mortality, 144, 157, 191
infrastructure, 165–66, 189, 201; investment in, 123, 197; sustaining, 197
institutions, investment in, 197
irrigation systems, 161, 167; annual cleaning and repair of, 165
Irwin-Williams, Cynthia, 83
Isleta Pueblo, 178(ph)

jacal construction, 53
Jackson's stairway, 100(litho)
Jay lance points, 17
Jefferson County, Mississippi, comparison of children born in, to children born in Marin County, California, 192–93

Jemez Pueblo, 43, 162
Judd, Neil, 115

kachina cult, 150
kachinas, 166
Keet Seel, 135
Keres, 180
Kidder, A. V., 159, 160–61
kidnapping, 190
Kin Bineola great house, 26
Kin Kletso great house, 89(ph)
Kin Lini great house, 74
Kin ya'a great house, 73, 98; controlling
   walls built at, 142; kiva at, 99(ph);
   tower kivas added at, 120
Kin ya'ii' clan, 74
kivas, 31(ph), 32(ph), 33(ph), 44, 59, 67,
   69, 81, 177(ph): growth in, 123;
   replastering of, 134; Rinconada, 85; and
   rituals, 117; single, 150; tower, 74
koshare, 163
Kuaua Pueblo, 161
Ku Klux Klan, 188
Kutz Canyon, 81, 84, 103(ph)

labor, 86–87
Laboratory of Tree Ring Research, 72
Lake Valley great house, 74
lance points, 13–14, 21, 40
land, extending a community's holdings
   of, 151–52
life expectancy, 157, 191–92
linguistic affiliation, 182(map)
literacy, 191
Little Ice Age, 134
longevity, 144

macaw skeletons, 115
maiz blando, 58
make-work projects, 123
malnutrition, 59, 110, 158
manos, 167; one-hand, 41; two-hand, 45
Manuelito Canyon: block tower
   overlooking, 105(ph); cliff-face site at,
   106(ph); residential expansion in, 120
Marcia's Rincon, 109
Marin County, California, comparison of

children born in, to children born in
   Jefferson County, Mississippi, 192–93
Marshall, Michael, 81
masked rain gods, 150
masonry, cobble-and-adobe, 138
masonry architecture, 72
McElmo-style pottery, 129
mealing bins, 44, 45, 60
meat, importation of dried, 61
mesa-top sites, 137–42; abandonment of,
   139
Mesa Verdeans, enemies of, 135
Mesa Verde pottery, geographical
   distribution of, 133
Mesa Verde region, scion communities
   in, 128–29
metates, 41, 60, 167; trough, 45
Mexico, 197; destruction of middle class
   in, 190
middle class, 189–201
Mimbres people, 116
Mississippi model of economic
   development, 48–49, 191
moieties, 164; convergence of interests of,
   165
Monte Verde site (Chile), 13–14
Montezuma Castle, 131
Morenon, E. Pierce, 81–82
mortality, child, 114–16
Mortenson, Thomas G., 193
Mug House, 131

Nambe Falls, 40
Navajo houses, dating of, 136
Navajo National Monument, 131
Navajo Reservoir district, 40, 41, 52, 61, 114
Navajo tales, 135
non-Indian Americans, dominance of, 8
Northern Ireland, sectarian violence in, 144
nutrition, 157, 158; and child-bearing, 20

obsidian, 151
Ojos Tecolotes, 70
ollas, 44, 46, 177(ph)
Oñate, Juan de, 180
oñaveno, 58
one-hand manos, 21

Oraibi, 171(ph)
Ortiz, Alfonso, 151, 185
osteoporosis, 45–46, 114, 115, 139, 158
Otowi, 160
outfits (Navajo), 70
outliers, 69
overwork, 46, 139

Pajarito Plateau, 140; settlement of, 130
Pale, the, 144
Paleo-Indians, 13; efficiency of late
    Archaic people compared to, 22; as
    efficient people, 16; increased
    complexity of society, 14; and
    population density, 14–15; and work, 15
palisades, 52
Peach Springs, 77, 79
Pecos Conference, 159
Pecos Pueblo, 159–61; abandonment of,
    181; diet at, 160; pattern of land-
    holding, 159
Peñasco Blanco great house, 27, 55, 77
Pepper, George H., 115; photos by, 169–
    78(ph)
Piedra phase, 52
pilgrimages, 166
Pima-Papago, 46
Pindi Pueblo, 133
pinnacles, 135
pit house B, deaths at, 111
pit houses, 31(ph), 33(ph), 46, 53, 147–48;
    and family size, 43; appearance of, in
    highlands, 134; dating of, 134; and
    efficiency, 126; farmers as founders of,
    129; increase in storage area in, 41; size
    of, 40; temperatures inside, 126;
    thermal efficiency of, 134
pit-house settlements, 128; common
    characteristics of, 41
Pizarro, Francisco, 179
plants: knowledge about, 18; processing
    sites for, 21; utilization of various
    species of, 18
Pojoaque Pueblo, 176(ph)
ponderosa trees, 78
popcorn, 35
population, 153–54, 180–81; factors

leading to increase of, among San Jose
    hunters and gatherers, 20; fluctuation
    in, 18; of Pecos in 16th century, 161; of
    Pueblo people in 16–18th centuries,
    180–81
Population Bomb, The (Ehrlich), 198
population decline, 183; infant mortality
    and, 143; and poorly nourished
    women, 120
population density, 22; and movement,
    21; and water, 142
population growth, 21, 43, 162; as liability,
    118
pots, efficiency of cooking with, 42
pottery, 42, 84, 110, 111, 130, 133, 134; broken,
    82; Chuska series of, 116, 117; cooking,
    138; exchange of, 54; firing of, 173(ph);
    glaze-painted, 148; importation of, 116;
    innovations in, 44; lack of, 40; reusing of,
    138; Sante Fe Black-on-white, 130–31;
    styles of, 72; trade in, 44
poverty, in United States, 144
power, 9, 48–49, 62, 87, 183; ritual as, 119;
    seduction by, 87; versus efficiency, 23,
    166
prayer sticks, 151
precipitation, 16–17, 46, 57, 133; in 1260s,
    139; between 1200 and 1250, 139;
    bimodal, 78; decline in, 52, 119; and
    elevation, 126; predictability of, 65;
    reservoir for storing, 137; summer-
    dominant, single-season, 69; two
    patterns of, 58; unstable, 37
Pueblo I period, 51–56; geographical and
    ecological setting of, 56; naming of, 53
Pueblo II period, 56, 56–61; geographical
    and ecological setting of, 56; inability
    of farming communities to expand
    during, 118; living space compared to
    storage space during, 60; structure of
    sites of, 58–59
Pueblo III period, 78, and distinction
    between Pueblo II, 137
Pueblo IV period, 147; and diet, 148; size
    of riverine sites during, 155
Pueblo Alto great house, 79
Puebloan society, 8

Pueblo Bonito great house, 11, 28(ph), 55, 72, 77, 92(ph, diag), 93(ph), 135; burials at, 115; completion of, 80; construction phases at, 79; and cosmology, 80; renovation of, 60; size of, 80 Pueblo culture, romanticization of, 162–63

Pueblo del Arroyo, 90(ph), 91(diag), 134

Pueblo feast dance, 155

Pueblo language: reluctance of teaching to outsiders, 184; and religion, 184

Pueblo people: assimilation of, into American society, 186; dualities in world of, 186; and loss of land to Spaniards, 185; as pragmatists, 187; and reclamation of lands, 185; survival of, for 1700 years, 187; tenacity of, 65

Pueblo Pintado great house, 97 (ph, diag), 119

Pueblo religion, 183–84

Pueblo Revolt, 166, 180

pueblos, 176(ph), 178(ph): above-ground, masonry, 130; construction of, on mesa tops, 136; Hopi, of Shipaulovi, 170(ph); and largest adobe construction, 161; mesa-top Hopi, 169(ph); modern times and, 182(map); and river, 150; seasonal occupancy of, 152; as self-contained units, 166; and survival, 183; unfortified, 130; unit, 60, 77, 109

punctuated equilibria, 52

raids: and larger communities, 153; and retreats to forested mesa country, 151

rainfall. See precipitation

ramadas, 41, 109

Red Mesa Valley, 60, 68, 69, 75, 77; inability of farming communities to expand in, 118; population growth a liability in, 118

religion, 44, 143; and change from dual to single kivas, 150; and earth, 81; as organizing principle in Chacoan society, 119; Pueblo, 183–84; rapid change in practice of, 130; religious life, not distinct from secular life, 81

residences, 53; Cochiti study of space in, 154. See also rooms

resources, scarcity of, 61

Rhine, J. Stanley, 112

Rinconada kiva, 85

Rio Puerco, 68

risk, 62

risk management, 58

risk pool, 54

rituals, 86, 88, 165, 183; associated with corn, 117; failure of, 120; increased space for, 119; interdependence of economy and, 125; as organizing principle in Chacoan society, 119

riverine period, 149

riverine pueblos, 150–55

rivers, and trade wares, 152–53

roads, Chacoan, 73, 85; two sizes of, 82

rooms: shapes and sizes of, 53; shedlike, 53. See also residences

Roosevelt, Franklin Delano, 189

Rosa-phase pit houses, 55

sacred formula, 122

safety in larger settlements, 52

Salmon Ruin great house, 81, 83–84, 104(ph), 119; abandonment of reoccupied, 136

salt, collection of, 166

Salt Road, 166

Sambrito Brownware, 42

Sandia Pueblo, 185

San Felipe Pueblo, 177(ph)

San Jose period, lessons learned in, 21

San Jose point, 19–20

San Juan basin, 203; northern, 80–85

San Juan Pueblo, 180

San Mateo district, residential expansion in, 120

San Mateo great house, 121

San Pascualito, 149

San Pascual Village, 149

Santa Ana Pueblo, and help given to Spanish families, 165

Santa Fe, as capital of Spanish colony, 180

Sapawe Pueblo, 161

scion communities, 125; founding of, by elites, 129; as islands of Chacoan

refugee society, 129; in Mesa Verde region, 128–29
Seaman, Timothy, 127
Sebastian, Lynne, 143
Sellers, D. K. B., 115
settlement pattern working in reverse during upland period, 126
settlements: expansion of, 57; overlapping of periods of, 56; size of Basketmaker and Pueblo I, compared, 52
Shabik'eschee village, 43
Shalako ceremony, 117
shale beads, 111
shipap, 81, 84
shrines, 81, 82, 151, 174(ph)
siege: defense against, 137, 138
Simpson, J. H., 9, 11
site CGP-54–1, 135
site CGP-56, 135
site LA 287, 150
site LA 415, 149
site 616, 138
site 627, long, unbroken history of, 109–110
site LA 757, 149
site 1360, 59–60, 110–32
site LA 6455, 148
site LA 11843, 127
site LA 12700, 137
sites, fortified, 149–50
Skunk Springs, 60, 77, 79
Smith Lake Navajo chapter house, 72
Spaniards, 185, 203
squash, 36, 38, 40, 42, 57, 84, 86, 110
Standing Rock, 78
status, downgraded, of Indians, 9
St. Johns Polychrome bowls, 133, 139, 141, 148; trading of, 130
stone boiling, 40
storage pits, 38; as seasonal dwellings, 41
storerooms, 53
surpluses, 65, 75, 77, 117, 139
survival, fundamentals of, 8, Pueblo arts of, 183–84
sustainability of communities, 200

talus, 68
Talus Unit, 94(ph)

Tano, 180
Taos Pueblo, 162, 176(ph)
tax policies (US), 199–200
tax revenue (US) as a percent of gross domestic product 1994, 196(gr)
Tewa, 180
Thoreau, 68
Tijeras Pueblo, 158
Tiwa, 180
tools, farming, 46
Towa, 180
trade, 54, 57, 111, 116, 153; in late 1300s and early 1400s, 152
trade networks: disintegration of, 125; drought disrupts, 141; growth of, 139; and narrow corridors along waterways, 152; new, 130
transportation, public, 197
trauma, 115
turkeys, 43; eating of, 129
turquoise deposits, 152
Tyuonyi, 141, 151

Una Vida great house, 55, 77, 95(ph, diag): renovation of, 60
underworld, 81
United States: child poverty rates in, 193; disparity of rich and poor in, 193; fragility of, 187; infant mortality in, 191; life expectancy in, 191; literacy in, 191; longevity of, compared to Puebloan society, 187; poverty in, 144
unit pueblos, 60, 77, 109
Upland Period, 125–45; decline of trade in, 125; and drought, 127; use of pit houses in, 125
uplands, 203
urban sprawl, 198

Valentine village, 40
Village of the Great Kivas great house, 120
villages, portability of, 168
violence, 121, 138; ethnic, 143; in Gallina highlands following collapse of Chacoan society, 128; sectarian, 144
Vivian, R. Gwinn, 55

wages, disparity in, 190–91
Wallace great house, 120, 128–29
walls: construction of, 53; controlling, 142
warfare, 143
warrior class, lack of, 118
water: excessive use of, 187; and
    population density, 142
water tables, rising of, 38
wealth, inequality in, 188
weather, 35
west-facing mesas, and precipitation,
    139–40
Wetherill, Richard, 25, 39, 77

Wijiji great house, 96(ph, diag), 135
Wimberly, Mark, 149

yucca root, 18
yuccas, transplanting of, 19
Yugoslavia, 143–44

Zia Pueblo, firing pottery at, 173(ph)
Zuni Indians, 180
Zuni Pueblo, 179
Zuni Salt Lake, 166
Zuni settlements, 162

Biographical Note

David E. Stuart is professor of anthropology and associate provost at the University of New Mexico. He is broadly trained in both anthropology and archaeology. His previous books include *Prehistoric New Mexico* (with R.P. Gauthier), *Glimpses of the Ancient Southwest,* and *The Magic of Bandelier National Monument.* His passion is undergraduate teaching.

Susan Moczygemba-McKinsey is the product of generations of small-site farmers, first in Poland and then in south Texas. Her ancestors had to abandon center place and seek life in a new world.